JOURNEY AMONG WARRIORS

THE MEMOIRS OF A MARINE

by

Victor J. Croizat, Colonel
United States Marine Corps (Ret.)

Foreword by P. X. Kelley
General, United States Marine Corps (Ret.)

WHITE MANE PUBLISHING COMPANY, INC.

All photographs not otherwise credited are from the author's personal collection.

This White Mane Publishing Company, Inc. publication was printed by

Beidel Printing House, Inc.
63 West Burd Street
Shippensburg, PA 17257 USA

In respect for the scholarship contained herein, the acid-free paper used in this book meets the guidelines for permanence and durability of the Committee on Production Guidelines for Book Longevity of the Council on Library Resources.

For a complete list of available publications please write

White Mane Publishing Company, Inc.
P.O. Box 152
Shippensburg, PA 17257 USA

Library of Congress Cataloging-in-Publication Data

Croizat, Victor J.
    Journey among warriors : the memoirs of a marine / by Victor J.
Croizat ; foreword by P.X. Kelley.
        p.   cm.
    Includes index.
    ISBN 1-57249-008-X (alk. paper)
    1. Croizat, Victor.   2. United States. Marine Corps--Biography.
I. Title.
VE25.C76A3   1997
359.9'6'092--dc21
    [B]   97-11296
                                                                          CIP

PRINTED IN THE UNITED STATES OF AMERICA

Le Lac

Ainsi toujours pousses vers de nouveaux rivages
Dans la nuit eternelle emportes sans retour
Ne pourrons nous jamais sur l'ocean des ages
Jeter l'ancre un seul jour...

The Lake

Forever driven toward new shores
Carried through the endless night without return
Will we never find anchorage on the sea of eternity
Even for a day...

Lamartine
1790–1865

To my wife, Meda, who shared my journey,
heightened its pleasures and
carried full measure of its burdens

TABLE OF CONTENTS

LIST OF ILLUSTRATIONS

Chapter Eight

Chapter Nine

LIST OF MAPS

FOREWORD

I first became aware of Colonel Victor J. Croizat while at anchor off Algiers during the summer of 1953. I was the officer of the deck of the USS *Salem*, flagship of the U.S. Sixth Fleet, when senior French army, navy, and air force officers arrived to make courtesy calls on our Fleet Commander. At the peak of these calls, I counted twenty-five *stars* either arriving or departing.

During a lull in these activities, a French army officer asked if I knew Lieutenant Colonel Croizat, who had been his classmate at the Ecole Superieure de Guerre. Although I admitted I did not, he nevertheless spent several minutes extolling the virtues of my fellow Marine, whom he referred to as "the most talented officer I have ever met." I later learned that, besides his personal attributes, Colonel Croizat's fluency in French had enhanced his reputation and that of the Marine Corps at the Ecole de Guerre. This tour gained him many lifelong friendships that proved invaluable later when he served in Vietnam, during his observations of French helicopter operations in Algeria, and when on a mission to French West Africa, all of which he writes about in this memoir.

Several years later I again heard about this extraordinary Marine officer, this time while serving as the Training Officer of the 3rd Marine Division/Provisional Corps, Japan. One evening, Captain James C. Breckinridge, a close friend and son of the legendary Marine general of the same name, came into my room to tell me he had orders to the new Republic of Vietnam where he would be working for his old friend and mentor, Colonel Vic Croizat, creating a Vietnamese Marine Corps. I believe that history clearly shows these two officers were directly responsible for the successful accomplishments achieved by that Corps during the two decades of its existence.

While Colonel Croizat and I served together at Headquarters, Marine Corps, during the mid-1950s, I knew him still only by reputation...and it was an enviable one indeed. As an early amphibian tractor officer, he was a pioneer in the development of the doctrine and techniques in the employment of amtracs. Then, as an amtrac battalion commander in four amphibious assaults in the Pacific War, he had proved their effectiveness.

This all leads me to my first direct personal contact with Colonel Croizat, which took place during the Marine Corps Survey Mission to Haiti in 1958, described in Chapter 6 of this book. During my thirty-seven years as a Marine, I have observed a number of truly superb diplomatic warriors in action, but never have I seen one who exceeded Colonel Croizat's skill and professionalism in his demanding assignment as the deputy Commander of this team.

My final contact with Colonel Croizat came while I was researching my thesis for the Air War College. Based upon my association with him and a Foreign Legion colonel I had known at Camp Benning, I wrote on the Algerian War and its political and military similarities with Vietnam. Both of these officers provided me with enlightening insights on Algeria which could not be found in any published form.

While I have selfishly allowed myself to talk about my relationship with this unusual Marine, I have really just touched the tip of the iceberg. Colonel Croizat was well known and respected in the Marine Corps of his time and has become a legend in today's Corps, not because of his many unique and demanding assignments, but more because his performance in each was *above and beyond*. This autobiography, like its author, is unpretentious and a warm and personal story of his many unusual assignments while on active service, as a Marine Corps officer in war and peace. The insights it provides into the military diplomacy of the mid-century and the colorful individuals involved will be of value to both historians and military professionals. *Journey Among Warriors* should be in the library of every professional military officer, not just the Marines.

P. X. Kelley
General, United States Marine Corps (Ret.)
28th Commandant

ACKNOWLEDGEMENTS

It all began with Colonel John E. Greenwood, an old friend and editor of the *Marine Corps Gazette*, who suggested I write up some of my more unusual assignments for his readers. I did so and, after these had been well received, John urged me to retell them and others in book form. Thus began what became a manuscript concerned largely with historical events I had witnessed and in which I had played a contributory role.

I gave a copy of my initial draft to Eugene and Natalie Jones, both professional foreign correspondents and documentarists, who had personal knowledge of many of the people and events I discussed. Their exhaustive critique and detailed comments encouraged me to revise my draft. My debt to these good friends is great.

Benis M. Frank, Chief Historian of the Marine Corps, has also placed me in his debt by reviewing the revised manuscript for historical accuracy and general content. I equally appreciate the recollections of General P. X. Kelley, 28th Commandant of the Marine Corps, in his Foreword on the crossing of our paths over the years. In addition, welcome guidance was provided by Dr. Martin K. Gordon.

Finally, the greater debt is owed my wife, Meda Fletcher Croizat, who shared so much of my journey, provided wise counsel as the tale unfolded and spent endless hours applying her professional competence as an editor to help bring the effort to its final form.

Although I am grateful for the contributions of the individuals cited, the story of my journey reflects my personal interpretation of the history through which I lived and must remain my sole responsibility.

PROLOGUE

Soldier, sailor, or civilian...who can resist the sound of the bugle? My first reveille, piercing the mists from Lake Champlain that shrouded my Army ROTC tent at Plattsburg, introduced me to a soldier's life. Later, when a Marine at Quantico, the call to colors each morning brought a moment of silent homage to flag and country. Then, during my Great War, the sound of taps over the fresh graves of comrades fallen at Guadalcanal, Kwajalein, Saipan, Tinian, and Iwo Jima seared images that will remain as long as life.

Such is the essence of the military profession, where duty and country are tangible realities and interdependence strengthens bonds among its members. Military service is also an endless learning process in which duty with troops is interspersed with formal schooling. My career began in the traditional manner, but involvement with the amphibian tractor in five landing operations in the Pacific began my less conventional journey.

Then, attendance at the Ecole Superieure de Guerre in Paris led to a succession of unique assignments. These began in Indochina in 1954 where I helped in the evacuation of North Vietnam, came to know President Ngo Dinh Diem of South Vietnam, and assisted at the birth of the Vietnamese Marines. In 1957, I was in Algeria observing French helicopter operations against insurgents. The following year I met with President Francois Duvalier of Haiti concerning his request for a Marine Corps mission to his poor country.

Two years later, an initiative by the French President to engage the United States and Great Britain in preparing the independence of African colonies took me to West Africa from Senegal to the Congo. The next year brought field studies in the Middle East. After that, it was back to the Pacific in time for crisis in Laos, followed by three years in Bangkok with the Southeast Asia Treaty Organization and a direct view of the intensifying conflict in that region.

In 1966, I returned to Vietnam to prepare an interim doctrine for riverine warfare. This, though not needed by the Marines, was used by Army units in the Mekong delta, thus aiding the service which had started me on my way. Most numerous among my companions on the journey were the warriors...some heroes, others legends, and many at the top of their profession. This roster, already lengthy, was augmented by civilian officials...presidents, kings, and lesser notables..all of whom added color to my days.

The tapestry of my twenty-six years in the Marine Corps is finely woven of these varied strands, many shared by my wife, Meda, who accepted hazards and long separations and made so many homes for us. Seeing the world as we did was a fascinating journey. Duty and service gave purpose to our lives, and our efforts to understand the subtle differences among the people that we met added to my professional effectiveness and enriched our experiences. For us, it is a tapestry to be cherished, a journey to be prized.

LIST OF ABBREVIATIONS

ABDA—	American, British, Dutch, and American forces/command
Amtrac—	Amphibian Tractor; also LVT
APB—	Barracks Ship, self-propelled (converted LST)
ARL—	Landing Craft Repair Ship (converted LST)
ASPB—	Assault Support Patrol Boat
ATC—	Armored Troop Carrier (converted LCM)
BOQ—	Bachelor Officers Quarters
CCB—	Command and Control Boat (converted LCM)
CCS—	Combined Chiefs of Staff
CINCPAC—	Commander in Chief, Pacific
DMZ—	Demilitarized Zone
E—	Engineer Battalion
FLEX 7—	Fleet Exercise 7
FLN—	National Liberation Front (Algeria)
HMS—	His/Her Majesty's Ship
JCS—	Joint Chiefs of Staff
JTF—	Joint Task Force
LCM—	Landing Craft, Mechanized (tank/artillery lighter)
LCVP—	Landing Craft, Vehicle/Personnel
LST—	Landing Ship Tank
LVT—	Landing Vehicle Tracked (Amtrac)
MAAG—	Military Assistance and Advisory Group
MACV—	Military Assistance Command, Vietnam
M.G.—	Marine Gunner (Warrant Officer rank, U.S. Marine Corps)
NATO—	North Atlantic Treaty Organization
NCO—	Noncommissioned Officer
OPLAN—	Operation Plan

P—	Pioneer Battalion
PBR—	River Patrol Boat
PBY—	Amphibian Patrol Plane (Catalina)
PCS—	Patrol Craft, Small
POA—	Pacific Ocean Area
RAS—	River Assault Squadron
RPC—	River Patrol Craft
SEATO—	South East Asia Treaty Organization
TERM—	Temporary Equipment Recovery Mission
TRIM—	Training Relations and Instruction Mission
USO—	United Services Organization
USOM—	United States Operations Mission
WPB—	U.S. Coast Guard Patrol Boat
YTB—	Harbor Tug

One

BY THE DAWN'S EARLY LIGHT

The weather had worsened as we steamed northwest from the Fijis. The previous two days had been particularly bad. A heavy overcast, frequent rain squalls, and pounding seas added to the misery of the 19,000 Marines crammed into a miscellany of twenty-three ships. Worst off were the Raiders corkscrewing their way on four old converted destroyers. But there was a consolation. The blustery, sodden gloom had kept Japanese reconnaissance aircraft grounded and allowed us to approach the lower Solomons undetected.

Sometime in the early hours of August 7, 1942, when our amphibious force turned eastward, I joined other silent shadows on the weather deck of the aging *American Legion.* Then, as our ships separated into two groups, each turning on course to its assigned transport area, the compound smell of earth and vegetation spread over the humid night air, and I became aware of a large land mass to starboard. We had reached our destination...the island of Guadalcanal.

The landings a few hours away were intended to block further Japanese expansion in the South Pacific and help secure the lines of communications between America and Australia. Our naval victory at Midway in June had interrupted the enemy's advance in the Central Pacific and dealt a severe blow to his naval power. Wresting control of the lower Solomons would extend his containment and set in motion the drive that, in time, would force him back to his home islands. The landings on Guadalcanal would also test the Marines' amphibious doctrine, some twenty years in the making, and introduce a novel vehicle, the amphibian tractor. Most important, the campaign would reveal a tenacity among American forces that would discourage whatever hopes for a negotiated peace the Japanese might entertain.

However, few of us present that morning were concerned with matters of strategy or doctrine and none could foresee the future. What we did know was that our division was fragmented and its training incomplete. Our embarkation

1

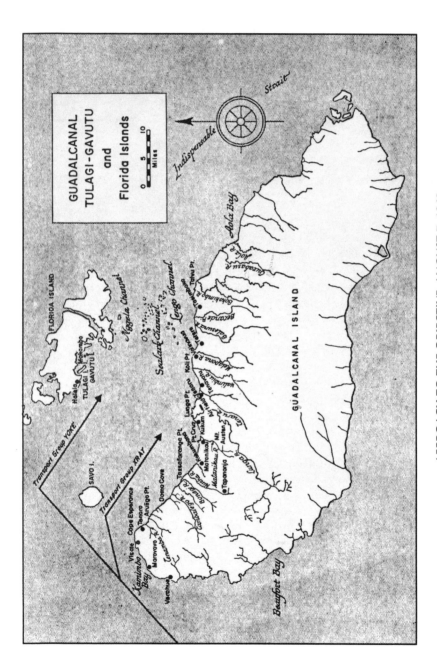

APPROACH TO THE OBJECTIVE, AUGUST 7, 1942

USMC Map

in New Zealand had been chaotic, and we knew little of our enemy and where we were to meet. As troubling as these uncertainties were, what was more important to many of us was how we would react to the reality of combat.

The 1st Marine Division, well below half strength when the Japanese struck Pearl Harbor, had been quickly fleshed out. Then, in March 1942, the 7th Marines had been detached for duty in Samoa, taking with it most of the seasoned noncommissioned officers and men. Five weeks later the remainder of the division had set sail for New Zealand where we expected to complete our training. Instead, we had spent the first two weeks unloading ships and moving into camps, and the following three weeks closing down the camps and moving back aboard ship. We had then sailed for Guadalcanal.

Fortunately, intermingled with the flow of new recruits joining us in North Carolina before we sailed had been a number of old-timers, who were often gamblers, scroungers, and heavy drinkers with little interest in libraries, organized athletics, or chapel. However, they had been in combat and possessed a well-founded knowledge of weapons and tactics. In the confused months that followed, they had passed on much practical knowledge to our young Marines...none more so than two gunnery sergeants, the loud and profane mortar expert Lou Diamond, and the quiet Shorty Smallwood, for whom machine guns held no secrets. The result was a cocky crowd in which personal concern over what lay ahead was suppressed by ceaseless banter.

Many of our senior officers were also combat tested. Cols. Clifton B. Cates and LeRoy P. Hunt, commanding the assault regiments that were to land on Guadalcanal, had met German infantry in Belleau Wood and on Blanc Mont Ridge during the Great War. Others, such as Maj. Gen. Alexander A. Vandegrift, our division commander, and Lt. Col. Merritt A. Edson, who would lead the 1st Raider Battalion ashore on Tulagi, had been blooded in the vicious firefights in Nicaragua and Haiti characteristic of the *banana wars*.

The rest of us, more numerous by far, were about to encounter our first enemy fire. Our predawn breakfast weighed heavily and the usual chatter had given way to silent introspection. The noxious odors of our crowded transports now seemed less offensive and even Capts. William Kaempfer and William Hawkins, the assault rifle company commanders who had been arguing loudly for days over who would first set foot ashore, were subdued. Then at 0613, our world turned violent in a roar of naval gunfire.

✳ ✳ ✳

This voyage on the *American Legion,* while different in purpose, was but another in a succession of seaborne travels begun in my early years. The first had started in Tripoli, Libya in 1920 where, the year before, I had made my undistinguished entry into the world. I am not aware that this event in the land where Marine Lieutenant Presley O'Bannon had planted the Stars and Stripes in 1805, an exploit noted in the first line of the Marine Corps Hymn, predisposed me to a career in the Marine Corps.[1] Neither do I remember my first sea voyage crossing the Mediterranean.

My first recollection dates from January 1922, when our home in a Turin suburb was thrown into confusion by the birth of my sister Georgette. Other memories of that year are of pleasant walks with my father to the river for a swim before supper and the welcome of local merchants. Vivid among

**FIRST TIME ABOARD SHIP
TRIPOLI HARBOR, JUNE 15, 1919
VICTOR (4 MONTHS), LUCIA, AND LEON CROIZAT**

these was an ample lady who owned a lumberyard where the marvelous resinous smells were matched by those of her cooking, which I was always invited to sample. For me, life was good; for my father, his opposition to the tightening grip of Mussolini's fascists was becoming too vocal.

By the fall of 1923, the worsening political climate convinced him to emigrate and he left for New York. While waiting to join him, my mother, sister, and I moved to my paternal grandmother's family home in Ceyzerieu, a village at the head of the Lac du Bourget, the largest of the French lakes below Geneva. This cross-border move from Italy to France was nothing new, for my family comes from the old Duchy of Savoy whose lands are now shared by France and Italy. My father's antecedents come from the French side, my mother's from both. My paternal grandfather, Victor, an engineer born and raised in French Chambery, moved to Turin shortly before the turn of the century to design and build the lighting system for that Italian city.

My father, Leon, spent his early years in both countries and was at the University of Turin when Italy entered the Great War. Commissioned in an alpine infantry regiment, he was in Turin on leave from the front in 1917 when Lucia, the daughter of an Italian railroad official, caught his eye. They married that

November. The following year he was posted to Tripoli, where I entered the world three months after the war had ended. We were soon back in Turin where my father, returned to civilian life, went on to gain a doctor of jurisprudence degree.

I had no problem shifting from Italian to French when we moved to Ceyzerieu, since the latter was the language we favored at home. I did, however, have trouble adapting to the formalities of a household presided over by an imposing great-aunt. Equally imposing was the 17th-century house with its inviting grounds, endless rooms, huge fireplaces, and a grand brick-floored kitchen, all made for exploration. Again, I must have impressed the local shopkeepers. When I returned twenty-five years later and asked where the Chaley house was located, the shopkeeper looked at me quizzically for a moment and exclaimed, "Mais vous etes le petit Victor."[2] For a moment, I was once more a small boy waiting for his father to take him to a land far away.

One of my vivid memories of our journey to America is of a violent storm at sea. Another is of the awesome Statue of Liberty emerging from a cold mist on the morning of February 29, 1924, a day made twice memorable by date and event. My early years in America were confining. I spoke no English, and our small apartment contrasted with the spaciousness I remembered in Italy and France. My world expanded in 1926, when I entered school and a dedicated Miss Daniels taught me English with unforgettable emphasis on phonetics. In 1928, family fortunes permitted an extended vacation at Aix-les-Bains, an elegant watering place only a few miles from Ceyzerieu. Shortly after the start of the new year, my father, sister, and I became American citizens and my English lost the flavor that had gained me the nickname of *Frenchy*.

My adjustments were as nothing compared to those made by my parents. Essentially a Renaissance man with keen interests in art and botany, my father found little pleasure in the legal profession or in the American business world. Yet, by 1929, his income allowed us to live comfortably. It also allowed him to pursue his passion for painting and begin entry into the art world. However, these happy circumstances were short-lived. The market crash of October that year brought an end to his business enterprise and extinguished prospects for developing his artistic talents.

In the spring of 1930, my father concluded that conditions could not be as bad in Europe, and we returned to France. There, he discovered the economy was no better. Moreover, as an American citizen, he was unable to get a work permit. After a difficult year during which my parents despaired of saving enough to return to the United States, news arrived that a watercolor he had dashed off one Sunday morning had been sold by his New York art dealer for the needed passage money.

Starting again in New York City in the 1930s was not easy. Nevertheless, my father found a job with the city's Department of Parks, thanks to the competence in botany he had developed as his opportunities in art had declined. He would remain a botanist and naturalist for the remainder of his long life. As for me, I was again called *Frenchy*. However, by the time I passed the examination to enter Stuyvesant High School in 1932, I had become just another American kid with a difficult last name.

Stuyvesant, a school with an exceptional curriculum in the sciences, was located on the lower East Side, and we then lived on the West Side in mid-Manhattan. Thus, for four years I was part of the mad throng traveling the sub-way in the heart of the city, an experience that encouraged me to look for an escape from the concrete confines of the city. The Boy Scouts provided occasions away from sidewalk and subway. Later, the Sea Scouts added the Hudson River to my refuges from city life. Books served as another outlet. The sea was my favorite subject and the Pacific the most absorbing. These interests inclined me toward a life at sea, but the College of Forestry at Syracuse University appeared to offer better career prospects.

My first year of college provided more stimuli than I could handle with comfort, but by my second year I had improved my study habits and expanded my start on extracurricular activities. During my third year at Syracuse, my family moved to Boston where my father had joined the staff of Harvard's Arnold Arboretum. While I was there preparing to depart for my last year of college, the Germans invaded Poland, and the British and French riposted with a declaration of war. Five days later, on September 8, 1939, President Roosevelt announced a Limited National Emergency. For my father, long familiar with European politics, these events were ominous.

Still, I was not surprised to find little excitement on campus over what was happening in Europe. My senior year began well. I was elected student body president and soon after received a graduate fellowship in botany. Then, in the spring, two fellow ROTC cadets, Victor Harwick and William Kaempfer, and I were told we qualified for regular commissions in the United States Marine Corps. Given developments in Europe, we concluded that an early call to active duty was likely and that a commitment to regular service was better than remaining a reserve waiting to be called. We submitted our applications to the Marines and accepted an Army offer of two weeks of active duty training. In June, I received my degree and reserve Army commission and closed the book on my days at Syracuse.

Vic Harwick accompanied me home, and we went together to the Boston Navy Yard to take our Marine Corps entry physicals. The visit gave Vic his first view of an ocean, and both of us our first sighting of a Marine officer in greens. We then left for Camp Dix, the Army's training base in New Jersey, where the shift from impoverished student to *officer and gentleman* was abrupt. Upon arrival, we were directed to a supply shed to draw equipment. There, when I reached for the stack assembled for me, my gesture was intercepted by a private who snapped, "I'll take that for the lieutenant." Surprised, I asked, "What for?" And the equally surprised private answered, "Sir, I am the lieutenant's orderly!"

For a youth accustomed to living on ten dollars per week, a lieutenant's salary three times greater was luxurious, even without an orderly. That I lived in a tent and spent much of my time standing on lines with other second lieutenants did little to lessen my enthusiasm. At the beginning of July, I received orders from the Marine Corps to report to the Basic School at the Philadelphia Navy Yard. My first discovery there was that Marine officers had no orderlies. I also found that most of my pay was needed to buy uniforms. The financial burden of this trousseau was among the reasons we were forbidden to marry for our first two years of service.

The hundred and fifty-four second lieutenants making up the Basic School Class of 1940 included some one hundred graduates of universities with Army ROTC programs and twenty-five graduates of the Naval Academy. This meant that most of us had received our initial military training at Army or Navy expense and confirmed the stories of Marine Corps frugality. We soon joined in the process of becoming Marine officers. We lived two to a room whose dimensions permitted only the austere furnishings needed for studying, sleeping, and the never-ending polishing of brass and leather. I found my roommate, 2d Lt. Wade Hitt, a tall soft-spoken Virginian, fascinating. I never learned whether my peculiar *Yankee* background proved as interesting to him.

The Philadelphia Navy Yard offered adequate classroom and parade ground facilities. But scouting and patrolling in League Island Park, just outside the main gate, had us dodging park benches, well-fed pigeons, and unwary strollers. We were more enthusiastic over our excursion to Cape May, New Jersey for small arms firing. Best of all were field exercises at Indiantown Gap where we blasted the Pennsylvania hills with heavy weapons and I enjoyed my first flight with 2d Lt. William Kellum in an aged dive-bomber.

A good part of our curriculum repeated much of what we had been exposed to during our ROTC studies. This included bayonet drill, in which I qualified expert. Despite that, I held that the spirit of the bayonet was an archaic concept. I said so one day when our instructor, Capt. Samuel D. Puller, younger brother to the legendary Chesty Puller, told us that if our bayonet became stuck between an opponent's ribs we could shoot it out. I asked why, if I held a loaded rifle, could I not simply shoot my opponent and avoid a contest of uncertain outcome. Captain Puller snorted, "Mistoh, youah fightin' thuh problem. Thuh training youah get heah, ef youah pay attention 'n git the right attitude, makes youah the best any time!" I remained unconvinced but let the matter drop.[3]

Two of our classroom subjects were noteworthy. The first was the wisdom of four decades of peacekeeping duties found in the *Small Wars Manual,* 1940. While the passage of half a century makes the technical information obsolete, chapters on disarmament of populations, armed native organizations, and supervision of elections contain guidance that remains relevant. The second subject presented in *Fleet Training Publication 167* reflected years of study and field trials in the complexities of amphibious warfare. But, where the drama of such warfare fired our imaginations, the resources needed to give it life were still lacking. Our amphibious training was more theory than practice.

We were addressed as officers and gentlemen but, lest that go to our heads, we were told that second lieutenants, like tent pegs, were expendable. We also learned that "Aye, Aye, Sir" was the only proper reply to an order, which might not always be clear or in the imperative. Beyond acquiring a code of conduct that disciplined the individual and furthered our social integration, we were impressed with the responsibilities of command, notably the importance of decision making and concern for our men's well-being.

Our director, Colonel Cates, overhearing us question the merit of an exercise, gathered us around him and explained, "The ultimate purpose of all training, even that which may appear frivolous, is to ensure that you respond correctly to situations as they arise. This is particularly important in combat, where there is seldom time for deliberate thought and reason yields to instinct." Then, looking at each of us, he added, "There will be times when you make mistakes. But, never let that keep you from acting. If you do nothing, the enemy gains the initiative and that invites disaster."

These subtleties and the more orthodox subjects having been mastered, we completed Basic School in February 1941 and proceeded to our new assignments. I was among the majority ordered to the expanding Fleet Marine Force units on the East and West Coasts. The more fortunate, or so we thought, were ordered to sea duty or to the 4th Marines in Shanghai. Among those assigned aboard ship, two were on battleship row in Pearl Harbor on the morning of December 7, 1941, when their war began and ended in a few tragic hours. 2d Lt. Harry Gaver, the well-liked number one man in our class was last seen on the *Oklahoma* trying to close a hatch to the magazines. Near that same time, 2d Lt. Carleton Simensen was killed by a bomb that struck the *Arizona.*

Less fortunate in the length of their agony were 2d Lts. Leon Chabot, Clarence Van Ray, and Mason Chronister who would die as prisoners of the Japanese. Only 2d Lt. John Winterholler among the four sent to Shanghai would survive the war. I had shared long evening hours in Basic School with boxer Chabot of the flattened nose learning how to spit polish shoes Naval Academy fashion and was doubly saddened when I heard he had died on a Japanese ship sunk by one of our own submarines.

When the war broke out in Europe in 1939, the Marine Corps had just under 20,000 men. That was still the Old Corps, and it lasted just long enough to welcome my class of new lieutenants. Soon after, the Organized Reserve was mobilized and the Marine Corps was on its way to becoming a different organization. By the time we left Basic School there were 65,000 Marines on active duty, half of them in the expanding Fleet Marine Force. On the West Coast, the recently designated 2d Marine Division was moving to Camp Elliott near San Diego. On the East Coast, 110,000 acres of pine barrens along the North Carolina coast were being readied to receive the 1st Marine Division, then on maneuvers in the Caribbean.

✳ ✳ ✳

My contingent of fresh lieutenants, assigned to The Training Center in Quantico pending the return of the 1st Marine Division, was housed in wooden huts built on the banks of the Potomac during World War I. These were little more than condemned shacks, but our lives were governed by traditional formality. We had to wear coat and tie to attend the movies on base and, if we ventured as far as the Army's Fort Belvoir, the dress for the movies there was blues or civilian black tie.

Our duties were scarcely onerous. This made it easy to satisfy my curiosity over a strange tracked vehicle I observed maneuvering in and out of the Potomac. On visiting the shed where the machine was kept, I met Sgt. Clarence H. Raper and Cpls. Walter Gibson and Harry Black. They had just returned from the Caribbean where they had tested it under the direction of Capt. Victor H. Krulak. After showing me the vehicle, Raper laughingly warned it might not have much of a future. He explained that when Captain Krulak had talked the commander of the Atlantic Fleet, crusty Admiral Ernest J. King, into taking a ride, it had thrown a track. The fuming admiral had last been seen wading ashore in his starched whites, a boiling wake of profanity marking his passage.

After wiping away his tears of laughter, Raper took me for a ride. The experience made me an enthusiast, although the vision that this slow, ungainly machine would play a key role in our Pacific offensive was not then evident. Shortly after, when a call came for volunteers to form an amphibian tractor detachment, Vic Harwick and I submitted our names. In April, Harwick received orders to Dunedin, Florida where the first production amtracs were being built.

Meanwhile, I stayed in Quantico where, in early May, the 5th Marines arrived and I was given command of the mortar platoon in M Company of the 3rd Battalion. Despite my position, I quickly discovered I had more to learn than to teach. The first time I was called upon to drill the company, I found the men in formation with their machine guns and mortars mounted on carts. These two-wheeled vehicles were each pulled by two Marines, who were now standing at attention with the cross bars, called drags, resting on the ground at their feet.

I had never drilled a unit with carts. My confusion must have been clearly evident to Gy. Sgt. Harold Smallwood when he saluted smartly and in a loud voice turned over the company to me. Then, in a quiet tone intended for my ears alone, the Gunny, whose glance could chill any lieutenant's soul, added, "Man drags, lieutenant, man drags." I returned his salute and repeated his magic words. To my relief, the Marines reached down and raised the drags to waist height ready to move at the next command. The drill went off without further incident.

In June, I received unexpected orders to the amtrac detachment at Dunedin. There, I would find a different approach to duty. Until now, it had been impressed upon me that everything I needed to know was to be found in manuals, orders, and other like documents. My short time in the 5th Marines had confirmed that knowing the book was the way to get ahead. Amphibian tractors,

THE ROEBLING "ALLIGATOR", CULEBRA, PUERTO RICO, 1941
First Roebling amphibian tractor procured by the Marine Corps undergoing tests under the direction of Capt. Victor H. Krulak prior to Fleet Exercise 7 (FLEX-7). The results of the tests were incorporated in the design of the militarized version which became the Landing Vehicle Tracked, Mark 1 [LVT(1)].

USMC Photo

LANDING FROM HIGGINS BOATS, NEW RIVER, JULY 1941

First Division Marines reembarking into 36-foot Higgins boat during exercises off Onslow Beach. The spoon bow and tunnel stern of the boat facilitated beaching and retraction, but the troops still had a long drop over-the-side and always got their feet wet.

USMC Photo

however, were too new and untried to feature in any publications. It was to be our task to uncover the capabilities and limitations of these machines and acquire the data that would eventually find their way into print. This process, which continued for much of the Pacific War, invited initiative and led to commands beyond what could normally have been expected.

✳ ✳ ✳

Research and development of landing craft had been hampered in the 1920s and 1930s by lack of funds. Little could be done to acquire landing boats until 1940 when the Navy tested a craft designed by Andrew Higgins for use in the Louisiana bayous and found it well suited to beaching and retraction. Later modified and fitted with a bow ramp, it became the model for the personnel and tank landing craft used throughout the war.[4]

During this same period, the Marine Corps became interested in a tracked vehicle built by Donald Roebling for rescue work in Florida's swamps. In 1940 he was offered $20,000 for a test model, which he built for $16,000. While he was trying to return the unspent balance, an unprecedented effort, the Marine

Corps tested the prototype and let an initial contract.[5] The first production unit was delivered in July 1941 to Maj. William W. Davies who, a few weeks before, had settled his Amphibian Tractor Detachment of four officers and thirty-seven men in the Dunedin Hotel.

* * *

Major Davies, affable and understanding, was perfectly suited to head a detachment rapidly expanding with regulars, reserves, old China hands, and fresh recruits. Capt. William Enright, who would command the first amphibian tractor company to join the 1st Marine Division, was a graduate of the Naval Academy. Capt. Henry Drewes, who would have similar responsibilities in the 2d Marine Division, was a reservist. Among the senior noncommissioned officers, 1st Sgt. Arthur Noonan had left a wife in China, while M. Sgt. Thomas Hunt had a family on Guam. This made for endless sea stories that added to the pleasures of our days and evenings.

The situation at the Dunedin Food Machinery plant was no less agreeable. I vividly recall Donald Roebling sitting on the floor surrounded by blueprints and pieces of metal discussing construction details with engineer James Hait and Marine Gunner Carl Cagle. Cagle, a wise old-timer who knew the ways of men and machines, had an uncanny ability to translate what we were learning in swamp, offshore waters, and rolling surf into terms that Hait could use to improve amtrac design. The outbreak of war would force retention of the original design to maintain production and delay the new model until 1943.

A break in this routine came in October when 2d Lt. Louis Saltanoff and I were ordered to New Orleans for a two-week indoctrination at the Higgins boat works. The time went by in a flash. We spent each morning on Lake Ponchartrain operating various types of boats and each afternoon observing how they were built. We spent our evenings together at New Orleans' renowned restaurants, having agreed we could not afford both fine dining and feminine companionship.

Near Thanksgiving, we received word that the 1st Division, established at New River, North Carolina since August, had been authorized to activate Company A of the 1st Amphibian Tractor Battalion with personnel from Dunedin. The roster, headed by Captain Enright, included 2d Lt. Charles Manterfield, myself, and forty-three enlisted men. The captain placed me in charge of the detachment that would leave Dunedin by train on Monday, December 8, 1941. My farewell calls on December 7 were progressing pleasantly until I arrived at Major Davies' quarters and found a stunned group listening to an excited voice on the radio repeating that the Japanese were bombing Pearl Harbor. Our conversation, when it resumed, was about friends in Hawaii and whether they were among the casualties being reported.

COLUMN OF LVT(1)S, DUNEDIN, FLORIDA, SEPTEMBER 1941
Column of LVT(1)s engage in a formation driving drill in a nearby coastal area. Victor Croizat left rear of vehicle No. 9.

USMC Photo

The next morning, still shocked by events, I marched the detachment to the railroad station where a large crowd had assembled in response to the word that the Marines were on their way. By the time our train arrived, we had kissed all the girls and many of their mothers and shaken hands with all the men. We also had packed away quantities of candy and cookies and a few bottles of good bourbon. It was a grand send-off, in sharp contrast to New River the next day, where a tent camp under the grey skies of winter silently awaited.

✳ ✳ ✳

I had not expected North Carolina to be so cold. To withstand the freezing temperatures we stacked newspapers under our thin pads, slept in our sheepskin coats, and bathed only for an infrequent night out. New River was remote and public transportation was next to nonexistent. I had a car and could get away, but few of the young enlisted men could break the routine of camp life. The division did what it could to provide movies and other entertainment in a tattered circus tent, and newly built shanties, clustered on the approaches to the base, provided more earthy distractions at a price. By the time the United Services Organization (USO) discovered New River, we were preparing to mount out.

The troops really never had time to worry about liberty. The war had intensified the efforts already being made to bring units up to strength, train, and prepare for deployment. This was being done in accordance with established practices, but these did not exist for amtrac units. The arrival of grizzled Coast Guard surfmen with three vintage landing boats added to my challenge when I was ordered to use them to familiarize infantry with the firing of boat-mounted machine guns. We also were to help clear brush for a separate camp at Peterfield Point, a wooded peninsula jutting into New River Inlet. This remote location typified the camps we would become familiar with during the war, close to water and far from anything else.

Sometime in this confused period, I obtained a short leave during which Sgt. John Morgan and I drove to our homes in Boston. There, I loaned him my car for his wedding and a brief honeymoon. In late January, 2d Lt. Glenn Maxon and I took two boats on a fifty-mile reconnaissance to find a suitable boat-firing range. We then obtained several Lewis machine guns dating from World War I and set about fitting our old boats for their new duties. When all was ready, I moved with my six crewmen into an abandoned cottage on the beach near our anchorage. We survived the bitter cold thanks to an enterprising surfman who found a supply of moonshine in nearby Fulchers Landing.

Our existence, though marginal, was bearable. What was not, was the sight of German submarines attacking our coastal shipping. The captain of the H.M.S. *Bedfordshire*, based at Morehead City, agreed that the twenty-four British trawlers assigned to augment our Navy's antisubmarine capabilities were gravely insufficient to protect our shipping.[6] When we later received several tank lighters, we naively asked the Navy about fitting depth-charge racks on their sterns. On being told how foolhardy that would be, we reluctantly abandoned our vision of supplementing the country's antisubmarine warfare forces.

While I was pursuing my semi-independent life on the beach, the amtrac community back at Peterfield Point was growing. On February 16 the 1st Amphibian Tractor Battalion was formed and I was called back to take command of its Headquarters and Service Company. Since the amphibian tractor was first looked upon as a seagoing truck, the amtrac organization was based upon that of a motor transport battalion, with its companies attached to the infantry regiments for operations. This allowed amtrac units considerable independence, even as their dispersal complicated the exercise of command.

Our work hours were long. My twenty-third birthday at the end of February was marked only by the loss of a ramp from a tank lighter I was bringing up New River Inlet. Despite such occasional adventures, my duties kept me far closer to battalion headquarters than I liked. Hence, I was pleased when I was given command of Company A on April 1. Shortly after, we were alerted for deployment overseas and my company was attached to the 5th Marines. Then in mid-month, while seeing to the loading of railcars with equipment and supplies destined for embarkation ports, I received a late birthday present, my promotion to first lieutenant. I thought this a fine going-away gift.

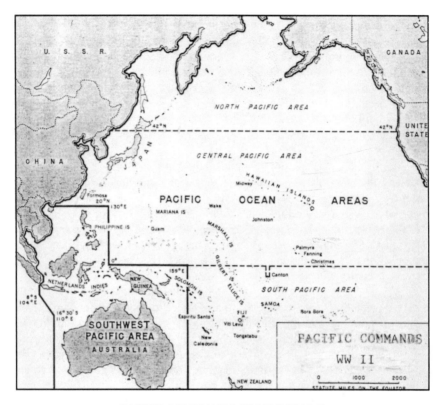

PACIFIC COMMANDS, WORLD WAR II

Shortly after the United States entered the war against Japan, American and British leaders met in Washington to chart the course of future operations. Among the decisions made was to create a supreme war council, the Combined Chiefs of Staff (CCS) which, on January 10, 1942, set up an Allied command comprising American, British, Dutch, and Australian forces (ABDA). But Japan's advances were already too sweeping for ABDA to be effective and it was dissolved on March 1. Two days later, the CCS divided responsibility for operations in the Asian-Pacific region between Britain and the United States by a north-south line running between Java and Sumatra. The United States Joint Chiefs of Staff (JCS), in turn, designated a Southwest Pacific Area under General Douglas MacArthur, and a Pacific Ocean Area (POA) under Adm. Chester Nimitz further divided into North, Central, and South Pacific Areas. Later, when it was decided to invade the southern Solomons with naval forces, the South Pacific Area boundary was shifted eastward.

USMC Map

When I boarded the *Wakefield* at Norfolk on May 18 with the advance echelon of the division headquarters and the 5th Marines, my first sergeant greeted me as captain. I refused to believe him until he produced the promotion list. Accompanying me were Charlie Manterfield, my easy-going executive officer, and ninety-five of my men; the rest were with our thirty amtracs loaded on other ships. Once aboard, I dropped off my gear in the two-person cabin I was to share with four other officers and went off to see to my men. I found them scattered about the ship and spent the rest of the day gathering them into one compartment. That was small comfort, however; all troop compartments had four-bunk tiers.

We sailed at midnight on the nineteenth. The next morning the sight of the cruiser and several destroyers that were to escort us to Panama eased my concern over German submarines and encouraged me to enjoy the present. The near future also appeared relatively calm. We looked forward to a sojourn in New Zealand, which rumor had as our destination. We crossed the equator on May 29. King Neptune imposed various indignities on all, with particular attention to General Vandegrift and our senior officers. This was one occasion when rank did not have its privileges.

As we left the spring of the northern hemisphere for the autumn of the southern, the weather worsened. Finally, on June 14, 1942, after a seemingly endless twenty-six days at sea, we arrived in Wellington. Once back on solid ground, we expected to assemble our equipment and supplies, settle into campsites, and get on with our training. The word was that we would be in New Zealand for the rest of the year. That was not unreasonable. The sorting out of division cargos commercially loaded on eleven ships was a big job. Then too the division's units needed time to hone their talents and become combat ready.

Despite the cold rain and mud, my company took to its new surroundings in excellent spirits. On June 19 we left Wellington to set up camp at Paekakariki, thirty-five miles away. By the twenty-third, I had all of my amtracs at Petone, a convenient site on the bay where I had been authorized to store my heavy equipment, safeguarded by a detachment of twelve men under Lieutenant Manterfield. The remainder of the company was busy getting our camp squared away and preparing defensive positions along the beach to allay New Zealand concerns over possible Japanese incursions.

On the twenty-fourth, I went to Petone to pay the men. Later, I joined Charlie Manterfield in an early movie in town and the added drama of an earthquake. Fortunately, we did not have to evacuate the theater, but a severe aftershock found me in the blacked-out city, its streets being littered by chimney bricks and shards of plate glass, with a frightened woman desperately gripping my forearm with both hands. In fiction this would have been the beginning of a romantic affair, but when the tremor stopped she melted back into the darkness without having uttered a word.

I started the drive back to camp, musing over her identity and smiling at the thought of how abruptly my first adventure in New Zealand had ended. A few miles on, I found the road blocked by a landslide and had a moment of panic because General Vandegrift was to visit our camp the next day. Then I remembered he was quartered in Wellington and would have to travel the same road in the morning. Relieved, I went back to Petone to spend the night. I was first on the road when it reopened and on hand to receive him when he arrived. His satisfaction at the way we were shaking down was evident in his parting remarks. The next day, he was to call on V. Adm. Robert L. Ghormley at his headquarters in Auckland and discover that our settling in was about to go into reverse.[7]

Two

GUADALCANAL: THE REALITY OF WAR

W inston Churchill called the Japanese attack against the United States an
act of suicide, and so it would prove to be. That truth was well hidden in
the first five months of 1942, when Japan was conquering an empire reaching
from Malaya to the Philippines and occupying a chain of island outposts to
protect its prize. In response, our Navy struck the Marshalls and Gilberts in
February, and in April, Lt. Col. James H. Doolittle led fifteen Army bombers off
the carrier *Hornet* and set course for Japan.

These actions, though daring, did little damage. The carrier air battles over
the Coral Sea in May and the American victory at Midway in June were more
significant, but even they did not end Japan's expansion. That would be accomplished at Guadalcanal in a campaign conceived in uncertainty, prepared in
haste, and launched with misgiving.[1] Fortunately, those of us who carried the
action never lacked confidence. We had been living with uncertainty since the
start of the war, and our time in Wellington had made us familiar with haste and
confusion. We also were largely ignorant of the events that had brought us so far
from home.

New River had been isolated and our time there filled with demanding
duties. The long sea voyage to New Zealand and our brief stay had added little
to our knowledge of the outside world. In addition, the Guadalcanal campaign
was a drama without script, where the trials of the landing force were multiplied
by lack of support from senior commands and an impossible time constraint.
General Vandegrift had first learned of the operation on June 26, twelve days
after his arrival in New Zealand with the lead echelon of his command; the
second echelon would not begin arriving until July 11, just eleven days before
we were to sail into combat.

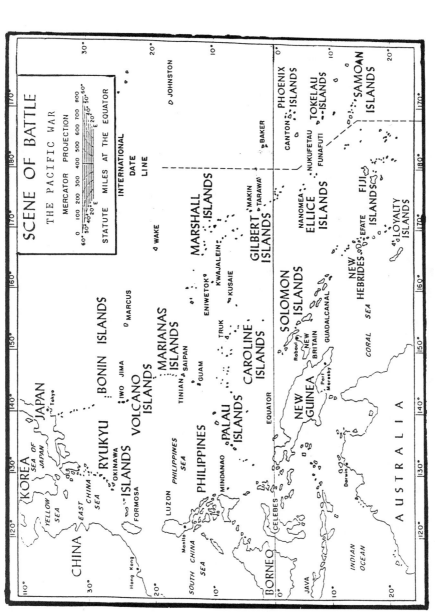

SCENE OF BATTLE

THE PACIFIC WAR

MERCATOR PROJECTION

STATUTE MILES AT THE EQUATOR

INTERNATIONAL
DATE
LINE

PACIFIC THEATER OF OPERATIONS, 1941–1945

USMC Map

This was a prelude to chaos. All arriving ships had been commercially loaded to make maximum use of their cargo space. Now, each had to be unloaded and its cargo sorted and distributed before being combat-loaded to meet the anticipated needs of the assault units. Much of this occurred around the clock on Aotea Quay in a cold rain after Marines replaced the stevedores who, not knowing our purpose, had balked at working long hours without their usual tea breaks.

My first warning of our impending move had come on June 30 at a meeting on the *American Legion* when we were told of an imminent amphibious exercise. The timing puzzled us since we still lacked equipment and had not yet settled into our camps. My suspicions grew when I heard my company with its amtracs was to be aboard ship by July 4. Lastly, instructions for drawing ammunition and storing our personal belongings left no doubt this was not an exercise. We made our schedule, though our amtracs lacked radios and machine guns. These were in second echelon shipping and were not issued until July 18. We had to complete our final preparations for combat in the crowded holds of the ships at sea.

Given the frenzied tempo of activities, I was not able to gain more than a superficial impression of Wellington's old world character, or a passing acquaintance with any of its attractive young women. In compensation, I was far too busy to think beyond tomorrow, and fatigue assured deep sleep even during several hectic nights when, too tired to find my billet, I slept on a pile of burlap bags in a dockside warehouse on Aotea Quay.

Lt. Col. Frank B. Goettge, the division's intelligence officer, had to gather what information he could from local sources. Unfortunately, data from Gen. Douglas MacArthur's headquarters in Australia were lost in transmission and the memories of former residents of the islands proved fallible. Goettge's frustrations were matched by those of our logistics and operations officers. It speaks well for the entire division staff that the impossible conditions under which they labored were so little evident at the briefing General Vandegrift held for his unit commanders on July 19, 1942.[2]

This tightly guarded meeting at the Cecil Hotel began with the general announcing the "privilege" accorded to our division "to mount the first American offensive against the Japanese." As the echo of that bombshell died away, he added, "Beginning on 7 August, we will land on the islands of Guadalcanal, Tulagi, Gavutu, and Tanambogo in the lower Solomons." Then, the murmurs began: "The Solomons? Where the hell are they? He can't mean the Solomons in Chesapeake Bay!"

Frank Goettge next shared his meagre information. His data on Guadalcanal provided only a general picture of an interior of abrupt jungle-covered heights cut by precipitous streams and coastal plains with orderly coconut groves and tall kunai grass. Maps were unreliable, even to mislocating a major elevation and confusing the Ilu and Tenaru Rivers. Knowledge of the Japanese was equally poor. We were told they had taken Tulagi on May 4 and started to build an airfield on Guadalcanal in July. Beyond that, it was estimated there were some 2,000 enemy in the Tulagi-Gavutu-Tanambogo area and perhaps 5,000 on Guadalcanal, numbers which, happily, were to prove excessive.

Lt. Col. Gerald C. Thomas, our operations officer, followed Goettge with the welcome news that the 2nd Marines plus the 1st Raider, 1st Parachute, and 3rd Defense Battalions would join us in time for a rehearsal. General Vandegrift would direct the landing on Guadalcanal; his assistant, Brig. Gen. William H. Rupertus, would direct the assaults on the lesser islands. Reassuring information on naval gunfire and air support was added. Lt. Col. Randolph McC. Pate, the logistics officer, ended by reminding us we would have only half our motor transport, few supplies, and little engineer equipment. Our landing force would indeed be lean.

Three days later we sortied in brilliant sunshine against a spectacular panorama of snow-clad mountains, a magnificent scene I looked upon as a happy omen. Once New Zealand had faded in the distance, we could collect our thoughts and turn to our unfinished tasks. We borrowed Navy paint and converted our shiny amtracs to a dull gray; we also tested and mounted our machine guns and installed our radios. Finally, each man turned to his personal preparations, accompanied by incessant chatter, usually about home.

Our calm seas were not to last. My diary for the twenty-third states, "Saw my first movie...all about South Sea Islands...I wish they were like Hollywood shows them...but, I know they aren't." On the twenty-fourth, I wrote, "Ran into foul weather...rain and heavy wind...sea rough. Going north, destination unknown. We have 26 ships together..." On the twenty-fifth I noted, "We are going to the Fiji Islands...sounds like a dream..." The next day I recorded our rendezvous with the remainder of our force "...about 50 to 60 ships together now. Carriers evident, also one battleship...ships as far as the eye can see." We shared a feeling of exhilaration from this majestic assembly, but the day would turn grim for our general at a conference for senior commanders aboard the *Saratoga*.

We of the rank and file were not aware of what transpired, which was just as well. Admiral Ghormley "found it impossible to give the time necessary for travel." This left the chair to Rear Adm. Frank Jack Fletcher, the Expeditionary Force commander, who repeated his opposition to the venture and announced his intention to withdraw his carriers two days after we landed. Vandegrift was aghast that he would lose air support so early and Rear Adm. Richmond K. Turner, our Amphibious Force commander, stormed that he could not unload the ships in that time. Fletcher, unmoved, remained adamant.[3]

The rehearsal on the twenty-eighth through the thirty-first was of mixed value. Navy gunners and airmen practiced on targets and Navy crews tuned up their boats. We Marines, however, found the beaches fringed in coral and only a scattering of troops got ashore before the Navy, unwilling to risk damage to its boats, cancelled further landings. The amtrac companies gained little from the exercise. I headed for the beach with four amtracs, but we were called back before we could land. The rehearsal's greatest value was the liaison it permitted among commanders and staff officers, many of whom were meeting for the first time.

On July 30, Colonel Hunt called the engineer company commander and me to meet with him. He was troubled by the river to the right of the beach where his regiment would land. It would hinder an enemy counterattack during the landing but become an obstacle when his troops pushed inland. "Couldn't we use amtracs as pontoons for bridges?" he asked. We discussed how to do so and decided to fit three amtracs with wooden platforms to serve as roadways. The next morning, I joined our volunteer crews and the engineers in the hold of the *Bellatrix* and got the project started.

Late that same day we set course for our final destination. The only excitement came from news that three Marines had unintentionally been left behind and we had gained a correspondent named Richard Tregaskis. The lanky Tregaskis, who later told his story in *Guadalcanal Diary*, was a welcome addition to our wardroom bull sessions. Even more, I enjoyed my quiet conversations with 1st Lt. Ralph Cory, our Japanese language officer, with whom I often toured the weatherdeck before turning in. Cory had been a consular officer in Japan and his commentaries lessened the profound ignorance I shared with many others about Japan.

✳ ✳ ✳

I was struck by the beauty of Guadalcanal as it appeared early on August 7, 1942. Years later, I was surprised to read that the dour Admiral Turner had also found the island to be "a truly beautiful sight." The serenity of the scene left me unprepared for the business at hand. Then, the opening salvo from the *Quincy* brought me back to reality. I suffered a momentary flashback to the romance of the South Seas when a sailing schooner on course for Tulagi emerged from the morning mist, to be blown out of the water moments later by a destroyer. The shore bombardment, meanwhile, intensified. Then, Turner signaled the classic "Land the Landing Force," and I went from observer to participant...my tension lessening with the activity.

The transports soon had their boats in the water and my amtracs were not far behind. Then, out of the congestion of landing craft circling in the transport area, three formed column and headed for shore; Sgt. Ralph Fletcher was making

INNOVATIVE AMTRAC BRIDGES, GUADALCANAL, SEPTEMBER 1942

USMC Photo

sure his bridge detachment would land just behind the lead units. At the same time, Sgt. Harry Elliott, who was to select and mark bridge sites with red target cloth, boarded a boat laden with riflemen scheduled to be in the first assault wave.

Our landing on Guadalcanal was unopposed, and Sergeant Fletcher soon had his amtrac bridges in position. I followed with my command group and found things ashore calmer than I had expected. There was little evidence of our bombardment. Some Marines were even enjoying a swim before moving off behind the cautious assault units. By noon the deceptive tranquility had begun to change. Colonel Hunt was urging his men forward as the 1st Marines streamed ashore, followed by artillery, tanks, trucks, and other equipment and supplies. Turner was by then doing all he could to hasten the unloading.

Vandegrift had a Pioneer Battalion to handle arriving cargo, but it was overwhelmed by the rapidity and haphazard way in which supplies were being dumped ashore and by the shortage of motor transport. All amtracs not being used to move artillery or keep the advancing infantry in water and ammunition were pressed into service to help clear the beach. The first air raid, near mid-day, and another two hours later were directed at the ships but would have been more effective if they had hit our beach. By then the congestion was so great unloading had been temporarily suspended. The hectic day eventually ended in a sleepless night, caused largely by trigger-happy Marines shooting at shadows and coconut crabs.

We returned to our duties at daylight. The infantry began encountering scattered resistance, but by evening they had overrun the unfinished airfield and main enemy camp and reached the Lunga River. The advance had also uncovered a windfall of supplies and equipment that would soon prove invaluable. Corp. Raymond Cantrell, whose amtrac was with the infantry, also found several cases of Asahi beer. After random sampling "to ensure it had not been poisoned by our wily enemy," he came to share his fortune with us. His manner left no doubt his testing had been thorough.

Late that second afternoon, Japanese planes struck again. A destroyer and transport were hit and later lost, as were seven of our aircraft. This convinced Admiral Fletcher to advance his withdrawal. Ignorant of this, I settled in for the night under an amtrac. The Japanese, meanwhile, approaching with a strong cruiser force, catapulted reconnaissance aircraft. The noise and beginning rain woke me. Then, soon after midnight, flares broke the darkness and the thunder of naval gunfire began. I watched with concern, but when the guns fell silent, I regained my poncho, believing our Navy had done well.

The bad news the next morning that one Australian and three American heavy cruisers had been lost, was partially offset by the failure of the Japanese to attack our transports.[4] My concern grew when I saw our ships getting under way, with unloading still far from complete. As the sea gradually emptied, I began to feel abandoned. That night, while I waited for sleep, I realized that our ships had represented safe havens and that this reassurance, though never voiced, had helped counter the uncertainties confronting us. Now, we were alone, with limited resources, in the midst of an enemy whose measure we had yet to take. Still, I did not question our eventual success; nor, in the months that followed, did I speak with anyone who did.

The only good news that day came from across the channel. The landing of the Raiders on Tulagi had been unopposed, but coral had kept their boats from beaching. After wading ashore and meeting the enemy inland, they had needed another twenty-four hours to secure the island. The later landing of the Parachute Battalion on Gavutu and Tanambogo had met an alerted enemy and casualties had been heavy. However, with help from the 2nd Marines, the islands had been secured on the ninth. We were left with 10,000 men on Guadalcanal and another 6,000 on Tulagi and the adjacent islands. These, with the supplies and equipment landed in two days, made up the force that was to defy the Japanese, whose abandoned materiel and provisions were now essential to us.

GUADALCANAL, SEPTEMBER 1942

Marine patrol prepares to move out in captured Japanese Army trucks to assembly point from where movement into the interior will begin.

USMC Photo

The withdrawal of the carriers made early completion of the airfield imperative.[5] Considering an attack from the sea the major threat, General Vandegrift assigned his infantry to defend the beaches and his support units to cover the inland approaches to our perimeter. Our amtrac battalion moved to outpost positions on the Lunga on August 15. This did not end requests for transport services. However, once units settled into their positions, such calls lessened. This was fortunate since our amtracs were rapidly breaking down. By then, we too were beginning to feel the effects of short rations, the absence of creature comforts, and an enemy whose ships and planes owned the seas and skies around us.

Zero fighters had looked us over on the tenth and, on the twelfth, the airfield was bombed in what became an almost daily event. The twelfth also saw the impetuous Goettge embark a lightly armed patrol of intelligence personnel to investigate a prisoner's report that there were Japanese near the Matanikau River who wanted to surrender. Landing after dark, the patrol had come under heavy fire and all but three were killed. The survivors had made their way back by swimming and crawling along the shore. When I heard of the tragedy, I was saddened to learn Ralph Cory and Capt. Wilfred Ringer, with whom I had shared shipboard life, were among the missing.

That memorable August 13 also introduced me to naval gunfire. A Japanese submarine shelled our area three times and two air raids added further excitement. The bombing, while earth-shaking, was impersonal. The sharp crack of the sub's gun, however, made me feel I was its chosen target. We suffered no damage, but it offended me to see off-duty Japanese sailors calmly doing their laundry, while their gun crew tormented us and we could not hit back.

Vandegrift's five Marine infantry battalions, deployed on frontages twice the normal, were now patrolling beyond the beachhead to gain warning of enemy moves. A particularly successful patrol led by Capt. Charles H. Brush, Jr. set out on August 19 to investigate reports of a Japanese force to the east. They surprised thirty Japanese laying telephone wire. As Charlie later related, a search of those killed yielded accurate maps of our positions. "Given the evidence," he concluded, "I assumed we had run into the advance party of a large force preparing an attack."

Brush's report caused the entire command to be put on alert. Our battalion was to reinforce beach defenses on the twentieth, but we were not called and I was at the airfield when Maj. John L. Smith landed his Wildcat and taxied to where I was standing. In the past thirteen days we had learned Japanese dominated skies were unfriendly and come to view all aircraft as hostile. Smith's arrival meant the monopoly was over. My enthusiasm was boundless until Smith opened his canopy and asked, "Where are the billets?" I was chagrined I could only reply, "You can dig your hole wherever you like!"

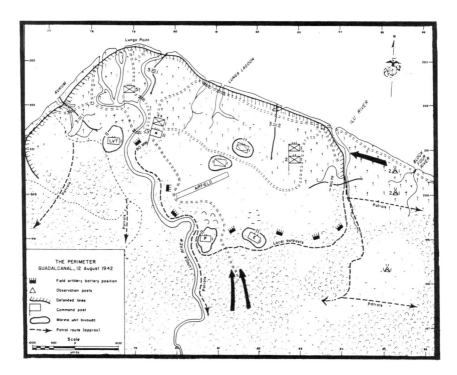

MARINE PERIMETER, GUADALCANAL, AUGUST 1942

The initial perimeter established on Guadalcanal had the 1st Marines deployed along the beach on the east, and the 5th Marines deployed on the beaches in the west. The Amtrac (LVT), Pioneer (P), and Engineer (E) Battalions covered the inland approaches. Note: Dark arrows indicate major Japanese thrusts as follows:

Night of August 20/21, Ichiki force struck 2d Battalion, 1st Marines on Ilu River (Misnamed Battle of the Tenaru)

Nights of September 12/13 and 13/14, Kawaguchi force struck at raider/parachute battalion positions on Bloody Ridge

Nights of October 24/25 and 25/26, Maruyama force struck at Bloody Ridge held by 1st Battalion. 7th Marines and 3rd Battalion, 164th Infantry

USMC Map

Sometime after midnight, listening posts across the misidentified Tenaru River (actually the Ilu), began to fall back before a strong enemy force whose presence was dramatically confirmed by a severely wounded native constable. Sgt. Maj. Jacob Vouza, tortured and left for dead, had staggered miles over jungle trails to reach the 1st Marines' positions to report just before the enemy struck. The Marines met the assault with an awesome volume of fire, in which a solo of sustained three-round bursts by a .50 caliber machine gun sounded strangely reassuring. The climax began at daybreak when Colonel Cates dispatched a force to hit the enemy flank and drive him into the sea. When the fight ended, the beach in front of the Marines was packed with enemy dead, a grisly monument to the code of Bushido.

The Marine air units had helped in the Battle of the Tenaru and, on the twenty-fourth, had joined carrier aircraft to turn back a Japanese force coming to reinforce Guadalcanal. Three days later, fourteen Army fighters moved to Henderson Field, followed by the remainder of Marine Air Group 23. This eased the immediate threat, but we had not been unscathed. Our beachhead had been bombed the twenty-fourth and twenty-fifth and, on the night between, several destroyers had hammered the perimeter, scoring a hit on my company bivouac and frightening us out of a night's sleep. Air raids were over quickly, but naval gunfire seemed to go on forever. It became nerve shattering when one was alone in a foxhole unable to fight back.

The importance of Henderson Field was now clear to both sides and battles for its control would rage through September, October, and into November. Although our situation remained precarious, I heard no voice of despair. Others beyond my hearing had some doubts over the outcome, however. In mid-September Vandegrift, on learning he could no longer count on support from Ghormley, asked Lt. Col. Merrill B. Twining, his assistant operations officer, to prepare a plan to withdraw the command to the hills. But Twining never prepared it, Vandegrift never asked for it, and we in the ranks never heard of it. The one thing we knew was that there would be no early reply to our question, "When is the Army coming to relieve us?"[6]

The men had landed with only their packs; the officers with a seabag. These, and minimal camp equipment, provided few amenities, none able to keep off the frequent downpours.

Most of us slept on a poncho laid on the ground under a rude shelter. A few had cots, but these were little better. The important decision each night was whether to sleep in a wet foxhole or unventilated dugout or to remain at ground level, knowing you had to run for a hole when the fireworks started. Whichever one chose, one slept fully clothed with helmet and weapon nearby. Fortunately, I had tennis shoes to wear at night, instead of my heavy boondockers.

MARINE CHEFS CONVERT JAPANESE SAFE INTO OVEN, SEPTEMBER 1942

USMC Photo

Eating was equally simple. Overcooked Japanese rice with a meat or vegetable complement was delivered to the troops on the line in containers or served at the company galleys twice a day. This was consumed with the spoons we carried in our breast pockets. A New Zealand ship once left us some canned sheep's tongue. I thought it a welcome change: those who did not, still ate their share. The menu was supplemented by heart of palm from trees blasted by shellfire. Some Marines tried fermented coconut milk but found the resulting dysentery disastrous when wearing one-piece utilities.

The only break in our rice diet came when we furnished working parties to unload the infrequent ship that slipped in. Proper timing could lead to a real meal; more often a can of fruit juice or candy was the prize. The alternative was to participate in operations outside the perimeter when individual rations were issued. My preference was the D ration, a chocolate bar treated to keep it from melting, which usually satisfied the day's needs of the tense stomach that went with such excursions.

The first mail arrived in September and the infrequency of deliveries that followed denied us the pleasures of anticipation. Still, shortages of food and mail were only inconveniences. The frequent casualties were tragic. One time, a damaged Japanese bomber jettisoned its load onto a luckless Marine working party. Another time, two inseparable amtrac crewmen occupying adjacent fox-holes died in a shower of fragments from a tree burst. Other losses were caused by Washing Machine Charlie, our name for the single planes that came at night to drop bombs fuzed to detonate on impact.

Such hazards were shared by all, but the infantry paid most heavily in the bitter battles for the airfield. Nor were the Japanese our only enemy. The coastal grasslands and densely forested interior were hostile, as were the humidity and heat. Even more dangerous were the insects. We did not all have mosquito nets and those who did found they hindered emergency runs for foxholes. Hence, we all fell victim to the Anopheles mosquito and, since we received no Atabrine until mid-September, malaria became virtually universal.[7]

❊ ❊ ❊

On September 6, I was ordered to the 5th Marines. Combat casualties and the adverse effects of our island paradise were creating vacancies in our infantry units. I was not surprised at the transfer. I was surprised, however, to find myself back in the 3rd Battalion commanding M Company, whose mortar platoon I had briefly led fifteen months before. My new beach front command post included a white bathtub and well. This singular luxury attracted many visitors who were welcome if they had their own soap. I also inherited a Japanese 75mm infantry howitzer and 400 rounds of ammunition which guests could fire at enemy troops taking their evening swim.

This accomplished little more than avenging Washing Machine Charlie's visits. A comfortable three-hole privy with overhead cover near a trail used by aircrews proved as attractive. It was relatively rainproof and a good place to gather scuttlebutt on the air war. In addition, the nearby regimental bulletin board posted summaries of naval, air, and ground actions. This official word, though helpful, was never as amusing as the endless rumors.

Because my weapons were deployed with the rifle units, I had few opportunities to get to know my men. I did better with the headquarters personnel and soon learned to appreciate burly 1st Sgt. Max Stamps, while renewing my respect for *Shorty* Smallwood, whose experience with machine guns in World War I served us well. I also was reminded that frontline troops just dig in and

OFFICERS OF COMPANY M, 3RD BATTALION, 5TH MARINES, WITH TRADE GOODS GUADALCANAL, NOVEMBER 1942

Rear Rank from left: Lt. Joseph Bishop .... anti-tank platoon
Andrew Haldane .... machine gun platoon*
Ralph Hornblower .... company executive officer
Howard Goodman .... machine gun platoon**
James Naylor .... mortar platoon
Front Rank from left: Lt. Frederick Gold ..... new replacement for Lt. James Barrett,
machine gun platoon
Capt. Victor Croizat .... company commander
Lt. James Flaherty .... battalion officer

*   *Haldane killed in action at Peleliu as rifle company commander*
** *Goodman killed in action at Cape Gloucester as rifle company commander*

keep their surroundings natural. The gun crews lived somewhat better in emplacements protected by coconut logs or dug under the jungle's larger trees. However, these too were fighting positions and contained little more than the prescribed water, rations, and ammunition needed for two days of unrelieved combat.

I was well pleased with my command, but increased Japanese activity indicated trouble ahead. Our conversations when we gathered for a final evening cigarette invariably turned to a discussion of our situation. We accepted that the Battle of the Tenaru had been but a beginning and expected the Japanese would soon make another try for our airfield. General Vandegrift confirmed this view when he ordered the infantry on Tulagi to Guadalcanal and increased patrols.

RAIDERS OCCUPY BLOODY RIDGE, GUADALCANAL, SEPTEMBER 1942

Native scouts lead Raider unit into ridge complex overlooking Henderson Field a few days before the attack by the Kawaguchi Brigade. Note the open nature of the ridges and the proximity of the jungle, which provides excellent concealment for all movement even in daylight.

USMC Photo

Our Cactus Air Force, using the code name for Guadalcanal, had grown to sixty-four Army, Navy, and Marine aircraft. These became the 1st Marine Aircraft Wing on September 3, when Brig. Gen. Roy S. Geiger arrived to take command. Geiger, a World War I aviator known to extract all that men and machines were capable of doing, would have ample occasion to live up to his reputation. The opening move was made by the Raiders and Parachutists under Lieutenant Colonel Edson, who landed east of our perimeter near Tasimboko on September 8, and drove off an enemy unit that abandoned quantities of supplies, weapons, and equipment. Edson judged it was the rear echelon of a large force moving inland. As later events confirmed, a Japanese brigade was then marching toward the airfield. Edson destroyed what his men could not carry and returned.

As evidence of an imminent attack continued to accumulate, Edson was directed to deploy the combined Raider and Parachute battalions on a ridge a mile south of the airfield. Late in the morning of September 11, a large bomber force blasted them as they were digging in. That same afternoon Admiral Turner arrived and delivered Ghormley's assertion that he could no longer support us on Guadalcanal. After dark, Japanese ships worked us over. The only happy note in that miserable twenty-four hours was the rumor attributed to Turner, that our 7th Marines would soon join us. We never learned of Ghormley's negative assessment.

My diary adds that two 5-inch guns were emplaced near my command post that day. Things worsened during the days that followed. Bombers again dropped their loads over the ridge at mid-day on the twelfth. That night brought heavy rain and with it a cruiser and two destroyers to support a series of probing attacks against Edson's position. The Marine line was dented but held. At daylight on the thirteenth Edson hit back, recovered the lost ground, and spent the remainder of the day strengthening positions to be ready for the coming onslaught.

My night had been less threatening, but the naval gunfire and reconnaissance aircraft had kept us all awake. The next day brought a succession of air raids and strafing runs by adventuresome Zeros. Worse arrived after dark when seven destroyers opened fire on the airfield, while a strong force hit Edson's positions. In the murderous night that followed, Edson's men, with reinforcements from the 5th Marines, broke five major Japanese attacks. This desperate action brought into play every weapon available; a sword-wielding Japanese officer even reached the division command post before being killed by the sergeant major. The Battle of Bloody Ridge ended at daybreak when the Japanese left the field and six hundred dead. Edson earned the Medal of Honor.

We were not initially aware of the critical nature of the action on the ridge, nor did we have much difficulty defeating the Japanese diversion against our positions on the afternoon of the thirteenth. However, the naval bombardment that night was unusually personal. It began with an opening round exploding over my shelter and showering fragments through the cot I had just left. The Japanese infantry resumed their efforts the next day and continued probing through the night of the fifteenth. Although they never penetrated our line, they inflicted thirty-five casualties on our battalion before being driven off. The acrid odor of wood set afire by our mortars and artillery and the sight of abandoned bloody bandages remain vivid memories.

At daybreak on September 18, I was on the beach to welcome Lt. Col. Lewis B. Puller's 1st Battalion, 7th Marines. I had only enough barbed wire for one double apron fence across our battalion front, so had opened lanes and stationed guides to direct Puller's people through it. But, as I feared, they were in a hurry to get into the action and my wire soon began to suffer. Much annoyed, I sought out Puller, explained the shortage of wire, and asked he curb his men. He cocked an eyebrow, turned without comment, and barked to his executive officer, "Go straighten things out!"

He then looked back at me and asked, "How're things going here?" "We had quite a fracas a few days ago," I replied, "but it's quiet now." Puller nodded, and I continued, "Of course, you can count on air raids during the day and naval gunfire at night." Turning toward the supplies piled up on the beach I added, "Those are likely to attract attention." The colonel, saying something like, "I suppose so," went on to other things. I too went on to other things. Toward evening I strolled to where Puller's men were bivouacked.

When I saw no foxholes, and the new arrivals setting up mosquito nets and undressing, I suggested a bit of digging might be worthwhile. However, they preferred the comfort of tough talk and ignored my warning. I shrugged off my concern, returned to my command post, and turned in. Shortly after midnight, an enemy destroyer opened fire and was promptly engaged by our 5-inch guns emplaced nearby. The duel was played out by the light of flares, which revealed Puller's half-naked Marines frantically digging with helmets, canteen cups, entrenching tools, or their bare hands. It is the only time I remember laughing while being shelled.

With the arrival of the 7th Marines, Vandegrift reorganized his defenses by deploying his infantry battalions on the flanks and inland limits of our perimeter and assigning the beach defense to the engineer, pioneer, and amtrac units. Our 3rd Battalion, already positioned to cover the western flank, was not moved. However, Colonel Edson, recently promoted and now commanding our regiment, directed adjustments in the trace of our front. A reconnaissance to determine where to reposition my machine guns revealed it would be difficult to obtain acceptable fields of fire.

I reported my concern to Maj. Robert O. Bowen, my battalion commander, and was told, "Colonel Edson decided where the front should be and I am not going to argue with him." When I insisted, he told me I could take the matter up with the colonel myself. The implication that I was a fool to do so was clear. Edson's reputation discouraged argument, but I had the innocence of the young and set off for regimental headquarters. Edson acknowledged my presence with an icy stare and I blurted out my misgivings. When I paused, he picked up his helmet and said, "Let's go look!"

In the hours that followed, we viewed the battalion front from the enemy's side, and I came to appreciate the difference made by a few strands of wire. On one side was the reassurance of being within one's own lines. The side I walked with the colonel was the unknown, where the unwary were targets for enemy small arms and the unannounced could easily fall victim to friendly fire. Yet, the colonel moved with confidence, and I could do no less. He impressed me with his eye for terrain, and I was pleased when my views survived his scrutiny. When I returned to report I had the colonel's approval to make adjustments to our line Major Bowen looked surprised.

That night, as I mused over my tour with Edson, I remembered asking Capt. Walter McIlhenney, of the Tabasco Sauce family, about the remarkable fire discipline in his rifle company. Walt had explained, "I just tell my Marines that whoever fires a shot at night without having blood or a body to show me in the morning spends the next night in front of the wire with only a knife!" I now understood why his way of enforcing discipline was so effective.

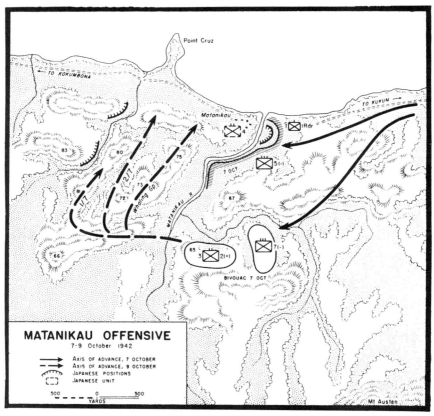

HAMMER AND ANVIL OPERATION, GUADALCANAL, OCTOBER 1942

USMC Map

Work on our new positions was demanding. The men were showing the effects of too many sleepless nights, too few meals, and never-ending tension. Yet, all turned to with remarkable willingness. The only grumbling came from Stamps and Smallwood who were unhappy when I insisted that our fire coordination role required that our command post be near battalion headquarters. They were relieved we had moved when Japanese artillery zeroed in on our former home in mid-October and leveled it, probably in retribution for the many swimming parties we had interrupted.

On the 2nd of October, our battalion was directed to prepare for an operation near the Matanikau River. This was cancelled before morning but four days later we were alerted again, and that time we went. The operation, to be coordinated by Colonel Edson, was in response to reports of 150mm howitzers being landed by the enemy near Kokumbona, a village east of the Matanikau, from where they could directly threaten our airbase. Division decided to clear the area by having two battalions follow the coast to the Matanikau, where they would form an anvil against which three other battalions on a wide sweep inland would drive the enemy.

Our battalion, part of the anvil, left at first light on October 7, advancing through untended coconut groves with our mortars and machine guns on carts dispersed throughout the column. We expected an easy walk, but in mid-morning, already heavy with humid heat, our advance guard began receiving fire. Two hours later, our lead companies were up against cleverly concealed positions, later identified as a bridgehead the Japanese had established for their forthcoming offensive. The fighting continued all day, the progress of sweat-stained Marines seemingly measured in inches. Yet, by nightfall the Japanese had been compressed into a pocket backed against the river.

Edson, questioning our slow progress, had come to our battalion command post to see what the trouble was. What he found caused him to call for a Raider company to strengthen our right and to stay the night so he could personally direct the action. That same afternoon, the battalion executive officer called for me. I found him well forward studying the sandspit at the mouth of the river. Pointing out its merits as a crossing site, he told me to send him two machine guns to deny its use to the enemy. I suggested the guns would be too exposed that far forward and recommended they be emplaced where they could be better protected. He reminded me that any Japanese move would be made after dark, so the gun crews needed to be close enough to hear.

I had misgivings but, accepting the validity of his point, I started back. While making my way through the brush bordering the beach, the smack of bullets cutting nearby twigs caused me to shelter behind a tree. When I cautiously looked around, I saw a line of haggard Marines making their way toward the enemy-held river. Nothing about the scene was spectacular, yet the memory of those weary men advancing steadily with rifles at the ready will forever bring to mind the determination that shaped the campaign.

Once the leading rank had passed, I continued on my way to the battalion command post where I arranged to send the gun section forward. Then, as it was getting dark and beginning to rain heavily, Colonel Edson called for me. I found him in the soggy gloom trying to use the telephone; our radios had been rained out and the battalion phones were working only intermittently. He told me to position four reserve guns to cover the clearing nearest the river to hold off any enemy attempt to break out.

While my supply sergeant went to the rear for the guns, I gathered four crews from headquarters personnel. The dark and rain delayed this simple task, but I was ready when the guns arrived. I assembled the men, gave one a gun, another a tripod, and a third two boxes of ammunition and repeated the process four times. I then told each man to hold onto the man in front and set off in the lead, feeling my way along the trail toward the river...the blind leading the blind.

I knew Japanese were nearby, and when I stumbled over a body my adrenaline hit a high; it lowered slightly when I identified a field shoe worn by a drenched Marine too startled to speak. I patted the foot saying, "Okay Marine, we're moving ahead," and continued until I thought I was at the edge of the clearing. I then turned left and peeled off my gun crews at regular intervals. That done, I returned to the command post, reported to the colonel, and settled into a waterlogged foxhole with my mortar platoon phone, the only wire link still working, to my ear. The colonel continued on the same circuit throughout the remaining hours of darkness.

That endless night was among the most miserable I have ever spent, on Guadalcanal or any place else. The drumbeat of rain on the jungle canopy was punctuated by the sounds of our Marines seeking to convince the enemy we were trying to cross the river and those of the enemy trying to break out of his encirclement. There was a great deal of stirring about and some deadly encounters. In one action, a Japanese officer rushed one of the guns I had sent to cover the sandspit, severely wounding two of its crewmen and killing the third. Such incidents were all too common during this night of terror and courage. Yet, I never heard Edson hesitate, raise his voice, or indicate he was not master of the situation. It was an incredible performance.

With morning, I returned to the guns I had positioned and was not surprised to find them badly placed and their crews woefully bedraggled. I resited the guns and had the men stand easy, anticipating the colonel would come by. However, Edson's concern was to drive off the Japanese remaining on our side of the Matanikau. That took the rest of the day. Finally, at nightfall, the surviving enemy charged the Marines and a vicious hand-to-hand fight brought matters to an end. Meanwhile, the envelopment force was preparing to sweep around the enemy rear.

As our operation neared its climax, Vandegrift learned that the enemy was preparing another offensive. He decided he could complete the envelopment but not set up the patrol base he had planned. The final maneuver, carried out the morning of the ninth, annihilated a large enemy force. We all then returned to the perimeter. Our battalion reached its bivouac late that afternoon. After seeing to my men, I lay down in our muddy dugout and slept a straight twenty hours. Our respite would be brief. The day we returned from the Matanikau, Gen. Harukichi Hyakutake, commanding Japan's 17th Army, had arrived on Guadalcanal to take charge of our funeral. We were soon to make sure he did not succeed.

Confronted with the enemy's continuing buildup, Admiral Ghormley ordered the 164th Infantry to Guadalcanal. When it landed on October 13, it brought Vandegrift's command to 23,000 men; Japanese forces were then nearing 20,000. Our Army's reception that Tuesday was remarkable, even for Guadalcanal. At noon, while the soldiers were still being ferried ashore, twenty-two bombers dropped their loads over Henderson Field and Fighter One, a newly completed airstrip nearby. Two hours later, fifteen bombers repeated the performance. Then, Japanese artillery opened fire. This was not unexpected but its timing could not have been worse.

When word spread of the Army landing, Marines with souvenirs had rushed to the beach looking to trade for candy, fruit juice, or that new delicacy called SPAM. The bartering and friendly banter was ended by the Japanese artillery fire. Despite the interruptions, all soldiers were ashore that afternoon. That night the Imperial Navy added its welcome in a lavish production. Just before midnight two battleships opened fire and spent the next ninety minutes blasting Henderson Field and vicinity with more than nine hundred 14-inch shells. It was a convincing demonstration of how well large caliber naval guns compete with thunder, lightning, and earthquakes. Not to be outdone, Japanese aviation added its fury to the angry night, but we agreed that the round went to the navy gunners.

I was in our dugout listening on the phone to our observer who called, "On the way," whenever the battleships fired. I would repeat his words for all to hear. We then would listen for the slow whoosh whoosh of the rotating shells passing overhead and brace for their earth-shaking explosions. After some time, I could hear an echo which sounded like "Over there, over there." I called out, "What do you mean over there?" An apologetic voice replied, "The shells are asking 'which way' 'which way' and I'm just telling them where." Despite this levity we were badly shaken. This was literally true, for many of us experienced uncontrollable tremors we could not conceal.

With daylight came the damage assessment. Henderson Field was out of action. Six pilots were among the forty-one American dead and two thirds of our planes were lost. Later that morning, another enemy force was sighted heading for Guadalcanal with six transports, but our battered planes were unable to keep them from reaching the island or save us from a bad night of pounding by eight-inch guns. Dawn brought groggy Marines the sight of enemy transports discharging troops and supplies at Tassafaronga.

I was at our observation post watching the activity when General Vandegrift appeared. My "Good morning, Sir!" was lost in the sudden roar of Zeros maneuvering over our heads and the crack of our antiaircraft guns. Suddenly, a Marine standing behind the general cried out, his finger split by a steel shard from a shell burst overhead. The general, whose bald pate had been shining in the sun, quietly put his helmet back on. A few minutes later when the wounded Marine had been led off, I told the general I had seen a small cache of aviation gasoline in a nearby ravine. He smiled, "That's good news!" and added to his aide, "Get it to the airfield at once."

Ground crews, meanwhile, worked feverishly to assemble enough aircraft for a strike and by mid-morning our dive bombers had sunk one of the Japanese transports. Next, Army bombers set two more ships on fire. Then came a remarkable performance by Maj. Jack Cram in General Geiger's personal amphibian patrol plane. I was startled to see the lumbering PBY pass at eye level heading toward the Japanese ships. Before my mind could accept what my eyes were seeing, the plane disappeared in a confusion of smoke and gunfire.

Seconds later, when a violent blast erupted, I assumed it had been hit, but I was wrong. Cram had scored. He slowly emerged from the black cloud and turned for home, leaving another Japanese ship ablaze. Jack Cram won the Navy Cross for his courage; I thought he deserved the Medal of Honor. Finally, that night we were visited by two Japanese cruisers and two destroyers bent on revenge. These pumped more than a thousand shells into our battered perimeter, leaving us only twenty-seven planes able to fly.

October, thus far, had been totally miserable, except for the arrival of the 164th Infantry, which enabled Vandegrift to deploy two Marine battalions to outpost positions on the Matanikau. Unknown to us at the time, the Japanese were planning to launch an offensive on October 18 with a main effort striking from the south and a diversionary attack at the Matanikau. Full of confidence, their main body marched off into the jungle to learn again that the adversities of terrain and weather made a shambles of their timetable. Inevitably, their attack was delayed, first to the twenty-second, and then to the twenty-fourth.

While the enemy was fighting the terrain, I continued daily visits to my machine gun positions. I set off on the nineteenth as usual, but was delayed by an air raid. When the ALL CLEAR sounded, I decided to cut through a ravine leading directly to our left flank. I was picking my way through the dense cover, when a shadow on the ground became a Japanese soldier with rifle and bayonet...who jumped up, turned, and ran. I was momentarily immobilized, then drew my pistol, fired, and missed what was again a shadow. The Marines nearby joined in a search but we found nothing, I hated to admit that, though the top pistol shot in my class, I had missed such a target. Later, I realized the incident was a convincing demonstration that indoctrination and training may limit, but not always dispel, human frailty.

The day of my adventure, the enemy main force was still out of range of our patrols. The only threat Vandegrift knew of was in the west, where we had driven off a Japanese probe on the twentieth. Still concerned with Japanese artillery and not realizing that the Japanese initiative in our area was a diversion, Vandegrift reinforced his Matanikau position. As a consequence, Chesty Puller's 1st Battalion was spread thin over the ridge that Edson had so ably defended the month before. That was precisely where the Japanese main effort hit on the night of the twenty-fourth. The enemy drove forward with his usual determination but the attack was disjointed, hampered by heavy rain and failed communications. The Marines, progressively strengthened by the 164th Infantry, held, but only just.

At daylight, the exhausted Japanese paused to regroup. For the equally weary Americans, that Sunday offered no respite. Our aviation was grounded because rain had made the runways unusable. Japanese bombers and fighters roamed overhead, but our planes could not take off to drive them away until evening. Nor could they deter the Japanese artillery or the destroyers that further contributed to our misery. After dark on the twenty-fifth, Japanese infantry, drawing on untapped reserves of strength, returned in a vigorous attack, but once again their lack of coordination doomed them. With daylight, the survivors faded away, leaving 3,500 dead on the battlefield. The American losses were one tenth those of the Japanese.

As this drama was unfolding ashore, a major Japanese naval force was heading for Guadalcanal to join in the Army's victory. The armada was intercepted by the *Enterprise* and *Hornet*. The engagement, though costly, was inconclusive, but the Japanese commander, on learning there was no ground victory to celebrate, prudently retired. October had been a trying month, yet no resolution was in sight, and the physical and emotional drain was telling. Then came the electrifying news that Vice Adm. William Halsey had relieved Ghormley on October 18. A week later, President Roosevelt directed the Joint Chiefs to reinforce Guadalcanal. The word that Bull Halsey was aboard did as much for our morale as the flow of resources that followed the President's directive.[8]

We were now moving toward a climax. November would bring the decision. It is of note that this was accomplished before the outpouring of American industry could reach the battlefield. The Japanese outnumbered us in ships and equalled our strength in the air and on the ground. Afloat, their gunner's night vision was as good as our early radar, and their torpedoes were superior. In the air the Zero was unmatched. On the ground, many of our weapons, beginning with the 1903 rifle, were older than the Marines using them, and we had neither the knee mortar nor the infantry howitzer of our opponent. Yet, the Imperial Navy was driven off, the skies cleared of enemy aircraft, and Guadalcanal secured.

Our battalion, within the perimeter since October 9, endured a succession of bombings and shellings. On the twenty-second, I had my first bout with malaria. The chills and fever abated without treatment, and I went with the battalion when it moved west of the Lunga on the twenty-sixth. There, we exchanged the beaten zone of bombs, naval gunfire, and shore-based artillery

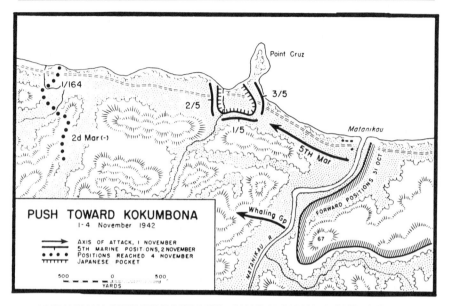

MATANIKAU OFFENSIVE RESUMED, GUADALCANAL, NOVEMBER 1942

USMC Map

for the relative quiet of snipers and discreet enemy patrols. Five days later, we were back on the Matanikau, preparing to move out on another attempt to drive the enemy's artillery beyond range of our airfields.

We crossed the Matanikau at daylight, following the 2nd Battalion on bridges our engineers had put in place during the night. Our progress was impeded only by a series of steep ridges, jungle-filled ravines, and enervating heat. However, the 1st Battalion advancing along the coast ran into trouble and we were ordered to help. By evening we had a strong Japanese force contained from the south and east and, at dark, we settled in for the night. I was happy I traveled light, with two canteens of water, a poncho on my pistol belt, and the usual chocolate bars in my map case.

The next morning, the 2nd Battalion was ordered to close the gap to the west. Then, while the enemy was pounded by mortars and artillery, we slowly moved in. During this maneuver, while on the phone with I Company, I heard wild shouting and exclaimed, "What in hell was that!" In reply, I was told, "Captain Wells is leading a bayonet charge!" When I later asked Erskine what had prompted his action, he said, "We were being held up and I was mad." Then, wryly, he added, "If I had thought about it, I wouldn't have done it." The Silver Star he received was deserved.

Our advance that day was overtaken by darkness, but by noon the next day the pocket was cleared. The way was now open for the move to Kokumbona, but once again General Vandegrift's plans were thwarted. Confirmation of a new enemy buildup near Koli Point to the east forced him to send a battalion to investigate. It arrived the evening of November 2 to see fresh enemy units coming ashore, vital information that could not be relayed until the radios had dried out the next morning. Vandegrift responded by reinforcing the battalion in the east and pulling the units in the west back, except for two battalions left near Point Cruz and our battalion ordered to outpost the Matanikau.

During this move I saw Lt. Harold Kepnes, our battalion doctor, among a truckload of wounded. Hal, known for attending the wounded where they fell, had been shot in the throat. Although we had become inured to death, there were few dry eyes when we learned Hal had died before reaching the field hospital. While we were on outpost duty, our forces in the east struck at the Japanese moving inland for yet another offensive. The encounters were costly for the enemy. Five hundred men were lost during the relentless pursuit by Lt. Col. Evans Carlson's fresh 2nd Raider Battalion over one hundred and fifty miles of jungle trails.[9]

When operations in the east neared the end, Vandegrift resumed his advance in the west. However, on reports of yet another imminent offensive, he called all units back to the perimeter. We went into bivouac near the airfield and started work on secondary defenses behind the beach on the twelfth. That same day, the Army's 182nd Infantry arrived; the 8th Marines had come in the week before. The Japanese greeted the Army with a massive air raid. More serious, they dispatched a heavy bombardment group to hammer Henderson Field and sailed eleven transports for Tassafaronga. The bombardment group was turned back after a battleship was damaged and two destroyers sunk. When daylight came, I watched our flyers finish off the *Hiei* with satisfaction.

We spent the day working on our positions while Bill Kaempfer, whose company was nearby, turned his time to a more interesting project. Using Mercurochrome, he converted an old sheet into four *genuine Japanese battle flags*, which he swapped to visiting aviators for an equal number of bottles of liquor. A visit to a lime tree and a stop at our Japanese-built icehouse to get ice for a "malarial buddy" completed the ingredients for a punch party. It was a grand affair, ending in the unwise decision to undress before retiring. We were deep in sleep when a Japanese cruiser force began shooting. Seconds later, we were huddled in a wet dugout uncertain whether we were shivering from the night chill, malaria, or the crashing thunder of its eight-inch shells.

Our pilots were off early the next morning seeking revenge. They found it, hitting the two cruisers that had ruined our sleep. Then, shortly before noon, our aircraft found the eleven transports and sank seven in a shuttle action that continued throughout the remainder of the day. That night a battleship engagement provided a spectacular light and sound show, which ended at dawn with four transports beached within sight of our five-inch battery.

I had joined Capt. Andre Gomez on his observation tower just as the range to the nearest transport was called as 17,900 yards. Andy explained, "My firing tables only go to 17,500 yards but when the tubes warm up they'll shoot the extra distance." Sure enough, he opened fire and when the paint began to smoke, the shells began to hit. The remaining transports were soon eliminated by a friendly destroyer and a succession of planes. Unfortunately for us, many of the troops were already ashore. I later asked a young Marine what he thought of more Japanese landing. Without hesitation he replied, "It's just that many more we'll have to kill!"

He was only partially right. The 1st Marine Division was soon to be withdrawn and whatever remained to be done on Guadalcanal would fall to others. Rumor of our relief became official on November 29 and, on December 9, General Vandegrift turned over command to Maj. Gen. Alexander Patch. That same day we boarded the *President Jackson* and left Guadalcanal without regret. It was hard to believe that for us it was over.

Three

SETTING THE RISING SUN

S omewhere in the unofficial annals of the Corps there is a song about the raggedy-ass Marines on parade. It could well have been written of the 5th Marines lined up on the beach at Guadalcanal early on December 9, 1942, waiting to board the *President Jackson.* We were indeed ragged, but four months on a bitterly contested island at the trickle end of a long supply line had given us the assured manner of seasoned troops. This was evident in the men's demeanor. A few cracked wise, more were serious, but all were wary, scanning the sky for enemy planes and the ground for folds that offered protection, just in case. No one wanted to be the last casualty on the last day on the island.

And so we embarked, quickly but without incident. Later, when Guadalcanal had disappeared, we could begin to think of what lay ahead. We believed we were returning to New Zealand, where we had left our personal effects and many of our illusions, but we soon learned Brisbane, Australia was our destination. We would have preferred Wellington but were glad to accept civilization wherever offered. Meanwhile, we were again eating with a knife and fork and sleeping without violent interruption, although I had put my mattress on the deck the first night when I found my bunk too soft. I had no trouble enjoying a hot shower.

Beyond these amenities, we gathered to talk of our experiences. Most revealing were the personal thoughts given voice in the gathering dusk when guards came down. We spoke of the tension we had lived with and of each day seeking the courage to fight our fears.[1] We repeated tales of our young Marines who had found the inner strength and will to prevail and agreed they surpassed the recruiting poster images of fearless fighters, who are rare in real life. We also spoke of our enemy's valor and thought it had been misused by their leaders, whose arrogance blinded them to our strength. In short, as we searched for meaning in what we had endured, we found our sea voyage a restorative.

44

✳ ✳ ✳

When our ship reached Brisbane, we were delighted to see a large gathering of young women and a fleet of trucks awaiting our landing. Our rush to the side caused the ship to take a serious list, which we expected to relieve quickly by going ashore. To our dismay, however, word was piped there would be no liberty. Our first day in Australia ended as it had begun...aboard ship. The next morning the trucks were back, not to take us on liberty, but to Camp Cable, a remote site forty miles from Brisbane.[2]

There we were issued Army khaki and introduced to huge ant hills, bounding wallabies, and not much else. The camp was primitive, the weather tropical, and the insects maddening. This, added to the debilitating souvenirs we had brought from Guadalcanal, soon had sickbays and hospitals overflowing. Happily, I was spared and able to devote myself to arranging a proper send-off for Gunny Smallwood, who was leaving for home. I was finding a solution elusive until I discovered that the Australian Army issued beer. Thereafter, all I had to do was borrow a U.S. Army truck from a rear echelon unit and draw the ration for the unit identified by its markings. I am confident our Army brothers would have been happy to help, had they known of our need.

My memories of Brisbane cannot differ much from those of other Marines. The only event worth sharing was on my first liberty, when I entered a pub and found Australian soldiers blocking my way to the bar. Their loud remarks about the bloody Yanks coming to enjoy their women were all in fun but impossible to ignore. I turned to the biggest of the lot and, in a voice for all to hear, announced, "I'm a Marine just down from Guadalcanal. I haven't spoken to any woman in over five months, but right now I have a helluva thirst." I then held up my hat with its Marine Corps emblem and added, "You can tell a Marine by this insignia and by his belt buckle, which opens beer bottles." The big Aussie roared in laughter, picked me up, set me on the bar, and called the bartender to "fill this Yank up."

The end of the year brought word our division would move to Melbourne, where the better climate would help restore its fitness. At the same time, sixteen of us from the 5th Marines received orders to the new Command and Staff Course at Quantico before going on to leaven new units. I had enjoyed Brisbane's laid-back atmosphere and warm hospitality; I was a reluctant passenger on the *West Point* when it sailed for Melbourne on January 8, 1943, with the division. Three days' liberty there added to my conviction that Australia was a suburb of paradise. We then began the long passage to San Francisco, which we reached the final day of the month.

We arrived wearing Army khaki, our winter uniforms and other personal effects somewhere in Wellington, never to be recovered. We bought new uniforms and, while waiting for a train to take us east, began to enjoy the city.

During this interlude, I noticed people staring at our newly authorized shoulder patch with the name Guadalcanal on it. When I reached home I discovered Guadalcanal had become an epic and those of us who had been there something between ghosts and gods. The clue was my father's greeting. My mother could generate tears at will, but, when my father met me with an unexpected embrace, I knew the occasion was special.

I knew no one in Boston and spent my leave enjoying my family. There were, however, two events of note. First, I called Bill Ringer's father to tell him of Bill's part in the ill-fated Goettge patrol. It was a difficult conversation. Mr. Ringer's voice was anguished and my answers halting as I sought to lighten his sorrow. Officially, Bill was missing in action and, when I could not affirm from personal observation that he was dead, his father said in a husky voice, "I still believe Bill will turn up." I was disturbed at the torment he would endure until he could accept that his son would never return.

The other event of note was an attack of malaria that thoroughly frightened my mother. When I found the strength to make it to the Navy Yard dispensary for quinine, the duty doctor wanted to know why. In reaction to my explanation he promptly drew a blood sample. Moments later, I was forgotten while he and the staff admired my plasmodia through the microscope. Eventually, I got my medication, completed my leave, and left Boston on a southbound train.

I was looking at the uninspiring landscape out of New York when I noticed a man studying my 1st Division patch. He came over and introduced himself as George Mead. The name immediately recalled an engaging lieutenant I had met on the *Wakefield* who had been killed in an early action. I replied, "I knew your son, we were on the same ship from Norfolk to Wellington." Obviously moved, he asked me to join him and his wife. Assuming they wanted to hear about their son's last days, I told them our story. I spoke of New River and how crowded we were on the *Wakefield*. I went on to mention the emptiness of the Pacific, the boredom, the welcome hilarity when crossing the equator, the granular texture of powdered eggs, and the endless speculation of what lay ahead. I recalled Wellington and the welcome prospect of six months there.

Then, when I spoke of our disbelief at orders to load out, the Meads leaned toward me, anxious to capture every nuance. I knew my story now concerned matters their son could not have written about because of security. I led them from New Zealand to the Fijis and Guadalcanal, and finally told them that George had been killed after he had gone forward to replace the fallen leader of a heavily engaged platoon. I ended, emphasizing how saddened we all had been by his death. In this way, I tried to replace some of the pain of their loss by pride in their son's deep sense of duty. I like to believe I succeeded.

✳ ✳ ✳

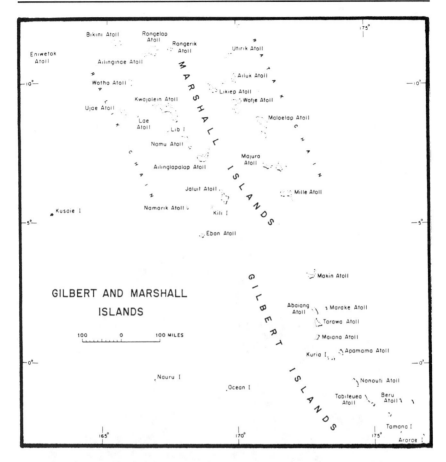

Bikini Atoll · Rongelap Atoll · Rongerik Atoll · Utirik Atoll

Eniwetok Atoll · Ailinginae Atoll

—10°—

Wotho Atoll · Ailuk Atoll

Likiep Atoll

Kwajalein Atoll · Wotje Atoll

Ujae Atoll

Lae Atoll · Lib I · Maloelap Atoll

Namu Atoll

Ailinglapalap Atoll · Majuro Atoll

Jaluit Atoll · Mille Atoll

Kusaie I · Namorik Atoll · Kili I

—5°—

Ebon Atoll

GILBERT AND MARSHALL ISLANDS

Makin Atoll

Abaiang Atoll · Marake Atoll

Tarawa Atoll

100   0   100 MILES

Maiana Atoll

Kuria I. · Apamama Atoll

—0°—

Nauru I

Ocean I · Nonouti Atoll

Tabiteuea Atoll · Beru Atoll

Tamana I

165° · 170° · 175° · Arorae I

GILBERT AND MARSHALL ISLANDS—GATEWAY TO THE CENTRAL PACIFIC

U.S. Army Map

The Command and Staff Course had the usual start-up problems, plus the insufferable wisdom of those of us just back from Guadalcanal. However, we finally admitted we had something to learn and the course continued in harmony. In June, I reported to the 23rd Marines at New River as a newly promoted major. The weather was better than it had been in late 1941, but the confusion was familiar. My duties were minimal. I had joined the regiment for its move to Camp Pendleton where it would become part of the new 4th Division and I would move to its amtrac battalion. We left on July 3 on a train with no priority and came to appreciate the hardiness of the pioneers as we slowly made our way to southern California, which we reached nine days later.

AMTRACS BECOME ASSAULT VEHICLES
TARAWA, NOVEMBER 1943

Eighty-two of the one hundred and twenty-five amtracs used to land assault troops and supplies across the reef fringing Betio Island were lost to enemy fire.

USMC Photo

Our camp was again remote and liberty difficult. However, I expected little free time. On August 19, I was ordered to form the 4th Amphibian Tractor Battalion at Camp Del Mar on the coast. Time telescoped as new personnel arrived, equipment and supplies were readied, and a flexible training program established. I was too busy to mourn when Lt. Col. Clovis Coffman superseded me in command. Then, on November 20, 2nd Battalion amtracs crossed the fire-swept reef at Tarawa with assault infantry. Its commander, Lt. Col. Henry Drewes, was among its seventy-nine killed and missing; another hundred were wounded in the action. Maj. Henry Lawrence, who took over the battalion, later summarized the experience saying, "We went from shit-troops to shock troops in a helluva hurry." That transition would have an immediate effect upon my fortunes.

The invasion of Tarawa in the Gilberts had been deemed a necessary prelude to our entry into the Central Pacific. In preparation for the thrust into the Marshalls, our 4th Division had sent observers to Tarawa. On their return, they reported that a minimum of two amtrac battalions were needed to land the assault units of a division. The Commandant agreed. The evening of December 5, a fortnight after the seizure of Tarawa, I was called to division headquarters where Col. Walter W. Wensinger, the operations officer, handed me a dispatch.

When I looked up from reading the message activating the 10th Amphibian Tractor Battalion with Company A of the 11th Amphibian Tractor Battalion attached, he smiled and said, "That is your new command." Then, he added, "You'll be busy. The ships with the division's amtracs will sail the first week of January." A vision of the chaos at Aotea Quay flashed before me as the colonel explained, "Personnel from the 4th Battalion will provide the nucleus for your command; all units will then be brought up to strength. Unfortunately, you will have to set up a tent camp at the boat basin because the barracks at Camp Del Mar are full."

I left with my mind churning. The news was startling, as was the immensity of the problem of organizing a battalion and sailing within a month. I thought of the crews to be trained; the hundred and fifty amtracs we had to armor, arm, and prepare for combat; the coordinated planning with the units we would land; and the preparations for our own embarkation.[3] By the time I was back in my office, I knew the task was impossible...so I promptly set to work.

All sense of time disappeared. The long hours at Camp Del Mar were extended by meetings with the units we were supporting based some dozen miles inland. Further lengthening duty hours were the eighty-mile round trips to San Diego, where our working parties were preparing our amtracs for combat. Then, as if this were not enough, my malaria returned and I had to seek treatment. The doctor insisted I remain in bed for forty-eight hours under medication. If the chills and fever abated, he would return me to duty. If I did not respond, I would

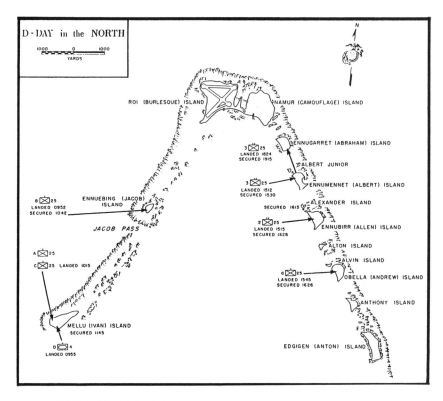

D - DAY in the NORTH

1000   0   1000
YARDS

ROI (BURLESQUE) ISLAND

NAMUR (CAMOUFLAGE) ISLAND

3 ⊠ 25
LANDED 1824
SECURED 1915

ENNUGARRET (ABRAHAM) ISLAND

ALBERT JUNIOR

3 ⊠ 25
LANDED 1512
SECURED 1530

ENNUMENNET (ALBERT) ISLAND

8 ⊠ 25
LANDED 0952
SECURED 1042

ENNUEBING (JACOB) ISLAND

SECURED 1615

ALEXANDER ISLAND

JACOB PASS

2 ⊠ 25
LANDED 1515
SECURED 1628

ENNUBIRR (ALLEN) ISLAND

ALTON ISLAND

A ⊠ 25

ALVIN ISLAND

C ⊠ 25 LANDED 1015

6 ⊠ 25
LANDED 1545
SECURED 1626

OBELLA (ANDREW) ISLAND

ANTHONY ISLAND

MELLU (IVAN) ISLAND
SECURED 1145

EDGIGEN (ANTON) ISLAND

D ⊡ 4
LANDED 0955

4TH MARINE DIVISION ATTACKS NORTHERN KWAJALEIN, 1944

Landings of 25th Marines by amtracs of the 10th Amphibian Tractor Battalion on islands in northern sector of Kwajalein Atoll, Marshall Islands on D-day, January 31, 1944. *Note: Main landings on D+1, February 1, 23rd Marines landed by 4th Amphibian Tractor Battalion on Roi Island, 24th Marines landed by 10th Amphibian Tractor Battalion on Namur Island.*

USMC Map

need prolonged treatment and lose my command. I settled into bed and two days later was back at work trying to make up the lost time.

Our administrative and logistic difficulties were but a prelude to the complexities of our operational responsibilities. These had their origins at Tarawa, where positioning artillery on lesser islands to support the main landing had been rejected because not enough amtracs were available. My battalion would make this possible at Kwajalein, our objective in the Marshalls. There, on D-day, we would land infantry to clear four small islands to which we would then

AMTRACS ON LST WEATHERDECK, CENTRAL PACIFIC, JANUARY 1944

LVT(2)s on weatherdeck of an LST en route to the Marshall Islands in January 1944. The early model LSTs were fitted with an elevator to give access to the tank deck from which vehicles were driven off the ship. These elevators were too short to accommodate an amphibian tractor, and a wooden ramp was built on the elevator up which the amtrac was driven to cant it sufficiently to clear the elevator opening. This was difficult to do in daylight, when the ship was alongside a dock, and far harder at night, when the ship was rolling in heavy seas several miles off an enemy-held beach. This was but one of the reasons why the D-day landings at Kwajalein on January 31 were delayed for several hours. *Note: Ramp on elevator (forward).*

USMC Photo

bring in artillery. The next day, we would join in the main landings on the islands of Roi and Namur.[4] This scheme, easy to summarize, would prove difficult to execute.

A rare light note sounded just after Christmas when Maj. Warren H. Edwards, a friend from Dunedin, arrived at my tent on the back of a grinning sergeant. The sergeant, noting Warren's low shoes, had offered him a lift to avoid the mud. Majors and sergeants we might be, but we were all young enough to enjoy occasional horseplay. I told Warren I was pleased to have him as executive officer but that time was too short for him to get involved at Camp Del Mar.

I had him go directly to San Diego and see to our embarkation. Because our hundred and fifty-four amtracs could not all be accommodated on the tank decks of our six LSTs, we had to stow some on the weatherdecks.[5] This required using the ships' elevators, but they were too short. Warren solved the problem by building wooden inclines to cant the amtracs enough to clear the elevator openings. Driving an amtrac onto an incline in daylight with the ship fast to a pier was difficult; doing so at sea in the dark off an enemy-held shore would be judged at Kwajalein.

Six days into the New Year I left San Diego as I had Wellington, exhausted and relieved to be on the way. Still, I was troubled. The battalion lacked cohesion and our amtrac crews had little driving experience at sea. Moreover, although the officers had briefed each driver on his specific mission, I was worried over the troop transfer and landing schedules, whose execution depended on units as green as we. Fortunately we were young...I was the old man, though a month shy of my twenty-fifth birthday...and shared the lack of self-doubt that had seen us through Guadalcanal.

My tranquility was upset midway to Hawaii when 1st Lt. Clifford T. Huntoon, my battalion adjutant and censor, reported reading a letter in which one of our beardless Marines had written his mother that his platoon so disliked their officer he would probably not survive the coming operation.[6] Huntoon ended his report, "I know nothing of any conflict. I wonder what the kid's thinking about." To this, I replied, "He may be masking his fear with tough talk. Let me think on it. Meanwhile, keep this to yourself." After confirming the situation was as reported, I decided to replace the young Marine's unspoken fear with a real one and had him brought before me.

When he was marched in and halted at rigid attention, I stared at him in silence, mentally confirming he was indeed a frightened youngster. Without preamble, I read from the Articles for the Government of the Navy the offenses punishable by death. I then read the relevant passage in his letter, and said, "This is a direct threat on the life of your lieutenant and is grounds for trial by General Courts-Martial." By that time he had turned white. I let him stand and continued, "However, I do not intend to divert officers from their combat duties to try you. Neither will I put you ashore for trial in Hawaii. I will set this aside on your understanding that if anything happens to your officer I will see you tried for murder. Do you understand?"

Unable to find his voice, he nodded assent, awkwardly faced about and marched off. I reminded Huntoon the incident should remain between us and concluded, "The lieutenant will have enough to do without worrying about covering his rear." The sequel to the tale came twenty months later when the war had ended. We were recalling our impossible December in California and the trip to Hawaii when the lieutenant, by then a captain, spoke of an unexpected bonus he had garnered thanks to his serious efforts to know his men. "A Marine in my platoon began looking after me as we neared Hawaii. He was always bringing hot coffee or a can of fruit and even dug foxholes for me on Saipan and Iwo!" I thought it best not to explain; illusions are too few in wartime.

The slow trip to Hawaii helped our units shake down, but our routing to Kauai, when the transports with the rest of the division went to Pearl Harbor, denied us the opportunity to update plans with the units we were to land. The arrival of a load of steel pipe, chains, and grapnels was less important but more annoying. We had been required to fit twelve amtracs with 4.5-inch rocket launchers in San Diego. This supplementary armament, inspired by the new tactical role of the amtrac and well-intended, interfered with its troop-carrying function. Now, we were again to fall victim to good intentions.

Instructions revealed the hardware was to fit four amtracs with booms projecting forward fifteen feet, at the end of which a yardarm dangled grapnels to set off mines. Our amtracs were already bow-heavy with the armor we had added, and the boom would worsen their trim dangerously. Moreover, when launched down an LST's steep ramp, they would almost certainly sink. As WO Roscoe Hibbard, our assistant maintenance officer, put it, "You have to be ashore to hang that gadget on your amtrac, and by then your worries about mines are over, one way or another." I reported the problem but was directed to comply with instructions. I did so by having the boom supports welded on four amtracs and, when we reached Kwajalein, dropped the hardware overboard.

Reveille the morning of January 31, 1944, came early. After a quick breakfast at 0330, I stepped out on the upper deck into a wind-whipped blackness. Gradually, as the dark yielded to an overcast sky, I saw we were some six miles seaward of Ivan and Jacob, the small islands controlling the entrance to Kwajalein lagoon. By then the LSTs were launching their amtracs into the choppy sea, where they awaited the guide boats to lead them to the transfer areas to embark the troops. This could not have been more conducive to delays. I was disturbed by the wind and rough sea, which reduced visibility from the amtrac and could drown out the engine upon which the bilge pumps depended. I was equally concerned over delays in lowering the amtracs from the top decks.[7]

Capt. Edgar S. Burks' amtracs were an hour late landing troops on Jacob and had to work their way to the lagoon side of Ivan to land. Still, both were secured before noon, when Capt. Harry T. Marshall's company began shuttling artillery ashore. Burks' amtracs then returned to pick up the troops for the landing on Albert, while Capt. George A. Vradenburg was doing the same for the assault of Allen. Both islands were secured by mid-afternoon and Harry Marshall followed with the remaining artillery. Our amtracs were then to return to their ships, but neither Burks nor I knew that Lt. Col. Justice M. Chambers on Albert had orders to also land on Abraham. This, though successful, confused Burks' crews.

With five islands secured and artillery ashore, the drama of D-day should have ended. However, just then Rear Adm. Richard L. Conolly ordered the LSTs into the lagoon to save the amtracs a long passage for the main landings the next day. The immediate effect was to make it difficult for our wet, bone-weary amtrac crews to find their ships. Many amtracs did get back aboard, but some LSTs failed to burn recognition lights or turned away amtracs from other ships. Numbers of these ran out of fuel and sank; the luckier found refuge on friendly islands.

My day had been frustrating. As commander of all amtracs used on D-day, I should have been with the assistant division commander, who was in overall charge of the multiple landings. Had I been, I would have fared little better. He was embarked on a small subchaser and unable to compensate for

INVASION OF THE MARSHALL ISLANDS, 1944

Namur Island, Kwajalein Atoll, February 1. Marines landing from LVT(2). Normally amtracs would move inland before off-loading their troops, but while this avoided wet feet, it still required a substantial drop to the ground. The 8-foot height of the vehicle also made loading and unloading of cargo slow and wearing.

USMC Photo

the inadequacies of the ship-to-shore control organization. In the absence of other instructions, I had set up my command post on my LST. My radios worked well but those in virtually all amtracs failed and, as the hours passed, I found it increasingly difficult to keep up with events. By nightfall I realized many amtracs were unaccounted for. I reported this shortfall and was directed to use Harry Marshall's as necessary.[8]

After passing the word to Harry, I spent the rest of the night looking for strays and getting a count of amtracs embarked. I lost my voice in the process, an unwelcome development when faced with repeated challenges from trigger-happy sailors spooked by rumors of Japanese suicide boats in the lagoon. The next morning, Coffman had the same problems launching amtracs and transferring the 23rd Marines that we had encountered the day before. Meanwhile, we had assembled sixty-two amtracs; enough to load most of the 24th Marines' initial waves. Finally, when everyone was ready, the execute order was given. Despite the delays and ragged execution, the landings on February 1 succeeded and Marines were ashore on both Roi and Namur shortly before noon.

Naval gunfire had done its work so well that the 23rd Marines encountered only light resistance and Roi was secured before dark. Namur, a command and administrative center with many concrete buildings and areas of heavy vegetation, was more troublesome. Preparatory fires had done much damage, yet the enemy stubbornly resisted. The Marines' advance was further hampered when a demolition team set off a torpedo storage site whose blast caused us a hundred and twenty casualties. Namur was not cleared until noon on February 2. Despite the complexity of the landings, the adversities of sea and weather, and the inexperience of the participants, the seizure of the northern sector of Kwajalein was accomplished at one third the cost of Tarawa.

After landing the 24th Marines, division authorized me to assemble my amtracs on Allen. Though the island was battered, we were happy to leave the ships. I also found pleasure in the surf crashing on the reef and the vivid colors in the lagoon. Early one morning while in solitary enjoyment of the scene, Lt. Perry Ayres, our medical officer, joined me and we began to speak of recent events. Responding to my question about the effect on the men, Perry said, "It's hard to believe how well they performed. Three out of four crews operated amtracs over twenty-four hours the first two days. They not only covered long distances at sea, where it was difficult to maintain orientation, they braved the reefs and surf to make repeated landings on enemy-held islands. Yes, they did well."

On February 2, the day after we had moved ashore, Capt. Wilson L. Peck's company was assigned to the garrison force.[9] Two days later, the Army's 7th Infantry Division secured Kwajalein island at the southern end of the atoll. That same day, Coffman's 4th Battalion sailed for Guadalcanal with Harry Marshall's company. Harry, however, remained with me to replace Warren Edwards, who was evacuated sick. The conquest of Kwajalein gave us the vast lagoon now sheltering the armada that had brought us there. I looked on this display of power with awe, recalling how modest our resources had been at Guadalcanal. Yet, I was sobered at the thought of the miles of ocean and the many casualties still ahead.

In the days that followed, we busied ourselves salvaging the amtracs scattered over the atoll. While doing so, we tried to identify the probable causes for each stranding to decide what spare parts we should plan to carry with us and how to improve driver training. Hibbard, who was in charge of this activity admitted, "It wasn't too hard to figure out the mechanical failures, but it's not easy to discover what caused an amtrac to swamp. All you know for sure is that it was a helluva frightening moment!" This work continued until February 15, when we were ordered to embark our remaining amtracs and sail for Hawaii.

We made slow progress because one of the ships accompanying us had another in tow and the line kept parting. The delay did not trouble us, but our ship was low on fresh water and short of food, and the same dish of gray dehydrated potatoes kept reappearing. Fortunately, Perry Ayres had a small hoard of medicinal brandy he could prescribe to ease our worst moments. He also discovered a space between the ships' ramp and bow doors where water sprayed inside, much like a Jacuzzi. We joined him regularly until the ship ploughed through a mass of jellyfish, and Perry, sitting on the turnbuckle that secured the doors, exploded in violent action, slapping at his backside where angry welts were appearing. The sounds of the sea drowned out his language, as it did our unkind peals of laughter.

We reached Pearl Harbor on March 2 and moved into the Replacement Center. Near four hundred strong, with much heavy equipment, we overwhelmed the authorities accustomed to orderly personnel drafts. We all made the best of an unsatisfactory situation, but our three weeks there were wasted. The only consolation was the liberty in Honolulu enjoyed by all despite the early curfew. One of my battalion clerks had a special moment in a house on River Street. I heard him tell a buddy, "I had a helluva long wait in the street but finally made it inside where an old broad on the sack said 'It's three bucks for three minutes, put your money on the table and hurry up.' It was over so quick I didn't realize she had only one leg until I was back outside."

At the end of the month we loaded back on LSTs and the next day came ashore at Maalea Bay on the island of Maui, where the 4th Division had reassembled. We were welcomed by Capt. William E. Lunn, who had brought out our rear echelon and made a start at building our new home. Bill admitted that our barren tent camp bordered by thorn bush and canefields on the shores of the bay "wasn't much." We added what we could to make our lives more agreeable by converting a warehouse into a club for the men and encouraging the officers and noncommissioned officers to build their own. We also respected tradition and lined our streets with whitewashed rocks.

10TH AMPHIBIAN TRACTOR BATTALION BASE CAMP, MAUI, 1944
USMC Photo

Until the war, Maui had enjoyed a tranquil plantation economy and an easy life style. This had changed when the Army brought in garrison troops and the Navy established two airfields. The Marines now were adding 20,000 men to the transient population. All this had little impact on us in our isolated camp twenty-five miles from the rest of the division. We had plenty to do in preparing to mount out again and incorporating the lessons learned in the Marshalls into our training. We were also busy reconditioning our amtracs and modifying two: one as a retriever, the other a machine shop. I still did not know where we would go next nor when we would leave, but I had learned that time for preparation was a luxury I had yet to know and worked accordingly.

✳ ✳ ✳

Within six weeks we were back aboard ship and again sailing west. The target this time was the Marianas, a fifteen-island chain more than 3,500 miles beyond Hawaii. Admiral King had long favored a move against the islands, but it was not until Gen. Henry H. Arnold urged the acquisition of alternate bases

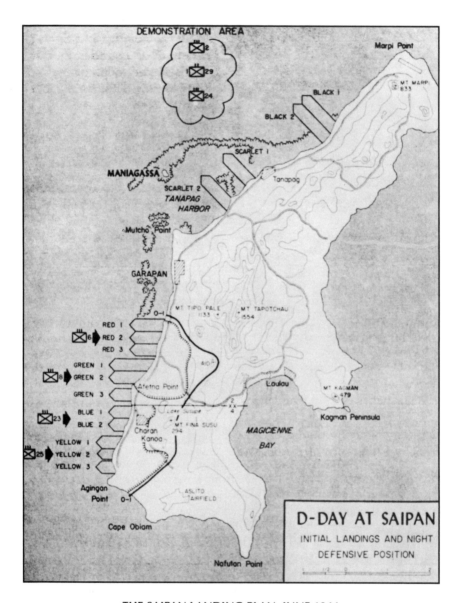

THE SAIPAN LANDING PLAN, JUNE 1944

The landings on Saipan in which 718 amphibian tanks and tractors from four Army and four Marine amtrac battalions carried 8,000 Marines across defended beaches in thirty minutes, represents the first mechanized amphibious assault in the Pacific War. However, the intent of reaching the high ground beyond the beach, the 0-1 line, in the initial movement ashore was not realized because the beach exits were blocked or could not be found due to heavy enemy fire falling on the landing areas.

USMC Map

for his B-29 bombers that the Joint Chiefs of Staff agreed. The campaign would begin with the 2nd and 4th Marine Divisions landing on Saipan on June 15 and later taking Tinian. Guam would be hit on the eighteenth by the III Amphibious Corps. Two Army divisions would be in reserve: the 27th afloat and the 77th on call in Hawaii.

Saipan's seventy-two square miles, one twentieth the area of Guadalcanal, ranged from broken wooded terrain in the north to rolling fields in the south, the whole dominated by Mount Tapotchau rising some 1,500 feet in its center. The Japanese garrison, estimated at 20,000 men, actually numbered 30,000. Even the lesser figure provided enough cause for concern. Saipan was the first line of defense of the Japanese home islands and would not be easily taken.

The assault would be made by four infantry regiments landing abreast on a 6,000-yard front across the reef-fringed beaches on the southwest side of the island. The 2nd Division, recovered from its bloodbath at Tarawa, would land north of the town of Charan Kanoa, while our 4th Division would land to the south. My battalion would land the 23rd Marines. Three amtrac battalions and one armored amphibian battalion were allocated to each division. This unprecedented number of amtracs, half of them Army, had led the command to propose a mechanized assault from the sea to the first commanding terrain inland. Maj. Gen. Thomas E. Watson, commanding the 2nd Division, thought this impracticable; Maj. Gen. Harry Schmidt was willing to have his 4th Division amtracs go for the high ground.

A greatly improved Navy ship-to-shore control organization, which included amtrac liaison officers stationed at key points, was most welcome. Also welcome was the assignment of support tasks to LSTs once their transport mission ended. All were to carry fuel for amtracs, one would provide maintenance facilities for each amtrac battalion, and three would serve as casualty reception centers for each division. These details reflected the lessons we had learned in the Marshalls and the two weeks of rigorous training we had shared with the 23rd Marines. A final two-day rehearsal with the 2nd Division, though marred by several accidents, straightened out remaining kinks.

At the conclusion of the rehearsal we were ordered to West Loch to make final preparations for departure. The LST I was on reached the Loch last. This did not trouble me, for I had earlier given orders to get all amtracs ashore immediately upon arrival for a final servicing. It turned out to be the best order I ever gave. When we got in, Bill Lunn and I set off for the 6th Service Depot for spare parts. When we were heading back in the late afternoon, we saw a cloud of smoke ahead which appeared to come from burning canefields. As we got closer Bill exclaimed, "That's not a cane fire, that's burning oil... something has happened!"

Our fears were confirmed when we reached West Loch. Six LSTs were burning and sinking in a scene of unimaginable violence. I remember the hours that
followed as a confusion of efforts to help dazed, oil-drenched sailors and Marines, get a muster of our men, and assess our equipment losses. My battalion,
its personnel and amtracs ashore, was largely spared, though we lost a precious
spare parts trailer. The Navy promptly replaced the LSTs and the 6th Service
Depot made up our equipment losses. We sailed on May 25, only one day later
than scheduled. Before departing, I shared farewell drinks with my battalion
officers in the Banyan Court of the Moana Hotel in Waikiki.

We made up the lost day during the long voyage to Eniwetok. There, in the
shelter of its vast lagoon, we transferred assault troops from the transports to the
LSTs carrying the amtracs in which they would land. This crowded the ships
well beyond their normal capacity but avoided the difficult transfer at sea on D-
day. As I surveyed our task force the evening before sailing, I sought words to
describe an armada of eight hundred ships carrying 165,000 men to strike at an
objective still a thousand miles away. A few days later when we heard of the
Normandy landing, I could not imagine how an Allied force, more powerful
than ours, could be engaged at the same time half a world away.

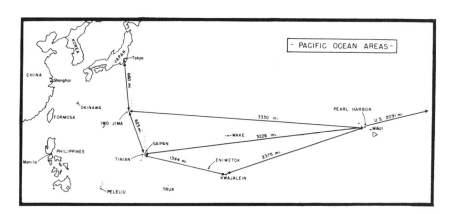

SAILING DISTANCES BETWEEN U.S. BASES AND OBJECTIVES

The Marianas operation, 1,200 miles from the nearest American bases, required more
than 800 ships to transport, cover, land, and support the invasion force of four divisions and one brigade. This vast assembly in the Pacific was matched in Europe where,
nine days before the landings were to begin on Saipan, an equally formidable force
struck at Normandy.

USMC Map

CURTAIN OF FIRE, SAIPAN, JUNE 15, 1944

Armored amtracs, LVT(A)4s, lead the way to Saipan as a curtain of fire begins to fall on the reef which the troop-carrying amtracs will have to cross. Of the 718 amtracs forming the assault waves, only 20 were hit or fell victim to the hazards of reef and surf.

USMC Photo

At 0542 on the morning of June 15, 1944, Admiral Turner ordered, "Land the Landing Force." Thirty-three minutes later my command group was aboard the control vessel off the beaches over which the 23rd Marines would land. Meanwhile, thirty-four LSTs were moving toward the line of departure ready to launch their troop-filled amtracs. Other control vessels displaying flags identify- ing the beaches for which they were responsible were also taking their stations. The scene took on added color as the morning sun brightened the calm sea and extended its dimensions to where the individual lost all significance.

The preliminary bombardments and air strikes started on June 11 had continued on a daily basis, then intensified at dawn that morning. Two battleships, two heavy cruisers, and seven destroyers had moved to within 2,500 yards of the shore to pound the defenses. Ninety minutes before the landing, the heavy drum beat of their guns was suspended, while carrier air delivered a roaring thirty-minute bomb and strafing attack. Then the guns had resumed their ponderous cadence until, at thirty minutes to landing, the full fury of their fires fell on the beaches.

On signal at 0812, twenty-four gunboats headed shoreward to saturate the landing beaches with fire once the Navy's big guns were masked. Then, as the thunder ended and the gunboats veered away, armored amtracs moved onto the reef to pick up the tempo with their lighter armament. Lastly, 8,000 Marines, loaded in six battalions of amphibian tractors formed in waves, started for the shore. Nearly all landed within thirty minutes. Seven hundred and eighteen amtracs headed for the beach that morning, all but twenty made it.[10]

Until they reached the reef, the enemy confined himself to occasional rounds fired at the control vessels. One hit close enough for Col. Louis R. Jones and me to duck behind a canvas windscreen on the bridge. Our sheepishness at this instinctive reaction turned to anguish when the amtracs arrived at the reef and were met by a fire storm. Yet, of the ninety-eight amtracs my battalion had in the assault only one was hit; the other battalions shared the loss of eleven more to enemy guns. Eight others were victims of mechanical failure, reef, and surf. Fire hitting the beaches destroyed three more of my amtracs and exacted a heavy toll of the infantry. Nevertheless, surviving squad and platoon leaders moved forward, calling the men to follow.

The landings on the 4th Division front were well executed, but the direct advance inland failed. Intense fires striking the right flank forced the 25th Marines to debark on the beach. On our front, a dozen amtracs got through the devastation of Charan Kanoa, but the thrust was unsupported, and the Marines were withdrawn to join in the later coordinated attacks. After unloading their assault troops, the amtracs began to shuttle reserve units and supplies ashore, routinely stopping at the aid stations to pick up wounded and carry them to the hospital LSTs. Within three hours, two of these had double their planned capacity and the third was nearly full. This flow of men and materiel to the beaches continued, while our crews gathered tales of near misses and shell splinters screeching off armor.

Late that afternoon, Colonel Jones called me ashore. I left my amtrac on the congested beach, though I missed its armor when a crescendo of mortar rounds heralded my arrival at his command post in a bomb crater. Voicing concern, he said, "I must be sure we have plenty of water and ammunition, particularly for the mortars, before we get hit tonight." I assured him there already were dumps of priority items ashore and I would see to his needs. Satisfied, he nodded dismissal with, "Fine! See to it and call if you run into trouble." I retraced my steps in the fading light across a landscape echoing with the discordant sounds of battle and vivid with images of wounded awaiting evacuation, shattered palms, broken boxes of ammunition and rations, and a miscellany of water cans and abandoned equipment.

That night, while sleepless Marines awaited the enemy counterattack, Vice Adm. Raymond A. Spruance received submarine reports confirming that the Japanese fleet in the Philippines could arrive off the Marianas by the seventeenth.

While he was evaluating this information, the enemy ashore struck hard at the Marine positions. These held until, at daylight, the few surviving Japanese abandoned their efforts. The Marines then resumed their advance. That same morning, Spruance decided to postpone the Guam landing but continue unloading until nightfall on the seventeenth.

The ships would then retire to the east, where they would remain on call. He further directed that the 27th Infantry Division begin landing immediately.[11] The unloading focussed on essential supplies, leaving most of the motor transport aboard. This multiplied calls on amtrac units and extended the range of their operations far inland. Our hard-pressed crews and maintenance people met the demands without murmur. However, the engineers and communicators complained bitterly at the damage our cleated tracks did to road surfaces and the miles of ground-laid telephone wire.

Much of our initial progress had been over fields of sugar cane that had been churned into a sweet mash by shells, bombs, tanks, and amtracs. The battered sugar mill in Charan Kanoa, whose smokestack had been used as an aiming point by Navy gunners, had also leaked sticky syrup into the streets. The ecstatic flies multiplied so quickly, it was soon impossible to open a can of rations without competing for its contents. Not until aircraft arrived to spray the island did the flies cease to supplement our diet.

My battalion moved ashore on the seventeenth. When I awakened the next morning to a canteen cup of hot coffee offered by Cpl. John Pretola, the empty sea brought me back to Guadalcanal. For a moment, I felt the intense loneliness I remembered from that distant August. But the memory faded; we had come far since 1942. This conviction was affirmed the next day in the Battle of the Philippine Sea, in which Japan's naval aviation received its mortal blow. That victory sealed the fate of the Marianas and precipitated the fall of the Tojo government, but the fighting ashore was not over.

Securing the southern part of Saipan and clearing it of bypassed enemy troops took until the twenty-first. The three divisions then began their drive to the north, which ended two weeks later at Marpi Point. The final scene of the drama began before dawn on July 7, when a last frenzied charge by the surviving Japanese cost them four thousand dead. This sacrifice inflicted over a thousand casualties on our forces. Two days later, several hundred civilians threw themselves off the northern cliffs in a tragic addendum to the 23,000 Japanese who had died in the bitter struggle. We had lost 3,000 dead. Four months later, a hundred B-29s lifted off Saipan and set course for Tokyo on the first raid since the Doolittle flight in 1942.[12]

My battalion's first bivouac was off a beach on whose reef a storm-battered Spanish galleon had scattered its treasure three hundred years before. I did not know this then but found another treasure in a farmer's hut, with laying hens under its floor and lime and papaya trees nearby. Though these breakfast makings

MY FARM ON SAIPAN, JUNE 1944

From left: Capt. Edgar S. Burks, Lt. Clifford T. Huntoon, Maj. Victor J. Croizat, Capt. George A. Vradenburg, Maj. Harry T. Marshall.

did not go far, I had the cooks bake biscuits and pies for everyone as soon as our welders could build ovens from salvaged armor. Such luxuries added to the morale of our men and visitors, whose numbers grew as the word spread. A chocolate cake I delivered on Colonel Jones' birthday touched him enough to return ten amtracs his people had "borrowed."

One day while in the mess tent with Perry Ayres, the chief cook told us of a large pig in the vicinity that would make a fine luau. I thought it a good idea but Perry countered with an oration on the dangers of eating pork. The cook listened with pained expression until, noting the doctor was wearing only a pair of torn drawers, he broke into a grin and said, "Doc, you're sitting on spaghetti. Will that make it bad to eat too?" I burst into laughter as Perry fled in embarassment. The pork was excellent.

My routine on Saipan occasionally allowed a change of pace. One such was a chance meeting with Evans Carlson who had led the 2nd Raider Battalion on Guadalcanal. I mentioned I had just learned how he had used amtracs for

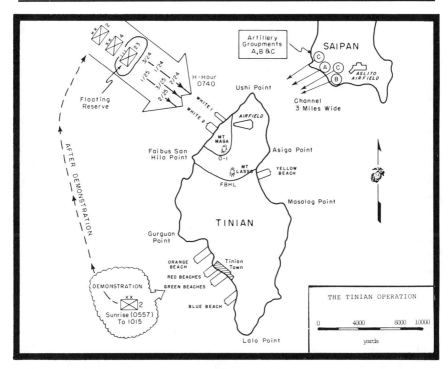

THE TINIAN OPERATION, JULY 1944

USMC Map

emergency resupply operations at Tarawa and added, "You set the precedent. Now, we can't keep up with demands for our services." Carlson laughed and we parted. The man had a warmth I had not found in Edson, who had led the other Raider battalion on Guadalcanal. On another occasion, a walk through the remains of Charan Kanoa and Garapan, the only towns I would encounter in my entire war, where bodies were decomposing in the rubble, left me troubled by thoughts of the many cities in Europe suffering a similar fate.

On a happier note, I was again impressed by the performance of my amtrac crews and maintenance company. Bill Lunn was everywhere, often working under fire to salvage disabled vehicles. In the first two days he and his men had returned twenty-seven amtracs to service, twenty-one of them holed by gunfire. He would have seventy-six of our original one hundred in serviceable condition for the Tinian landing, an exceptional accomplishment considering the hard use to which the vehicles had been put.

※ ※ ※

The island of Tinian, two-thirds the size of Saipan and just three miles away, was regularly subjected to harassing fires, including those from an Army 155mm gun battery near our camp. The artillerymen, though noisy, had a projector, and we joined them happily for movies until the memorable night that featured *The Fighting Sixty-Ninth*, a classic movie on World War I. As the story unfolded, the battery maintained its schedule of fires. The crack of the 155s, now echoed by the movie's soundtrack, was familiar. Then, enemy gunners on Tinian opened counter-battery fire. We thought the first rounds were part of the entertainment, but in seconds fantasy yielded to reality and we scurried for foxholes. The movies continued, but the audience was never as relaxed.

The invasion of Tinian was unique in that the 4th Division landed over two beaches whose total width was usually assigned to a single battalion. These had been selected after a reconnaissance revealed them to be lightly defended. Moreover, they were near enough to Saipan to preclude the need for a separate supply base. Once the decision was made, the four hundred and fifty-three amtracs remaining in serviceable condition were assigned to the 4th Division.[13] My battalion received sixty Army amtracs to add to our seventy-six to land the 23rd Marines.

The 4th Division began loading on July 15. Last to embark were the 2nd Division units tasked to simulate a landing off Tinian Town early on July 24. This deception succeeded, but a concealed Japanese six-inch gun exacted a high cost. Meanwhile, our 4th Division amtracs headed shoreward covered by smoke and fires from seven warships and thirteen battalions of artillery on Saipan. The 24th Marines began landing at 0747; the 25th Marines followed. By early afternoon the Marines' beachhead was a mile deep and half again as wide. Pleased at the progress, Major General Cates, now commanding the 4th Division, directed his reserve to land. In response, my amtracs had the 23rd Marines ashore by late afternoon. At nightfall, 15,000 Marines were dug in, waiting for trouble.

They were not disappointed. The Japanese began probing Marine positions soon after dark and launched the first of three violent attacks two hours past midnight. The thrusts were pushed with fanatic abandon but, thanks to Cates' preparations, their effort came to naught. At daylight, when the firing stopped, there were twelve hundred dead before the Marine wire. We shuttled supplies ashore until ordered back to Saipan two days later. By then the 2nd Division was entering into the fray, making the end inevitable. Tinian was declared secured on August 1.[14] On August 7, I received orders to return my battalion to Maui.

Admiral Turner reportedly thought the Saipan landing the most difficult of any he witnessed. I agree. Yet, despite the curtain of fire that fell between reef and beach during the assault and the enemy resistance that followed, my amtrac crews were miraculously spared heavy losses. We had three crewmen killed, another three missing and seventeen wounded, plus six more evacuated sick. Tinian cost us a further three wounded. These losses, though statistically light, were painful. Purple Hearts never come easy.

✳ ✳ ✳

Before completing our embarkation, I was offered a flight to Oahu. I asked Harry Marshall to get the outfit back to Maui and took off. The next day I reported to Fleet Marine Force Headquarters where I learned of plans to seize bases in the Carolines to cover the invasion of the Philippines. Operations were to begin on September 15 with the invasion of Peleliu and Angaur, followed by that of Yap and Ulithi. Yap was a cluster of islands surrounded by a triangular reef, through which a channel had to be blasted. Because the explosives cable needed was too massive to be positioned by swimmers, I was asked to provide three amtracs with volunteer crews to handle it.

When my battalion returned to Maui, I assembled the men and called for volunteers to depart immediately on a hazardous mission in the Western Pacific. All had just returned from four months of confined shipboard life and hard campaigning, and all were familiar with the dictum never volunteer. Yet, after I finished speaking, there was a brief silence and everyone stood up. Deeply moved, I stammered a "Thank you men, those of you selected will be notified." Later, several corpsmen asked to accompany the volunteers, "just in case." Gy. Sgt. Jack F. Tracy, nine men, and three amtracs were soon sailing west. When the Yap landing was cancelled they landed with the Army on Leyte. I got them back only in time to leave with us on our next operation.

Shortly after I returned to Maui, the division's Red Cross director asked me how his people with us were doing. To my reply that we had none, he promised to take care of our needs. My assurances that our needs were not a Red Cross responsibility fell on deaf ears; four Red Cross women soon ended our monastic life. Providing a social center and transportation for them posed no problem. Toilet facilities were something else. As expected, they found our eight-holers terribly smelly. The officers, touched by their distress, purchased a flush toilet which elicited smiles of appreciation until they realized we had no sewer. It remained in their office as a symbol of their hardships at Maalea Bay.

✳ ✳ ✳

In early October we began receiving new ramp-type amtracs to complete our allowance of a hundred machines.[15] Then, on November 12, we were again assigned to the 23rd Marines, now under command of Colonel Wensinger, and began planning the invasion of an uninviting place called Iwo Jima. That island, an eight square-mile pile of ash and rock, lying precisely halfway between Tokyo and the Marianas, was needed to support our bomber campaign. Its importance was equally appreciated by the Japanese who, in June 1944, had sent the brilliant Gen. Tadamichi Kuribayashi to defend it.

Despite steady losses to American submarines and aircraft, the Japanese had built up its garrison to 20,000 men, equipped with a formidable array of heavy guns, mortars, and rockets, some able to launch projectiles weighing

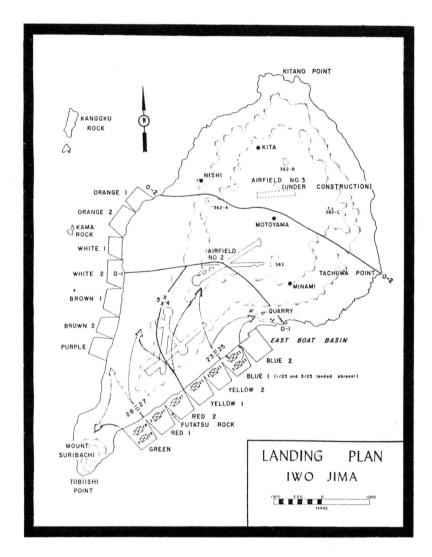

IWO JIMA LANDING PLAN, FEBRUARY 1945

The assault landings on Iwo Jima used four Marine amtrac battalions and one armored amphibian battalion. Because the beach approaches were clear of reefs and other offshore obstacles, it was anticipated that once the infantry was ashore and the priority cargo carried on designated LSTs had been landed, no further amtrac services would be required. However, the volcanic ash made the movement of wheeled vehicles impossible and of other tracked vehicles difficult. Accordingly, amtracs were retained to keep combat units supplied, help position artillery, evacuate wounded and satisfy all urgent transport requirements until the island was secured.

USMC Map

over five-hundred pounds. Our estimate of the enemy strength on Iwo Jima was low by twenty-five percent. More serious, the maze of tunnels and caves in which they had buried their weapons would not be discovered until the fighting began, nor would Kuribayashi's decision to confront us with a flexible defense.

The resources on our side were also impressive. The conquest of Iwo Jima was to engage a quarter million men, half to man our ships, and the remainder, including 70,000 Marines, to take the island. Our plans called for the 4th and 5th Marine Divisions to each land two infantry regiments to the southeast in four battalions of amtracs screened by sixty-eight armored amtracs of the 2nd Battalion. The 3rd Marine Division, which had been chasing die-hard Japanese out of Guam's jungle, would be in reserve. The control organization would be similar to that used in the Marianas, except that I would be on the division control vessel to coordinate the operations of its two amtrac battalions.

One Sunday during this planning period, two civilians came seeking help in getting their sailboat off a sandbar. I was ready for a break and drove an amtrac to the rescue. After the job was done, one of them offered refreshments at his home; an idyllic setting a short walk from our camp. My appreciation of it must have been evident for he offered me the small beach cottage on his property for my quarters. I was delighted to accept, as was Harry Marshall when I invited him to join me.

Near the same time, the officers planned a dinner dance and elected Harry, our handsome Virginian, to persuade the few eligible young women on the island to attend. I accompanied Harry on his challenging quest one evening when he visited the Nanikai Club where several of them lived. While watching Harry knock on doors, I glimpsed a small attractive brunette I arranged to have at my table. The party was a success, and I later invited Meda Fletcher for a drive to Hana. The wild ginger and waterfalls on the outbound journey were a delight, but a tropical downpour so delayed our return, she had time only to wash off the mud and rush to work. I thought our friendship doomed, but three years later we were married.

My battalion embarked on six LSTs on January 5. I went with the division headquarters on the *Bayfield* and our liaison teams joined the headquarters of the units we were supporting.[16] 1st Lt. Donald Kramer who, having headed the rear echelon during the Marianas campaign, had asked to accompany us "to be able to have a tale to tell the children I hope to have," was among these. The landing we were to undertake was not complicated. There was no reef and, though the surf breaking directly on the beaches and the volcanic ash might be troublesome, there were terraces to provide cover.[17] Once the troops were ashore, we had twenty-eight loads of cargo to land, after which we expected to go to Okinawa where landings were to begin on April 1.

My battalion's embarkation at Maalea Bay was routine. However, the division loaded at Kahului and was bid a proper farewell by a Hawaiian band and hula girls. Meda witnessed their loading out since she passed the dock area crowded with waiting Marines each morning on her way to work. She remembers how the usual whistles that followed her about on Maui were missing when she walked by the men preparing to embark. Their usual exuberance was stilled and they responded with only a nod or quiet smile to her good luck wishes.

BEYOND HANA, MAUI, 1944

The rehearsal paralleled our earlier experiences, but this time our stay in West Loch was uneventful. Again, we met for farewell drinks at the Moana's Banyan Court and on January 22 sailed for the Marianas. There, on February 10, the assault infantry transferred to the LSTs and I went aboard PCS 1452, the small patrol craft that would control movement over the 4th Division beaches. We held a final rehearsal on the twelfth, during which we had our first view of B-29s forming up for their long flight to Japan. The impressive sight helped me accept the cost of the Marianas campaign. Three days later, it was our turn to head north.

The four-day trip to Iwo Jima was an unusual experience. We control officers occupied a deckhouse that had replaced the ship's after 40mm gun tub. We were so close to the water we could flip cigarette butts over the side without leaving our bunks, and the wardroom was so small we had to file in and fit ourselves around the table before it could be set. More impressive, our hundred-foot ship repeatedly disappeared below the crest of the long Pacific swells and we lost sight of the LST group we were helping to screen.

Our routine was interrupted just before darken ship on the eighteenth, when our lookout spotted a free-floating mine. The captain reported to the screen commander and requested permission to leave station to destroy it by gunfire. Somehow the message was garbled and he understood we had sighted an enemy submarine. By the time things were straightened out we had lost sight of both the mine and the convoy and it had become dark. A lonely few hours followed while we chased after our traveling companions, all the while hoping the mine was well behind us.

I was on the bridge at first light the morning of February 19, 1945, to see Mount Surabachi emerge from a calm sea under a clear sky. Behind me our ships spread beyond the horizon. At 0640, six battleships began the pre-landing bombardment. The cadence, quickly picked up by cruisers and destroyers, featured an occasional ripple of rockets from our forty-two gunboats. At 0800, that measured thunder yielded to the violence delivered by fifteen B-24 bombers and a hundred and twenty carrier-based fighters and bombers.

Five minutes before the Navy planes appeared, our LSTs had started launching their amtracs. Within fifteen minutes, nearly five hundred were afloat and heading for the line of departure 4,000 yards from the shore. At 0830, just as the naval guns resumed firing, the central control vessel signaled the execute and the first wave of armored amtracs started shoreward. They were preceded by a line of gunboats that spewed rockets and veered away. Then, exactly on schedule, the armored amtracs touched the black sand. Two minutes later, at 0902, the first troop-carrying amtracs landed. Nine minutes later, 4,000 Marines were ashore.

ASSAULT LANDING, IWO JIMA, FEBRUARY 19, 1945

Sixty-eight gun-mounting armored amphibian tractors lead 380 cargo amphibian tractors loaded with the assault units of the 4th and 5th Marine Divisions toward the black sand beaches dominated by Mount Surabachi.

USMC Photo

Until then there had been virtually no enemy reaction. The Navy was keeping him down with a rolling barrage in a first-time attempt to provide assault infantry with a curtain of fire paced to its advance. The major difficulties were the high surf, the volcanic ash into which the men sank, and the unexpected height of the terraces. Then, our hope we would be lucky this time was shattered by a deluge of mortar rounds. These first hit the beaches on the right, but by 0930 all landing areas were being blasted. Nonetheless, the scheduled waves maintained the momentum of the landing.

On the left, 5th Division units crossed the 700-yard neck of the island in two hours of vicious fighting. The 2nd Battalion, 28th Marines then began its advance up Surabachi. Five days later it would reach the summit and immortality. On the right, the 4th Division discovered its own hell-on-earth. We had landed the 23rd Marines in good order, but they then had eight hours of hard fighting to reach the airfield, a third of a mile inland. The division's toughest test was the seizure of the "quarry" by Col. John R. Lanigan's 25th Marines whose advance required diverging movements in terrain dominated by cliffs from which

MARINE HOWITZER AND BURNING AMTRACS
IWO JIMA'S INHOSPITABLE BEACH, FEBRUARY 1945

USMC Photo

devastating fires rained down. The objective was taken before nightfall, but the cost was appalling. Joe Chamber's battalion had but a hundred and fifty left of its original nine hundred men.

The 4th Division's tanks were also badly mauled. I saw several of the landing ships carrying them hit on the way in and watched the tanks ashore flounder in the volcanic ash, while drawing enemy fire. Tanks did not become effective until proper beach exits had been prepared. The landing of artillery was equally troubled. Reconnaissance parties were decimated, previously selected battery positions were beyond reach, and the amphibious trucks carrying the artillery had difficulties with the surf and ash. Still, despite the many tribulations, two battalions of artillery were brought ashore and helped into position by the ubiquitous amtracs.

My station on the division control vessel allowed me a panoramic view of the violence. I had never before seen a shoreline so encumbered with the debris of battle, yet the activity appeared familiar. Off our control vessel, amtracs loaded with priority cargo were awaiting the call to land; others ashore were helping position artillery and clear boat beaching sites and vehicle exits. All returning amtracs were stopping by the aid stations for wounded to take to the hospital LSTs. Our battalion medical section was also ashore to help ease the effects of the carnage.

Perry Ayres had proposed to have his medical section supplement that of the shore party until our battalion set up ashore. Thus, in the early afternoon of D-day, Ayres and his party had landed in a shower of mortar shells. All were spared and had set off looking for the aid station they were to assist. They found it destroyed by shellfire and had taken its place. Perry later reported two hundred and forty Marines treated from February 19 to 24, noting that data for the first twenty-four hour period were incomplete.

At 1600, I received orders to start landing priority cargo. The shuttle to shore continued under the eerie light of star shells until 2300, when the beaches were closed because of the volume of fire falling on them. By that time 30,000 Marines were ashore, 1,500 of them already wounded and five hundred dead. Don Kramer later admitted, "When I reached the beach I was sure I would never live to have children to hear my story." With a wry smile, he continued, "I was carrying everything regulations prescribed. But, with the world exploding around me, all I could think to do was scuttle into a hole and cut straps to lighten my load. Then, when my mind began working again, I carried on my duties in the state of constant terror shared by everyone else."

By the evening of the second day we had almost finished unloading our LSTs, but it was evident we were not going to leave. With wheeled vehicles of little use, only amtracs could provide reliable transportation. They would continue to do so until Iwo Jima was secured. The effort cost us thirty-three amtracs

BEACH CONGESTION AT IWO JIMA, FEBRUARY 1945

Combat supplies flow to the beach where they are organized into dumps from which they are delivered to the frontline units by amphibian tractors which continued as the most effective means of transport throughout the campaign.

USMC Photo

just in the first four days. Bill Lunn had been doing all vehicle maintenance and repair aboard ship, but the demands for service soon exceeded the space available afloat. I requested permission to move ashore but was denied. Our beachhead was still too shallow, and no one wanted the lucrative target we represented close by.

MINE-SHATTERED AMTRACS, IWO JIMA, FEBRUARY 1945

Amphibian tractors destroyed by mines on the beach at Iwo Jima. Japanese laid "yard-stick" mines over buried aerial bombs which, when detonated, were powerful enough to lift a 15-ton loaded LVT and blow a large hole in its bottom.

USMC Photo

Time again lost meaning. Then on the morning of February 23, I was startled to see the American flag flying over Surabachi and hear wild cheers, ships' whistles, and bells. I later learned this moment of exceptional emotional impact was shared by Secretary of the Navy James Forrestal. I used the occasion to ask again to land my battalion; this time division agreed. As we landed and headed for our area, we heard a sharp crack and stopped. A small mine had broken our vehicle's track. When the crew dug down to expose the damaged section they uncovered a large bomb that had split instead of exploded. I stared at it a long time, a cold sweat forming on my brow.

Later that day, I settled into a roofed-over bomb crater and, that night, en-joyed my only amusing moment on the island. As the war had progressed, the use of passwords had been simplified because people who needed them were often too wrought up to remember what they were. To avoid the consequences of such memory lapses, higher authority had decreed that passwords should be things rather than specific words. The password in effect that night was "trees"; anyone challenged would call "oak" (or another tree) and the challenger would reply with "elm" (or another tree). Dark had fallen when, above the growling transmission of an amphibious truck coming toward me, I heard the loud voice of its driver shouting, "Trees, trees, any kind o' trees...ah's a friend...doan't shoot!"

My twenty-sixth birthday at the end of February passed with little notice. A visiting observer who had shared my shelter had left me a bottle of rum, saying, "Thanks for the hospitality, you can probably use this more than I." He was right. The rum made my coffee taste better, though the day was far from festive. The endless bombings and shellings on Guadalcanal had been enervating, but the island was not unattractive and there had been moments when life was tolerable. Iwo, in contrast, had no redeeming qualities and, with 100,000 men locked in battle on its eight square-miles, the air was seldom free of passing bullet or shell.

For me, Iwo Jima will always be the sight from my command post of our dead laid out in tiers, waiting for the living to win the ground for their burial. Time to mourn them would come later. Our energies were absorbed in helping the infantry make its way through the labyrinth of Japanese defenses. As cited in a V Corps report, "Supplies and equipment were hauled from ships directly to the front lines, and had it not been for the LVTs the troops ashore could not have been supplied..."

The nature of this service is exemplified by an urgent call one night for mortar ammunition. 1st Lt. Lyman D. Keown answered and, knowing that his route lay across a mined area, walked ahead of his laden amtrac under the light of flares, prodding the ground to find safe passage. He received the Silver Star for his exploit. Perry Ayres, recommended for the Navy Cross for organizing his emergency treatment facility, was awarded the Bronze Star. The valor of many others equally deserving went unrecognized.

There were other occasions calling for qualities less easily explained. One evening as Ayres and I were quietly talking, we heard an explosion and cry of pain nearby. We rushed toward the sound and found a Marine who had just had both his legs and an arm shredded by a mine. Perry saved the young man's life while I got an amtrac to evacuate him to a hospital ship. When the man was gone, I asked if he would live. Perry paused and said, "Probably, but if he does he won't have much of a life." Then he added, "I thought when I was tying off his blood vessels that perhaps I should just have loosened his tourniquets, but I decided playing God was not for me. Was I right?" Neither of us could answer.

Other questions concerning Iwo Jima remain unanswered. I was at the airfield early in March when a B-29 skidded to an emergency landing. The incident seemed to justify why we had gone there but, when I later learned that the Marines lost in taking Iwo equalled the aircrews saved by it, I had trouble reconciling the balance.[18] The question of why chemical weapons were not used is equally puzzling. Long after the war I read that there were over fourteen thousand chemical bombs available to the Pacific Command. These were enough to incapacitate the Japanese on Iwo Jima, where no civilians remained. All that prevented their use was President Roosevelt's aversion to gas warfare. Yet, the next President authorized the use of nuclear weapons against two Japanese cities where civilians shared in the devastation.

On March 15, 1945, we were ordered to reembark and return to Maui. The next day, on my way to the *Lander* in an amphibian truck, we unexpectedly came under fire from a surviving Japanese gun. My luck still holding, the gunner missed and I went aboard without further incident. We sailed, mourning the battalion's nine dead and twenty-two wounded. A few days later, the remnants of the 4th Division gathered at Eniwetok, where General Cates met with unit commanders to review After Action Reports and announce that our next task would be the seizure of Miyako Jima, an island southwest of Okinawa. We then set course for Hawaii.

Back at Maalea Bay, we were joined by the 3rd, 5th, and 2nd Armored Amtrac Battalions and settled into the familiar routine of cleaning up equipment, replacing losses, and beginning preparations for the next operation. The calm was deceptive, however, for events elsewhere were moving toward a climax. On April 23 the invasion of Miyako Jima was cancelled and we were told our next landing would be near Shanghai. This, too, was cancelled. Then, on May 31, we began preparing for the invasion of Japan. Meanwhile, the war had ended in Europe and the final action in the Pacific was approaching. Hiroshima was destroyed with a nuclear weapon on August 6, Nagasaki followed on the ninth. Hostilities with Japan were suspended on the fourteenth.

This period was also marked by changes in my own fortunes. By this time, the Marine Corps had thirteen amtrac battalions and two group headquarters, the 1st Group Headquarters was now on Maui to control the four amtrac battalions based there. I viewed my orders to join it on July 14 with mixed emotions. The 10th Battalion had been the center of my life for twenty months. Yet, responsibility for planning and coordinating the operations of several amtrac battalions appeared a move in the right direction. Before I had a chance to find out, a family emergency called me home.

I left on July 16 for Boston and was returning by way of New York City when I unexpectedly found myself in the midst of a wildly jubilant crowd in Times Square celebrating the end of the war with Japan. It was a unique location for an unforgettable moment, yet I felt detached from my surroundings. For me, reality was the waters and islands of the Pacific that had absorbed my thoughts and energies for more than three years. I would have preferred to share the joy of victory with my battalion on Maui.

Four

FROM ONE WAR TO ANOTHER

The abrupt end of the Pacific War brought a loss of focus to my life. For three and a half years it had been dominated by the demands of five amphibious operations, for which time for training, planning, and preparation had been adequate only for the last, Iwo Jima. Now, suddenly the emotional high that had sustained me was gone, I knew only that my beaches henceforth should be friendly.

After the frenzy at Times Square I welcomed the relative tranquility of Maui. Throughout the Pacific, however, Marine units were on the move. In September 1945, the 2nd and 5th Divisions were bound for occupation duty in Japan, while the 1st and 6th Divisions were en route to China. The remaining two divisions were being held in readiness should any element in Japan's four-million man army question the surrender instructions. But the Japanese were as cooperative in peace as they had been brutal in war. The disbandment of many Marine units was accelerated accordingly.

The responsibilities of the amtrac group I had just joined had ended with the war and I was assigned to escort Brigadier General Edson when he visited Maalea Bay. He had just taken over the Service Command, the supply organization of the Fleet Marine Force, and was getting acquainted. I had not seen him since Guadalcanal and was pleased that I was remembered, albeit not clearly. His brief orientation ended, he returned my parting salute with, "I'll be seeing you." Had I remembered he never wasted words, my transfer orders to his headquarters at Camp Catlin, near Pearl Harbor, would have been less surprising. I reported on November 2, to find Edson replaced by Brig. Gen. E. O. Ames, who was soon relieved by Col. Henry D. Linscott.

I was uncertain what my new duties might be but glad I would be seeing Meda, who had left Maui for the public relations department of the Hawaiian Electric Company in Honolulu. The matter of my responsibilities was settled when I became assistant to Col. Bert Bone, the Service Command's ordnance officer, who had been a Marine before I was born. This arrangement lasted just long enough for a brief orientation before he left for home and I assumed his duties. My title was imposing, but I had a lot to learn.

At the time Japan surrendered, there were a quarter million Marines serving overseas, including 20,000 in the Supply Service. Fourteen months later, the newly named Service Command had less than 4,000, and we had disposed of half the property we held in the Pacific.[1] I was intimately involved in this process, which was aggravated beyond reason by the United States' precipitate demobilization. The gathering of resources for our invasion of Japan had suddenly gone into reverse while the men needed for the disposal process, including the crews of the ships and planes, were fast disappearing into civilian life. The problems were many; occupation forces in the Far East had to be supplied, stocks had to be set aside in permanent depots to support peacetime forces and the remainder disposed of as prescribed in complex regulations.

Added turmoil was assured by frequent changes in the policies affecting the duration and mission of occupation forces, peacetime force levels, and the regulations governing property disposal. By the end of 1945, the 3rd and 4th Divisions had been disbanded and our supply units consolidated on Guam, the Hawaiian Islands, and China, where the occupation promised to last for some time. I would eventually visit all of these installations but my immediate concerns were with the nearby 6th Service Depot and the two service battalions on Maui and Hawaii.

Nature took a hand on April 1, 1946, when I received a dispatch stating, "Hilo struck by tidal wave; ordnance disposal program accelerated; details follow." I dismissed the message as an April Fool's joke. When a dispatch from Maui repeated the same information in much the same language, I began to wonder. Then, a news bulletin removed all doubt. The Hawaiian Islands had been hit by a tsunami! The next morning, I flew to the Big Island, where I viewed the havoc along Hilo's waterfront. Our materiel losses were indeed substantial and we closed the facility shortly after. Damage to the battalion on Maui was less extensive and it was retained for several months. The depot on Oahu, with ample covered storage, was undamaged.

The 5th Service Depot on Guam was not affected by the tidal wave, but the island climate was hard on property stored in the open. When the depot reported it could no longer maintain its amtracs, the 1st Amphibian Tractor Battalion was reactivated and assigned the year-long task of processing them for storage. The battalion commander, Maj. Hank Lawrence, was not surprised at the size of the job when he arrived in August, but was upset that anyone who wanted to bring out dependents would have to build his own quarters. Maj. Eugene Siegel later told me with some feeling, "I didn't mind building my Quonset hut but I was mad when the Marine Corps decreed it, 'adequate' quarters and cut off my housing allowance."

I visited Guam several times in 1946 and found the amtrac processing going well. However, I was appalled at how much other equipment was disappearing under tropical vegetation. I had just returned to Oahu when a report crossed my desk detailing the difficulties the Marines were having providing security for the rail lines from Peiping to Tientsin and Chingwangtao. The area was infested by communist forces and tanks were being used, in the absence of more suitable armored vehicles, to support the Marines' patrols. I went to our newly promoted Brigadier General Linscott and told him I knew of half-tracks on Guam that appeared in good condition. He agreed I should find out whether they could be quickly prepared for service in North China. When Guam replied affirmatively we contacted the Navy, which sent destroyers to provide the lift.

Other than the rare occasions when my duties had such positive results, much of what I did was distasteful. It is gratifying to be part of a building process, but the reverse holds little satisfaction. Fortunately, Honolulu was a pleasant place to live and I had a congenial classmate in Maj. Alexander M. Benson with whom to share a Quonset and occasional afternoon breaks at Waikiki landmarks. My evenings were most often shared with Meda. I introduced her to military circles; she provided access to civilian ones.

One of my introductions began when General Linscott found me listening to her radio program describing the advantages of cooking with electricity. Puzzled, he asked, "What's this, Vic, taking cooking lessons?" I stammered an explanation which he followed with, "I'd like to meet her. She could probably help me get ready for Mrs. Linscott's arrival." Not long after, Meda invited the general and a friend of his to dinner. It was a success. She provided them with a touch of home life they had not known for several years and encouraged them to monopolize the conversation. She also graciously acquiesced when they insisted on washing the dishes.

The Marines' participation in the occupation of Japan was relatively brief.[2] The return of the Marines to China was more enduring. The III Marine Amphibious Corps, which arrived in North China in October 1945, had soon become embroiled in a politico-military situation that would prove beyond resolution. My concerns, however, were limited to supporting the Marines, whose mission was to assist the Nationalist Government occupy key areas and repatriate Japanese troops, while avoiding "participation in any fratricidal conflict in China."

As in Japan, relations between the Marines and the Japanese troops in China were good from the start. Indeed, they quickly became allies when they shared the task of denying areas to the communists pending the arrival of the Nationalists. In contrast, relations between the Americans and Chinese Nationalists were difficult, sometimes even adversarial. As an example, Chiang Kai-shek had wanted to reoccupy Manchuria as soon as possible, but the Americans had opposed the move as an over-extension of his forces. This impasse was unintentionally resolved by Soviet troops, whose looting of the industrial infrastructure transformed Manchuria from an economic asset to a liability.

Chiang's plans to use the Marines in his struggle against the communists made it evident that an early decision had to be made regarding American involvement in China's civil war: the Marines could not be both neutral and partisan. President Truman thought the problem could be resolved by having Gen. George C. Marshall negotiate a cease-fire between Chiang's Nationalist forces and Mao's communist levies. He accomplished this in January 1946, soon after his arrival in China, but the Marines were not convinced it would work.

Their first clash with communist forces had come just six days after they had landed. Relations had improved slightly when the Marines helped distribute relief supplies in communist areas, but the encounters had continued, including among them a raid on the Hsin Ho ammunition dump in October. By then, Marshall was informing President Truman the truce was failing. Still, he persisted as mediator until January 1947, when he left to become Secretary of State.

The Marines, expecting the truce to collapse and American support for Chiang to become limited, had disbanded the 6th Division in March 1946 and, the same month Marshall left, the first unit of the 1st Division left China. Three days

MANUAL LABOR DEFINES TIENTSIN, NORTH CHINA, FEBRUARY 1947

later, on January 21, Linscott and I left Oahu for the Far East to review the effect of these moves on the supplies to be retained and the disposal of the surplus. We had been closely following events in China, where the 7th Service Regiment had been the principal supply agency for the III Marine Amphibious Corps. Now, with the 1st Division withdrawing, the regiment had been assigned to the rear echelon with responsibility for disposing of all excess property. The Marines remaining to safeguard Seventh Fleet facilities ashore would be supplied by the service battalion in Tsingtao.[3]

Four hours after our plane lifted off we arrived at Johnston Island to refuel, and I got off to stretch my legs. When the fueling was finished in less time than anticipated, the flight was called early. I returned to find General Linscott urging the impatient plane commander to wait for me. I would have been embarrassed to miss a flight on an island barely large enough for a runway. Fortunately for my self-esteem, I was able to reciprocate when we reached Guam. As we taxied toward the terminal, General Linscott saw a Marine honor guard and asked who

TIENTSIN-HSIN HO ROAD, NORTH CHINA, FEBRUARY 1947

was on board deserving of such reception. I replied, "Sir, the guard is for you." Nonplussed, he muttered, "Being a general takes getting used to." I helped straighten out his uniform and he made a properly dignified exit; I followed with his brief case.

We spent the afternoon and the next day at the depot on routine matters and left just before midnight for Shanghai. No layover was scheduled, but I hoped to get a good aerial view of a city that had featured so prominently in Marine Corps lore. The 4th Marines had moved to Shanghai in 1927 and remained fourteen drama-filled years. Seven future commandants had been schooled there, and a generation of Marines had gathered tales of privates with personal servants, lovely White Russian girls, and two-cent beer. Unfortunately, we landed in a snowstorm and left for Tsingtao in the same weather. I saw only the plane's wings.

Our two days in Tsingtao were spent working with the service battalion. I also managed a brief tour of the city, made familiar by its German-built forts and European aspect. I reacted differently to Tientsin, whose streets defined the term manual labor. Everywhere I looked people were pulling, pushing, and carrying heavy burdens. Many wore quilted cotton clothing, but others were too lightly clad for the bitter cold. The bodies in the gutters awaiting collection attested to the difficulties of survival in that cruel environment.

As in Tsingtao, our meetings in Tientsin were useful, and my visit to our ammunition dump at Hsin Ho, thirty miles away, most interesting. Because of communist harassment, all Marines traveling out of the city had to be armed, each vehicle had to carry an automatic weapon, and only point-to-point travel was permitted. Thus equipped, four of us left in a jeep on the sunny morning of January 28. I was enjoying glimpses of mud hut villages when we blew a tire. Repairs were quickly made, while a chattering crowd gathered. Though all appeared in good humor, I kept close to the Thompson submachinegun by the front seat. The trip impressed upon me that occupation duty in China now was a far cry from what service there had been before the war.

When I rejoined Linscott, he directed I leave for Peiping the next day and start the 5th Marines disposing of their surplus ammunition. The next afternoon I was being entertained by a stunning White Russian secretary while waiting to meet Col. Julian Frisbee. The young woman spoke perfect French and English and admitted to fluency in Russian, Chinese, and Japanese; the last acquired as secretary to the previous occupant of the premises.

Despite my willingness to linger, I was soon shaking hands with the grizzled regimental commander. His cordiality exhausted, Colonel Frisbee declared that the instructions I had issued on the ammunition he was to dump at sea were absurd. "Do you realize," he glared, "that you're telling me to dump more ammunition than the 5th Marines took to Nicaragua in 1927 and expended in the six years they fought rebels there?" I started to explain but decided I was in a no-win situation. I concluded my call with the remark, "General Linscott will be here tomorrow afternoon and I am sure he will clarify the situation to the colonel's satisfaction."

PEIPING, MAJESTIC CITY, NORTH CHINA, FEBRUARY 1947

I went back to his secretary, who was willing to take me shopping, but not join me for dinner. I later learned a Chinese banker provided funds for her to live comfortably while educating a younger brother. That evening I dined with a friend from the regiment. I was surprised when we arrived at the restaurant to see him chain the wheels of his jeep to the chassis. This, he assured me, was an essential precaution, for unattended motor vehicles were regularly stripped. I was equally surprised at our $50,000 (Chinese) tab for two vodkas and Chicken Kiev dinners. I asked about the rate of exchange and was told not to bother, any figure would be invalid by the time I heard it.

A two-bedroom suite had been reserved for the general and me at the Peiping Grand Hotel, whose European style was faded but still elegant. I greeted the dawn by throwing open the French windows and looking at a dusty pink sky, below which the city emerged from a yellow-gray haze of smoke from countless soft coal fires. Peiping, my third city in China, was again different. The boulevards I could trace from my balcony were broad and tree-lined. The quiet was most striking.

The throngs of people on the streets made little noise in their soft footwear, and the cyclists added only the tinkle of their warning bells. The vast square leading to the Forbidden City was equally silent. I had arranged for a guide to take me there and, although my winter service uniform was not suited to the bitter cold of North China, the occasion was not to be missed. My guide and I were virtually alone and I was able to ponder how man could conceive such magnificence, yet be unable to devise a social order to lessen the misery I had seen beyond the walls.

That afternoon I was back in the colonel's office with General Linscott. He opened with, "Well, Julian, I understand you have some questions about the ammo to be dumped." To that the colonel replied, "Goddammit, Henry, we used to fight a war with less than what your major here wants me to throw away." And so it continued through many cups of coffee until, near dusk, a placated colonel invited us to have Peiping duck that evening. We ate in a simple dirt-floored restaurant dominated by a beehive oven in which the ducks were suspended for cooking. A United Nations representative added to the occasion with insights on what was happening in the country.

The next two days were a combination of work and shopping. I was attracted by the arts and crafts and wondered how objects of such grace and elegance could be made in dark, ill-equipped shops. I left China on February 3 with renewed respect for its people and a deepened concern for the outcome of their civil war. The next day, during a layover on Guam, I made a quick visit to Saipan. It was nineteen months since our landing and I found its tranquility strange but reassuring. I was pleased at its recovery.

Soon after my return, we received authority to transfer 6,500 tons of ammunition in China to the Nationalist forces. We also were informed that agreement had been reached to turn over all surplus Marine Corps stocks on Guam to the Chinese for one million dollars, which we loaned them. This was done by replacing the Marine guards by Chinese. It seemed an unusual way to discharge our responsibilities. My involvement in a disposal effort without precedent or antecedent had also ended. I had finished my war in the Pacific.

✳ ✳ ✳

I left Oahu on the *General Anderson* on August 1, 1947, shortly after the National Security Act creating a single Department of Defense and a separate Air Force became law. Preoccupied with affairs in the Pacific and Far East, I had been little aware of the battle for survival the Commandant and a handful of Marine officers had been waging for two years. Their efforts had succeeded and recognition had been given in the Act to the Marine Corps' singular capabilities.

Important as this was, my thoughts were elsewhere. My orders to Camp Pendleton granted thirty days leave, during which Meda and I planned to marry. Three years of shared experiences had helped her decide to set aside her independent life and share mine in the Marine Corps, and she had flown ahead to her parents' home in Washington State. I had never been to the Pacific Northwest and welcomed Meda's suggestion that I take the afternoon train east through the Columbia River gorge. I was equally pleased at her plans for us to marry in the garden of her parents' home in Kennewick, honeymoon on Mount Rainier and the Olympic peninsula, then make our way south along the coast to my new duty station.

I boarded the train in civilian clothes carrying a bag with my sword strapped outside. When the conductor came by, he eyed my sword case and asked, "Where are you from?" I explained I was a Marine returning from four years in the Pacific on my way to get married and ended, "I'm planning to use that sword to cut my wedding cake." The conductor asked to see it. I opened the case for him and, after looking it over, he said, "That sure is a fine samurai blade." Not wanting to contradict him, I nodded assent. He rewarded me by saying, "You'd better come with me to the engine. You'll get a better view of the country and can make sure the engineer gets you in on time." Meeting my future father-in-law after descending from a locomotive was an unusual beginning.

Francis Fletcher was a small, quiet man whose family had arrived in the New England colonies of the early 1630s and moved west with the frontier. He had married a young woman whose Swiss family had fought blizzards and locusts on the northern plains in the mid-1800s before seeking greener mountains to the west. Meda was born in northern Idaho. They later moved to eastern Washington where her father had developed orchards and managed an irrigation district. He was then involved in lengthy litigation with the federal government over the farmers' water rights. Being city bred, I was ignorant of such things, yet I was made to feel at home by Meda's family. I continue grateful for the warmth of my reception.

✳ ✳ ✳

Camp Pendleton in 1947 was not the place I had known in 1943. Then, I had joined in the formation of a new division and had shared in its preparation for combat. Now, I reported to a quiet post where the veteran 1st Marine Division was preoccupied with returning to peacetime practices. Maj. Gen. Graves B. Erskine, who commanded both the division and the base, reportedly destroyed colonels with frightening regularity. As a major I was less vulnerable but, as commanding officer of the Tracked Vehicle Schools Battalion, I became consumable. Fortunately, my command at the Boat Basin was far enough from the general's headquarters to lessen my visibility.

My job was to run a school to train tank and amphibian tractor operators and mechanics. With a staff of combat veterans and well-equipped shops this offered the promise of a pleasant, if not exciting, tour of duty. On the personal side, the absence of quarters on the base and the few rentals in nearby communities made housing difficult. We solved the problem by buying a small house overlooking the Pacific in the town of Del Mar, twenty miles from the Boat Basin.

My second problem was a return to strict accountability. For three and a half years of war, accountability had been set aside. Then, during my two years in the Service Command I had given away or destroyed mountains of equipment and supplies. Now, I found myself accounting for light bulbs and toilet paper and serving on Boards of Survey for housekeeping items used up long ago but still on inventory lists. Yet another trial was the general's insistence that a commander was responsible for all that happened to his command, including venereal disease. I was perplexed when, after a vivid film on the horrors of such disease, one of my men was apprehended in *flagrante delicto* with a prostitute behind the barracks. According to the general, it was my fault.

A lighter moment came when one of my officers, almost the age of my father, formally requested permission to marry. My surprise at this traditional courtesy was heightened upon learning the bride-to-be was only seventeen. With serious mien, he confessed, "Life in the bachelor officers' quarters is a bust. There's grass growing through the cracks in the floor and

READY FOR SATURDAY MORNING INSPECTION, DEL MAR, 1948

mice gnaw the starch in my shirts. That's just no way to live." Then, he brightened and added, "My girl is a sergeant major's daughter. She grew up in the Corps and is young enough to become a proper wife." Convinced by the logic I gave the captain my blessing.

Another light moment came when one of my company commanders and his wife made their formal call on us. I thought a flash of recognition passed between Meda and the captain, but nothing was said. When they left, Meda exploded in laughter. She had known the captain on Maui, where he, not expecting to see her again, had importuned her for dates with the story of an unfortunate marriage to a woman of indifferent qualities. The truth, as we had just seen, was that his wife was a blond beauty with intelligence and charm. A less complicated reunion was with Bill Lunn, who had directed the demanding maintenance activities of my amtrac battalion during the war and was now heading a research project on amtrac survivability in surf.

I was happy to have Bill nearby and welcomed his advice regarding my schools' activities. I also appreciated his opinions in the aftermath of an amphibious training exercise in which a Marine had drowned. I was on the Board of Investigation, which found that the armored amtracs with gun turrets had passed through the surf without trouble, whereas water entered the open hold of the troop-carrying amtracs. The one in which the Marine had drowned had lost power and capsized, trapping him inside. Bill contributed the findings of his studies to our board, which recommended that a quick-release cover made of light armor be fitted on all cargo tractors. These findings were approved and Bill helped design and install the cover.[4]

In late 1948 with sixty days' leave and a year's savings, Meda and I drove to Miami, from where we flew to Caracas. My father had happily left Boston's deadly winters the year before to accept a position as botanist and university lecturer with Venezuela's Ministry of Agriculture. The contrast between Meda's family home and my parents' was striking. Conversations in her home were carried on in low voices; in mine, the loud chatter reached a climax each noon with the arrival of the mail. Meda was amused at the frenzy of speculation the event created. Even more amusing was my mother's unknowing mix of French, Spanish, English, and Italian words, often in the same sentence.

We were in Venezuela when Perez Jiminez came to power, a political process we found as interesting as the city and countryside. We wandered Caracas, surprised to see modern office buildings and lovely villas sharing space with shanties. We took the old German-built train to the lowland town of Valencia and were dismayed at the panorama of barren farms abandoned by people drawn to the oil fields and cities. The results of the disrupted economy were evident in a small neighborhood store where people from

ECOLE MILITAIRE FRAMED BY THE EIFFEL TOWER, PARIS, 1949

the mean shacks built against garden walls bought a meagre handful of rice or beans, while the shelves sagged with imported foods. It was Meda's first view of such contrasts.

✳ ✳ ✳

In February 1949, we learned that Meda was pregnant. Less stirring, but also pleasing, was news we had reached the top of the waiting list for a new car. These welcome developments would complicate our lives. Early in August, I received a call advising I was being ordered to Paris. I at first thought we were speaking of the Recruit Depot at Parris Island but quickly discovered my destination was the Ecole Superieure de Guerre in Paris, France. I had heard of the prestigious French war college and knew this would be a unique experience, for it had been the only foreign school to which Marines had been sent before the war.

But then I was told I was to be in Paris prior to August 25 and was to fly from the West Coast, via Washington, for briefings. I explained that we had a house to sell and had just bought a new car. I pleaded for time to settle my affairs and drive to New York, the only port from which the government would ship our car. This was reluctantly granted, but we were allowed only five days for the cross country trip. I had argued this was too tight, but when I learned Meda would not be allowed to fly beyond her fast approaching seventh month I surrendered. Our drive across country was hectic, but we kept to the schedule and in Washington I was greeted with a promotion to lieutenant colonel.

Early on the twenty-second, we were in New York arranging to ship our car and preparing to leave that night on a TWA Constellation. The next evening 1st Lt. James T. Breckinridge, commander of the Marine Guard at the Embassy, and his wife Judy met us at Orly and saw us to the Continental Hotel. After a long night's sleep and a call on Capt. H. H. Smith-Hutton, the naval attache, I went to the Ecole Militaire, to find a surprised caretaker who explained that August was reserved for *les vacances* and suggested I come back in September. I wondered how Meda would take the news that we need not have hurried. When I told her, she gave a newly acquired Gallic shrug with her "C'est la vie." We used the time searching for ways to stretch our inadequate living allowances in France's postwar economy.

With help from the Breckinridges, Smith-Huttons and the Naval Attache staff we eventually found a place to live and a doctor to assist in Meda's confinement. We also kept our sense of humor and found Paris a magnificent city. Traffic was mad but not yet overwhelming; theaters and restaurants were well attended. We gazed respectfully at the Mona Lisa in the Louvre; I gazed appreciatively at the Follies Bergere. After the relative isolation of Camp Pendleton and the focus on Asia that we had shared, Europe in 1949 was exciting. Now, it was the Pacific War that was remote; the only reality was Europe, the effects of the war still much in evidence in many cities and its security and well-being its principal preoccupations.

The communists represented an important political force in France at that time. Yet, the press and radio made much of the menace of the Soviet Union, whose year-long blockade of Berlin had been thwarted by the American-led airlift. The confrontational foreign policy of the Soviets had persisted, and the West had responded with the Atlantic Alliance just formalized. This had been paralleled on the Soviet side by the creation of the German Democratic Republic and the explosion of an atomic bomb. While Europe was being divided by the Soviet leadership, the Marshall Plan was beginning to restore the war-depleted economies of countries in the west.

When I returned to the Ecole Militaire in September, I learned that classes would start in November. Until then, foreign officers would tour training facilities to become familiar with French military organization and terminology. The orientation program was flexible enough to meet personal needs. John Stockton, an Army captain who was to attend the Ecole d'Etat Major (Staff College), had a car arriving in Germany at the same time as ours. He suggested we take the train to Bremerhaven and drive back in convoy. John had served in General Patton's Third Army and proved an excellent tour guide as we traveled over recent battlefields. The devastation in Germany, where a carton of cigarettes remained a precious medium of exchange, accented his narrative.

Back in Paris, I began my orientation visits. Despite Meda's minimal French, she had us moving to suburban La Jonchere by the end of September. There, we would share a duplex with our Embassy's cultural attache and be within walking distance of the Stocktons and Lt. Col. Edward Bechtold and his family. Ed, an artillery officer who had participated in the landings in North Africa and Normandy, was also to attend the Ecole de Guerre. La Jonchere, on the heights west of Paris, lay between the Seine and the auto route to Normandy, the only such road in France at the time. Wealthy Parisians had built homes there before the turn of the century when royal land became available. The Bechtolds and Stocktons had each rented one of these. Meda and I were satisfied with our modest duplex.

Our son, John, was born on the cold misty morning of October 31 at the American Hospital in Neuilly, under the concerned attention of Doctor Yver, a paternal gentleman who spoke no English. We never found an American on the staff, although Meda had an English-speaking Dutch nurse for two days. Largely as a result of our precipitate move, Meda had a difficult time. However, she was able to help remove the swaddling clothes of our first-born to verify he had all the proper parts. I gave the doctor's bill, the equivalent of fifty dollars, to John on his twenty-first birthday. The hospital charges, which we also paid, are better forgotten.

There was another expense that remains a delicate point. When I registered John's birth at the *Mairie* of Neuilly I spoke French and his name was recorded as *Jean*. Later, when I filled out forms at our Embassy to confirm his American citizenship, I wrote his name as *John*. That spelling was refused because *Jean* was the spelling of record. Meda, already unhappy I had failed to include her family name, insisted *Jean* should be officially changed to *John*. I had that done in Washington, for another fifty dollars.

The beauty and history of Paris is readily apparent when looking across the Pont d'Iena through the arch of the Eiffel Tower and across the grounds of the Champ de Mars to the gray stone buildings of the Ecole Militaire. Louis XV was king when their construction had started in 1751 for a school to "furnish France with an officer corps drawn from the impoverished sons of noblemen who had served the crown." Cadet *Napoleone Buonaparte* had spent his sixteenth year there. Later, they had served as a hospital, military headquarters, granary, stables, and barracks. In 1878, they had become the home of the Ecole Superieure de

2ND STUDY COMMITTEE, FRENCH WAR COLLEGE, 1949

Center: Colonel Labouerie, committee chairman; flanked on his right by Lt. Col. Christian de Castries*; left, by Lt. Col. Victor Croizat.

* *De Castries would command the defense at Dien Bien Phu in Indochina in 1954.*

Guerre, established two years before in the nearby Invalides. The Ecole had occupied the buildings since that time, except for the years of the First and Second World Wars.

Marine Corps participation, begun in 1926, had ended in 1940. I was the first Marine to return. My class was the sixty-third in the succession and the third since the school had resumed classes in 1946. It was made up of forty-three French officers, ten government officials, and twelve foreign officers. The French were a highly select group chosen from among two hundred and fifty candidates who had taken rigorous qualifying examinations. Beyond their professional attainments, several had titles of nobility and many were well-born. Yet, nearly all shared a genteel poverty due to the impact of the war on family fortunes and their low pay. Only two French officers had automobiles.

Our days usually began with conferences related to national defense presented by military and civilian authorities. The afternoons were spent in committee work on map exercises at division, corps, and army level. This routine was periodically interrupted by visits to factories, research laboratories, government facilities, and battlefields. I was impressed by the scope and organization of our curriculum and found it noteworthy that our commandant, Major General Bertrand and his deputy, Brigadier General Demetz, often joined in our activities.[5] The facilities were less impressive.

The two-hundred-year-old Ecole Militaire had magnificent rooms and a full share of history and tradition. What it did not have was reliable plumbing and heat. We kept our overcoats on in the lecture hall, where our steaming breath often obscured the speakers. The mess was slightly more hospitable, but the toilets were frigid and the paper cut from old map exercises. I usually walked to our Embassy for lunch with a classmate as guest. One such time, Commandant James Thiebaud, my Swiss classmate, stopped on the Champs Elysees and, looking toward the Arc de Triomphe, said, "I never cease to admire such magnificence. Do you realize Paris would not be as lovely had not kings and emperors imposed their taste on the people?" I agreed that architecture by committee seldom yielded such pleasing results.

My infrequent exchanges with Lt. Col. Stefano Coisson of the same *Alpini* corps in which my father had served were more thought-provoking. The graying, distinguished Italian was friendly, but I could not penetrate his reserve and wondered if it came from having fought on the other side. I asked the question of Lt. Col. Christian de Castries and was told, "Coisson is a professional who did his duty. The Germans who made me prisoner in 1940 were also professionals and treated me well. It was only later when reserves and conscripts filled the ranks that courtesies were forgotten and the war went to hell."

Neither Meda nor I ever settled into a routine since there was too much to experience. She had found a woman to help with the housework and care for John. This allowed her to study French and left us free to enjoy an active social life and travel as the occasion permitted. Europe is compact and our new car and open roads brought many sights within easy weekend range. In this manner we saw the gutted center of Rotterdam and the remnants of Cologne, ate sauerkraut

MEDA WITH FRENCH-BORN HEIR, PARIS, 1950

overlooking the cathedral at Strasbourg, had M. Haviland help us select our china in Limoges and bought a coffee service from a silversmith in Florence. I also enjoyed introducing Meda to the regions of Savoy and Piedmont where I had lived as a small boy.

My name and fluency in the language encouraged my French classmates to bring Meda and me into their social circle, despite their straitened circumstances. We were often invited to dine off delicate family china with crested silver at a table set in austere surroundings. Not all the French were living tough; de Castries had an exquisite apartment on the fashionable Rue Montaigne. With his red Spahi vest, polished boots and long cigarette holder he outshone all other cavalrymen in the class. The clipped poodle that shared his car added to the image of a dandy, a vision belied by his war record and decorations. Paradoxically, this officer who had made his reputation as a master of mobile warfare ended his career commanding the static defense at Dien Bien Phu.

Another among the favored minority was Lt. Col. Jacques Langlois de Bazillac who had ridden with Maj. Gen. Philip Leclerc when the 2nd Armored Division liberated Paris. While on a school visit to the sites of the 1944 landing in southern France, Langlois, who took pride in being a French Marine, arranged a picnic for us with a Madame who had been good to poorly paid Marine lieutenants in the old days. Upon retirement, she had purchased a bar that continued to cater to young officers. The picnic, which included two attractive assistants, was truly a *Never on Sunday* affair.

When our field trip in the south ended, de Castries suggested we spend the weekend in Vichy where the International Horse Show was in progress. Meda drove down from Paris to meet us. I knew de Castries had been a member of the French riding team before the war but had no idea of the prestige that attached to his person until Meda and I found ourselves in the midst of an elite gathering bathed in his lustre. Her love of riding allowed her to relish the experience. I, however, had not enjoyed equitation classes in Quantico as much as a horse meat filet I had once eaten, a preference not to be mentioned in that crowd.

Back in school, the roster of speakers who filled our mornings continued to be impressive. Among these was a retired general who had soldiered in Morocco. He recalled *l'oeuvre civilisatrice de l'armee* (the civilizing role of the Army) and the merits of the *tache d'huile* (oil spot) tactic to gain control over dissident populations. His narrative evoked visions of starlit desert skies, the austere grandeur of the Rif mountains and village elders pridefully wearing French decorations earned in long forgotten battles. I was listening enthralled when Bechtold whispered, "Translate his words into English." When I did, I found them amusing exaggerations. I later noted this in polite toasts or introductions. The French words touched emotions, the English translation invariably sounded stilted.

Our committee work revealed an innovative and flexible approach to combat operations. Map exercises were usually sited in Europe, though several were cast in North Africa and in the Middle East, where Israel's triumph in its first war for survival was opening a new chapter in Arab-Israeli relations. Indochina also received our attention. That conflict had started late in 1946 as a colonial war to restore France's prestige. When the communists gained control of China, it had become part of the West's opposition to communism. This perception was reinforced by the outbreak of the Korean War. Still, the Indochina War continued to be fought with volunteers from the regular forces attracted by a sense of adventure and the substantial allowances that helped restore an acceptable standard of living for their families. These benefits were paid for by the hazards of combat and long separations.

One memorable exercise was a replay of the Battle of France in May 1940, wherein original French dispositions were altered by a mechanized corps in reserve. The accompanying discussion revealed the emotional burden the French military were still carrying from the defeat of 1940. This had been attributed to a crushing superiority in German military power but, later, it was learned that the only serious imbalance was in attack aviation.[6] The comforting idea that the French had been overwhelmed by German materiel was dispelled. The fault clearly lay in their High Command. The innovative French thinkers, who had seen the battlefield of the future as clearly as German General Guderian and the British writer Liddell-Hart, had been insufficiently authoritative to alter the course of events.

The collapse of France had shocked the officer corps. The Army's need to regain its self-respect was straightforward, but the making of the new French Army had to be accomplished with officers like my classmates, whose war experiences differed widely. How to decide what measure of loyalty should be applied to officers serving in the colonies in 1940, who had continued to obey orders from the government after it moved to Vichy? How did their patriotism and service differ from that of those who escaped over the beaches of Dunkirk and joined de Gaulle's Free French? What of the many prisoners of war? Were those who failed to escape less worthy than those who succeeded? Then, too, how to differentiate fighting in the Maquis or other Free French units from membership in the First French Army?

Underlying this diverse patrimony was evidence that the French Army of 1949 reflected the image of the American, from which its sustenance had been drawn after the Allied invasion of North Africa in 1942. The final derivative of this complex and emotional situation was that the French colonies which had supported Gen. Charles de Gaulle's Free French during the war now were demanding a new relationship. These calls were poorly timed, for loss of empire was contrary to France's efforts to again become a great power.

Particularly striking in the turmoil of these cross currents was the goodwill and admiration the French displayed toward the Americans. This appeared during a class visit to Marseille. I had been reading the morning paper headlining President Truman's commitment of American forces to the defense of South Korea. While walking back to my hotel, alone and in uniform, I was stopped repeatedly by Frenchmen who took my arm or shook my hand exclaiming, *"Truman est magnifique!" "Vive les Americains!" "Nous sommes avec vous!"* The performance was all the more amazing in that Marseille was a communist stronghold where military shipments to Indochina were often delayed, when not damaged outright.

My visit the next day to our naval attache's office was even more amazing. When I neared the entrance on Rue Boetie I found a large crowd blocking the street and sidewalks. It was friendly and I had no difficulty in making my way into the building. Once inside Captain Smith-Hutton confirmed what I had deduced; they were veterans seeking to serve in Korea. As the captain put it, "Given the authority, we could form a division from general to private with those people in the street!"

This exhilarating episode was offset by sober warnings from our Embassy that the Soviet reaction to United Nations intervention in Korea could be an offensive in Europe. I thought it prudent to prepare an evacuation plan for Meda to get herself and John to Spain if that happened when I was absent. I stocked the necessary gasoline and cash and prepared road maps showing an itinerary using secondary roads to the border. Lastly, I stressed she leave immediately if Soviet forces crossed the Elbe. This was the first of several international dramas that would enliven our lives.

I was now in my final weeks of school and sad that this unique experience was ending. We brightened a bit when I obtained excellent seats from which to enjoy the pageantry of the Bastille Day parade down the Champs Elysees. The full panoply of Empire was on display that warm 14th of July: the Foreign Legion in its slow cadence, the Chasseurs Alpins in their quick-march, the Spahis on prancing white horses, the steady beat of Moroccan Goumiers and Algerian Tiralleurs, the measured pace of the black Senegalese battalions, all interspersed among the Metropolitan formations. It was a spectacle from an era that would soon be gone.

Ed Bechtold was slated to join General Eisenhower's new SHAPE Head-quarters in the North Atlantic Treaty Organization and I had hoped that the Marine Corps, having invested in qualifying me for such assignment, would keep me in Europe. However, I was to have three months after completion of the Ecole de Guerre to "study and observe the different arms, services, and military installations of France" and then proceed to Washington for further orders. All visits to French military facilities after the end of my studies were to be cleared with the appropriate authorities. Accordingly, Captain Smith-Hutton and I agreed that the travels authorized by my orders could be used to meet requirements of the Office of Naval Intelligence. Current information on the ports of Algeria and Tunisia was most pressing among these. '

French Navy clearance for my mission was readily obtained, and I left for Algiers to report to Vice Adm. Pierre Ronarc'h, commanding French Naval Forces, North Africa. Upon arrival, I checked in at the St. George Hotel, where it was claimed General Eisenhower had taught the bartender to make martinis, and called the flag secretary at naval headquarters to schedule my call. I reported the next morning, anxious to meet the admiral, who had become a legend in 1940 when he sailed the unfinished battleship *Jean Bart* out of the shipyard at Saint-Nazaire hours before the Germans arrived and brought it to Casablanca. Naval headquarters was in an old Turkish fort forming a breakwater, at the end of which the admiral's office was located.

Promptly at 1000, I entered Admiral Ronarc'h's office and found a modest room with austere furnishings and open windows, below which breaking waves brought the sounds and smells of the sea. The admiral, a craggy Breton, waved me to a seat. I sat forward, chatted for the duration of a cigarette, thanked him for receiving me, and rose. He waved me back and resumed talking. Two hours later, I was overlooking the city from the garden of Admiralty House enjoying a drink while his daughter was seeing to our lunch. After coffee, the admiral and I retired to his study where he continued with stories until, just before eight, his daughter came to remind him he had a dinner to attend.

The next morning, after arranging for delivery of flowers to Admiralty House with a thank you note for Mlle. Ronarc'h, I called the flag secretary and asked why he had not alerted me to what I should expect. The lieutenant explained that the admiral had few duties and spent much of his time interfering with those of his subordinates, all of whom had heard his stories many times. Thus, when my visit was announced, the staff had decided that I was a proper audience for the admiral and would ensure them a free day. I was not displeased. The admiral's cordial reception set the tone for my visit and assured the success of my mission.

I had also found much of interest in his conversation. To hear the story of the *Jean Bart* from the man responsible was a rare privilege, and his comments on French resistance to the landing of American and British forces in North Africa in November 1942 provided an important historical perspective. At that time, only the northern half of France was occupied by the Germans; responsibility for the rest of the country and its North African possessions remained with the French. Thus, when Allied forces appeared off Morocco and Algeria, the French felt obliged to resist in order to discourage the Germans from extending their occupation. Resistance would also measure Allied intent. If their intervention was simply a raid or demonstration, the French would win; if the landing was in strength, the French could capitulate without giving the Germans cause to intervene.

After gathering documentation on the port of Algiers, I proceeded to Oran, where I was given plans of the elaborate facilities being added to the naval base at Mers el Kebir. My last stop in Algeria was Bone, where I asked the port director to have the data I needed ready right after lunch because I was taking the train to Tunis. When I appeared, he was still at lunch. Annoyed, I sent for him. He arrived in bad humor and gave me the papers with little grace. I told him I thought him discourteous. Back in our car, my escort laughingly told me, "The director is a communist. He will have a stroke if he ever discovers you are American." After a moment he added, "You really are a threat to French security. It is too easy to forget you are not a countryman."

In Tunis, I was met by Commander Vaillant, the resident representative of the naval command at Bizerte. He asked about my schedule and I replied it was up to him, as long as we included a visit to Carthage. This was a fortunate comment. He was greatly interested in archeology and took me to several digs not open to the public. Our shared interest quickly put us on a friendly basis, and Vaillant confided that the one unwelcome aspect of his duties in Tunis was to help restore order whenever the American consul made a speech. The consul seemed unable to talk without referring to the evils of colonialism, which immediately fueled disturbances.

My sojourn in North Africa yielded information on thirteen major ports of sufficient merit to earn me a letter of appreciation from the Director of Naval Intelligence. It also ended an exceptional tour of duty that had enabled me to learn a great deal about the French, including specifics on operations in Indochina which I forwarded in official reports.[7] At the end of October we started the tedium of packing and the sadness of farewells. We were dismayed when our packers expanded our possessions with sufficient excelsior to fill forty wooden boxes. We were even more dismayed when the truck carrying them crashed into a stone wall and scattered its entire contents across the main road from Paris to St. Germain. Whether excelsior or miracle, only the truck was damaged.

We left Paris with reluctance, driving our car to London via the Calais-to-Dover ferry. Upon arrival, I confirmed our passage aboard the *Alexander M. Patch* sailing for New York. We then had two days to discover that austerity with a flair was continuing in Britain. We noted with a mix of compassion and amusement that our modest meat portions were invariably accompanied by two or three tired brussel sprouts, served with a flourish from an ornate silver dish. Rationing still existed and dining out in London in 1950 remained something less than an occasion.

We sailed from Southampton on November 20 into a wintery North Atlantic and were relieved to see the Statue of Liberty after a stormy trip. The morning after arriving in New York, I was at Marine Corps Headquarters in Washington, where I was inexplicably offered sixty days of unwanted leave and told I was assigned to the Marine Corps Schools in Quantico.[8] Europe was suddenly a remote part of a distant past. We were not happy to be back.

Quantico was a riverside village in George Washington country and part of the early colonial history of Virginia. Its association with the Marine Corps had begun in May 1917. At the time we arrived on a gray December day, the three-tiered Marine Corps Schools had been functioning for some thirty years. The Basic School, moved from Philadelphia, was at the bottom. Above it was the Junior School for captains and majors. Finally, the Senior School at the top was reserved for lieutenant colonels and colonels. I was assigned to the last as an instructor in the Tactical Operations Group headed by Col. Wallace M. Greene, Jr.

Housing was difficult and there was a six-month wait for quarters. Meda again handled the problem. We started in shabby temporary lodgings in the town of Quantico where the landlord, despite rent-control, raised the rent because I was of higher rank than his last tenant. After Christmas, she found us a better, though still drab, apartment just outside the main gate. This unsettled period, aggravated by severe morning sickness, was a less than pleasant introduction for her to a post where we developed many enduring friendships.

Shortly after arriving I called on Franklin Hart, then Commandant of the Marine Corps Schools. We talked of the difficult landing on Namur and of our days on Maui until, just before I left, he asked me to tutor his son in French. Unable to think of a diplomatic refusal, I agreed. Years later I learned Hart had just rejected a request for my services with the United Nations mission to Palestine without mentioning the matter to me. Had I known, I might have been less compliant with his request for personal tutoring.

In early summer we moved into quarters on the base, a top floor apartment in a building occupied by lieutenant colonels, all with young families. Shortly after, on September 14, our daughter, Suzanne, was born at the naval hospital, completing our family. Meda found carrying a baby plus managing a two-year-old up the three double flights was a challenge. Still, by our second Christmas we were well settled. Meda had friends with whom to enjoy the museums and theaters in Washington, when I could not join her. I was finding my professional responsibilities stimulating. No military subject was ignored and no problem escaped the continuing search for improvement.

The services were then seeking to understand the role of nuclear weapons on future battlefields. As a tactics instructor I took part in a number of study groups at the Infantry School at Fort Benning. During these sessions I became aware of how handicapped the Army was by its dependence on the Air Force for its air support. We Marines had our own aviation and, with it, a nuclear weapons delivery capability; the Army had to rely on an Air Force concerned with strategic bombardment. The Army sought to satisfy its needs by acquiring its own tactical aviation and developing long-range artillery to fire nuclear projectiles. But the Defense Department imposed limitations on fixed-wing Army aviation, leaving only the helicopter, which it exploited spectacularly in the concept of sky cavalry.

I was sympathetic to the Army's difficulties; dependence on another service for the support needed to accomplish one's mission is dangerous. Moreover, the devastation in Europe had strengthened my discomfort with the values of strategic bombardment. While nuclear weapons now made the heretofore inflated claims of the bomber enthusiasts possible, I still could not accept a radioactive wasteland as an asset. This attitude made me savor the embarrassment of the Air Force during a demonstration at Eglin Air Force Base for one of the periodic Joint Civilian Orientation Conferences hosted by the Secretary of Defense. These featured prominent figures in defense industries and related organizations, who were organized into *flights* for visits to service facilities where demonstrations of specialized skills were intended to reveal how effectively the military was spending their taxes.

I had been assigned to escort the Gold Flight. After being awed by night carrier operations in heavy seas off the Virginia Capes and deafened by the Army blasting the Georgia countryside with shot and shell, we flew to Florida to give the Air Force its chance to gain new friends. The climax of the show was to be a demonstration of carpet bombing contrasting the modern B-36 with the B-17 of World War II. Following band music, the B-17s flew by and dropped impressive numbers of 500-pound bombs. After more music the announcer proclaimed in reverential tones, "And now, gentlemen, the B-36!" We all leaned forward and looked up, Then, we waited, and waited, and waited, but the sky remained empty. Neither the announcer nor the band was prepared for the contingency. The long, awkward silence was at last broken by an extended rumble in the far distance. The B-36s had dropped their loads...but, on the wrong range!

Back in Quantico, I found my request for duty in Korea had been turned down. This was not unexpected for I had been told that my recent overseas service made it unlikely my tour in Quantico would be cut short. Still, I had felt compelled to submit my letter when I found myself in the reverse of the situation I had enjoyed in 1943. I was a tactics instructor who had not been to Korea, teaching students fresh from the battlefields. With that option denied me, I took on the full range of instruction from historical lectures to tactical exercises and extended map maneuvers. This led to a pleasant interlude in southern Italy where I verified the accuracy of the model of the Bay of Naples we used to demonstrate amphibious assault operations.

Another set of temporary duty orders sent me to Arzew, Algeria for a two-week NATO amphibious orientation course. The curriculum based on Marine Corps doctrine was hardly onerous; what was, however, was the noonday meal. Captain Patou, the commander at Arzew, had a superb cook whose labors we were always ready to honor because French breakfast never quite satisfied. The ritual began with an aperitif, after which we were wined and dined for never less than an hour. We then returned to the bar for a quick coffee and brandy before making our way to the lecture hall, where we slipped into a post-prandial stupor that defeated every lecturer, no matter his subject. An added tragedy was that when we regained consciousness we faced a long evening with nothing to do; a situation I failed to resolve when Patou told me that having our main meal in the evening would violate tradition.

I was now in my fourth year at Quantico and well versed in the curriculum which I thought needed a problem set in Indochina to familiarize students with an area of growing interest. The director agreed. With access to quantities of aerial photos of the Indochina coast provided by the Office of Naval Intelligence and my own personal notes and related documentation, I prepared a problem sited near Quang Tri below the 17th parallel, where Marines would fight years later. The problem ran in April just as my French classmate, Colonel de Castries, was making his last desperate effort at Dien Bien Phu. This stimulated student interest, already encouraged by our excellent Naval Intelligence material and my familiarity with the Indochina war. It was a satisfying way to end forty-two months as an instructor.

In early June, I received a call from Headquarters in Washington informing me I was to be assigned to the Navy Section of the Military Assistance and Advisory Group, Indochina for liaison duties with the French. I was delighted until I learned no dependents were allowed. Neither Meda nor I were happy at breaking up the family, but we turned our energies to planning and packing. This was not easy. Meetings in Geneva were at that moment deciding the fate of Indochina and we thought it possible she might be permitted to join me later. It seemed best for her to await developments at her parents' home. We thus separated our worldly goods into three lots: one for storage, one for Meda and the children, and a third for me. We packed and cleaned in the sticky summer heat, said good-bye to our friends and, after the usual white glove inspection of our quarters, began the long drive west.

**STOP ON LONG DRIVE WEST,
GENERAL CUSTER MARKER, MONTANA**

Meda's parents assured us she and the children were welcome for as long they wished to stay. These were comforting words, but Meda and I both knew a lengthy stay with two active children would be an imposition. Equally important was that, while I was off to an exotic land, she was returning to the home she had left after college, when she had decided to "go west" on her own. While promising adventure for me, our separation was a long step back for her. Already saddened by prospects of losing the camaraderie we shared, our farewells were further affected by the unspoken concern that Indochina was still a war zone. Altogether, this was one of our most difficult partings. I began my return to the Pacific with a deep sense of loneliness and uncertainty.

Five

INDOCHINA: UNEASY ARMISTICE

Indochina, for me, was first fantasy, then reality.[1] The fantasy had begun in 1930 at the Colonial Exposition in Paris, where I had been awed by a partial replica of the temple of Angkor Wat. Reality had begun near twenty years later when Ecole de Guerre classmates somberly received news of casualties among friends and colleagues. Reality had become personal at Quantico with my exercise on Vietnam. It had remained so in Washington during briefings on my new assignment, when I discovered that the French had denied our military mission, in Saigon since 1950, a voice in any operations and training deliberations. Then, in January 1954, Lt. Gen. Henri Navarre, the French commander-in-chief in Indochina, had agreed to receive five American liaison officers at his headquarters in Saigon.

The other services had promptly sent their selectees. The Marine Corps had delayed its decision and I had only ten days to settle my affairs. This, while inconvenient, was not disturbing. My French war college classmates in Indochina included the chiefs of the intelligence and operations sections and I was confident they would provide me access in Navarre's headquarters. However, the surrender at Dien Bien Phu had precipitated a crisis that heralded the end of hostilities and could eliminate my job before it began. Meda and I set these concerns aside as we drove across country and endured the sadness of parting. But, my disquiet returned in Hawaii when I learned the French had signed an agreement on July 20, ending the war.

The tedium of the trans-Pacific flight failed to calm my troubled thoughts. The end of the fighting in Korea the year before had not resolved differences there, and developments in Indochina appeared no more conclusive. I expected the confrontation between the Western and communist worlds to continue and wondered what my role would be. I had as many questions as there were miles across the Pacific. However, by the time we lifted off Clark Air Force Base and

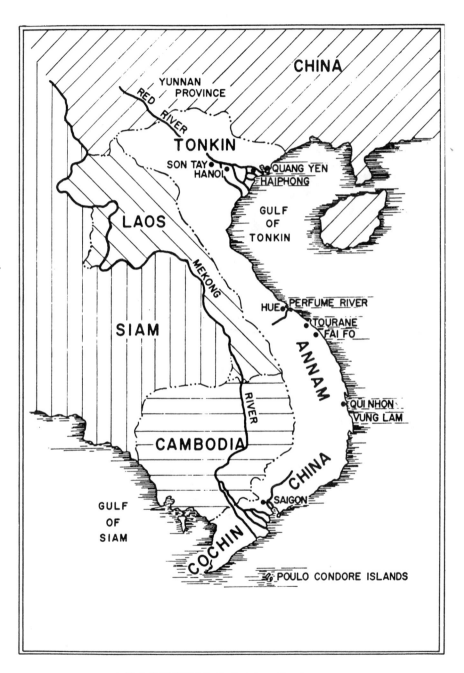

INDOCHINESE PENINSULA, 19TH CENTURY

U.S. Navy Map

headed west over the South China Sea, I had regained my sense of adventure and was fascinated when we made landfall and a brilliant mosaic of rice fields unfolded below me.

Tan Son Nhut Airport was no hotter nor more humid than Washington. On the drive to the Majestic Hotel, I traveled streets whose names honored the heroes of France's colonial past, then entered Rue Catinat to reach the Saigon River and the hotel. Saigon, with its tree-lined streets, open buildings, and profusion of flowers, reminded me of southern France. The people were nearly all Asian and the costume of the women unusual, but the general aspect was definitely French. The traffic, in particular, was confused enough to be Gallic, though the cyclo-pousses and buffalo-drawn carts added an exotic touch. Evidence of the eight-year war just ended was unobtrusive. Wire grills protected the sidewalk cafes from grenades, but the military presence was modest.

My sense of familiarity lessened on the way to the Military Assistance and Advisory Group (MAAG) compound, when Boulevard Gallieni took the name Tran Hung Dao and French Saigon yielded to Chinese Cholon. The drab compound, in a maze of narrow streets, included a main building and several small shelters crowded behind a high wall. It was in striking contrast to the French facilities I had just seen. Capt. James D. Collett greeted me with the news that the liaison agreement with the French had not materialized. He then took me to meet Maj. Gen. John W. O'Daniel, whose courteous reception belied his gruff appearance. He did little to ease my mind over my duties and Collett did not help when, on our way back to the Navy office, he told me to "take a few days off while we decide what to do with you."

I first sought to familiarize myself with the city during the long siesta but found everything closed down. I did better getting acquainted with our MAAG, aid mission, and Embassy personnel and calling on my French classmates, all of whom provided welcome insights of the current complex situation. The commitment of United States forces in Korea in 1950 had transformed the struggle in Indochina from a colonial war to an anti-communist struggle supported by increasing American aid. The Geneva Agreements had ended the fighting, but the French were to remain until elections in mid-1956 ended the temporary partition of the country.[2] The United States was to fund these French forces. However, that decision was complicated by the fighting in Algeria and pending negotiations on a regional collective security pact.

The Vietnamese in the North, with a victorious army of 230,000 veterans backed by 100,000 militia, confidently awaited the outcome of the elections in 1956. In the South, an army of one hundred and twenty-five separate battalions under French command was disintegrating, while French-supported Sect forces prepared to fight for their fiefdoms.[3] Superimposed over this faltering structure was the newly designated Premier Ngo Dinh Diem, inexperienced,

deeply suspicious of the French, and a well-born Catholic in a land of predomi-
nantly Buddhist peasants. The Americans, meanwhile, were debating whether
to take on supporting the South Vietnamese Army before the Diem government
proved stable, or to do so in order to strengthen it.

I was grateful, as I went about absorbing this flow of facts and impressions,
to find lighter moments. Lt. Col. Eugene Guibaud, the French intelligence chief,
told me the note I had sent from Quantico had been parachuted to de Castries at
Dien Bien Phu. I had enclosed a *Washington Post* article stating Eisenhower
thought he should be made a general. He had been, but only in time to surrender the garrison.[4] Later at dinner, Guibaud's garden prompted me to mention
how attractive the trees and flowers made the streets. Saigon, he replied, had
become dirty and ill-kept and was no longer the *Paris of the Orient.* I would
remember his sentiments when, years later, I returned to a city overwhelmed by
teeming multitudes and a blue fog of motorscooter fumes.

While on my routine of discovery, I noted large numbers of refugees on the
streets. The flow had begun when the French in North Vietnam consolidated
their forces in an elongated perimeter extending from Hanoi to Haiphong. That
had abandoned much of Tonkin, including the Catholic provinces of Bui Chu
and Phat Diem, to the Viet Minh. Then, with the signing of the Geneva Agreement, the flow of people to the south became a flood of half a million civilians,
plus a quarter million members of the French Expeditionary Corps. It was a
drama of unexpected magnitude which, five days after my arrival, settled the
question of my duties.

Michael Adler of our American aid mission had gone North in July to monitor the situation, and O'Daniel had sent Lt. Col. Rolland Hamelin to look things
over. On his return, Hamelin reported the French had thirty-one reception centers filled near Hanoi and an additional 35,000 refugees were gathered between
Haiduong and Haiphong. The French, he added, were bringing some 3,000
refugees south each day, but the sealift to move heavy equipment and vehicles
was inadequate. Calls for help came from Diem on August 5 and from the French
the next day. President Eisenhower responded promptly. Task Force 90 under
Rear Adm. Lorenzo S. Sabin was assigned to provide sealift and on August 7
O'Daniel was appointed coordinator of all American evacuation support, with
Collett as his deputy. I, too, was soon involved.

As I began my second week in Saigon, refugees were crowding into schools,
the municipal theater, and the many tent cities that had appeared in open lots,
parks, and on the race track. General O'Daniel was everywhere, as were French
Brig. Gen. Gambiez and other American, French, and Vietnamese officials, who
labored to receive and resettle the ever-growing numbers. The miracle was that
so much was accomplished by agencies that were overworked even before they
were properly organized and staffed. My responsibilities centered on serving

General O'Daniel as interpreter and action officer. Thus, I was not surprised when he called early on my second Sunday in Saigon to say a camp for 12,000 refugees had to be built in two weeks at Cap Saint Jacques, on the coast below the capital, to help relieve the Saigon reception centers.

He directed I go to the Vietnamese headquarters and ask Maj. Gen. Nguyen Van Hinh, the Chief of Staff, to have two battalions of infantry at the Cap by Monday morning. I was then to join Lt. Col. Jack Blades and CPO William Azbell and proceed to the Cap by boat. There, we were to contact the French authorities and get the work started. My exposure to generals at the chief-of-staff level was limited and I did not think that early Sunday offered the promise of a warm welcome. I was wrong. General Hinh received me cordially, agreed

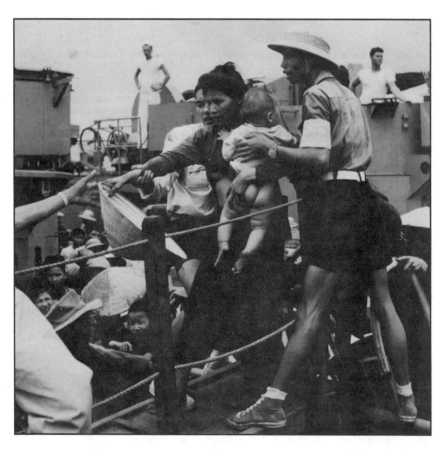

REFUGEES ARRIVING, CAP ST. JACQUES, SOUTH VIETNAM, AUGUST 1954

to my request, went on to tell me of his interest in refugee affairs, and added an informative background on Vietnam's naval forces.[5] I would happily have prolonged my call had I not needed to start down river.

We reached Cap Saint Jacques, now Vung Tau, and checked in with the French colonel commanding the sector, who offered to help in any way he could. Earlier that week, Admiral Sabin had offered General O'Daniel the use of Seabees to build camps and control beach operations. O'Daniel had refused, explaining that would violate the Geneva Agreements' provision prohibiting the introduction of additional forces into the country. I did not know of that meeting but was about to learn of it. While Blades and I met with the French, I sent Chief Azbell to find out if there were any Seabees aboard an American landing ship in the bay. There were, and they were eager to help.

No sooner had they landed and started to clear brush than the colonel came to tell me to call MAAG immediately. When I did, I was told the International Control Commission had reports of American landings and was coming to investigate.[6] I explained the situation and said I would have the Seabees return to their ship, but did not add I would arrange to have them paint their equipment any color other than Army khaki or Navy gray and return that night in civilian dress. Thanks to these *civilians* and my Vietnamese troops the camp was ready on August 29. By then 177,000 Vietnamese had been evacuated by the French with the beginning of American help, reception facilities were in place in the South, and resettlement had started.

That done, I asked General O'Daniel if I could move north and work that end of the evacuation. He agreed, and I flew to Haiphong on September 17 and joined Adler and Hamelin in the dreary Hotel de Paris. The city, built late in the 19th century seven miles up the Cua Cam River, reminded me of drab garrison towns in northeast France. The port was limited to ships with less than thirty-foot draught, but Haiphong was important because of its industries and rail-link to China, which the Japanese had severed in 1940. Echoes of its past were still evident, but the bustle was lessening perceptibly day by day. I found the evacuation there being pursued with the same vigor as in Saigon. Adler was rapidly depleting our tent stocks in the Far East to provide the tentage for camps which the French were building with black Senegalese, brown North Africans, and blond German Legionnaires.

The Legion also provided the security for the Briqueterie, the open area where the refugees boarded French landing craft for the four-hour trip to the transports anchored in the spectacular Baie d'Halong. Our Navy, concerned with health and sanitation, had landed a medical team to help in the camps. Lt. (jg) Thomas Dooley, an amiable young doctor with the team, was most energetic in caring for the refugees, and his engaging manner soon made him a popular figure. This encouraged him to publish a lavishly embroidered version of his services which did not endear him to the people and agencies who had done most of the work.[7]

**REFUGEES EMBARKING, HAIPHONG,
NORTH VIETNAM, SEPTEMBER 1954**

In addition to the Navy medical team, I was usually present at all embarkations, as were Lieutenant Colonel Blanchet from the Saigon headquarters and Major de Champeau from the Haiphong base command. Mme. Querville, the wife of Rear Adm. Jean Marie Querville, commanding naval forces in the North, and Mme. Vu Thinh Ngai, head of the An Lac Orphanage, were there with the Vietnamese Red Cross to dispense necessities to the embarking families. Lastly, the Vietnamese Refugee Committee assigned interpreters and nurses to sail on our ships. These resolved many problems but could not solve that of flush toilets. Drawings explaining them were distributed, but only the paper proved useful. Yet, despite such difficulties, the evacuation was going well and medical problems were rare.

The communists did not interfere initially with the movement of refugees but, as the numbers grew and the loss of face became evident, the Viet Minh vilified our efforts and sought to block the overland movement of refugees to the reception centers. As a result, refugees put to sea on rafts trusting the French to pick them up. When Admiral Querville learned of these desperate measures, he sent landing craft to ferry them to French and American transports offshore. Meanwhile, our combined information services worked diligently to get word to the Vietnamese of their option to move south. But Father Joseph Khue, who maintained an underground information net extending deep into Viet Minh areas, proved the most effective.

Quiet and unassuming, Father Khue's enthusiasms were contagious. I found his reports useful once I learned to discount his optimism. I also learned about the temporal power of local priests. When the communists came to a Catholic village, they usurped the authority of the priest, who then led his flock away. Because of this, eighty-five percent of the refugees from North Vietnam were Catholics. I did not question encouraging the North Vietnamese to leave, since the Viet Minh regime was oppressive. But I was uneasy and, recalling General Hinh's allusion to the political implications of a massive infusion of Catholics into the South, wondered how much this was influencing the exodus.

One day, while walking with a priest who shared my concerns, we came upon several unhappy women bathing in a pond. Their distress, they explained to the priest, was that the American soap would not lather. This puzzled me until I remembered the delivery of relief packages containing bars of American processed cheese, identical to the blocks of soap sold in village markets. Not surprisingly the women, unfamiliar with cheese, had thought it was soap. It was hard to keep a straight face while the Father explained.

My office in the city hall was next to that of the port director, a duty Admiral Querville delegated to a Navy rating from Marseille named Yvonne Negre. Since I arranged berthing for our ships, I was a regular visitor. One morning Mlle. Negre arrived late, her face unusually pale. I offered her coffee and, as her color returned, she confided, "I went to an opium den last night and, surprised that a pipe was consumed in one puff, I had several. Instead of dreams, I spent the night vomiting." Her story discouraged experimentation. On another occasion she tested my interpreter ability saying, "A word I'm sure is not nice has puzzled me for years. When the Americans landed in southern France, they were friendly but when things went wrong they would blame the *fucking* French. What does that mean?" My translation was labored.

Shortly after arriving I had happily accepted an invitation to join the Haiphong base command mess. The meals were excellent and the contacts useful. I discovered the French were no better at understanding our motives and attitudes than we theirs, and neither of us were particularly perceptive when it came to understanding the Vietnamese. My contacts with Admiral Querville were equally rewarding. At first my conversations with the cocky Breton dealt with ship movements, but these soon expanded to riverine warfare, which had been one of his major concerns, and to a place in his social circle. I was also welcome at Madame Ngai's dinner table and at Governor Le Quang Luat's residence, where the traditional tea was replaced by whiskey and soda, all the more appreciated because it was so rare.

Wine is part of the French military ration and was readily available. Whiskey was not. We were thus pleased when we received a case of Canadian Club from Saigon. It arrived as an Indian, a Canadian, and two Polish officers of the

International Control Commission moved in across the street, so we invited them to share in its opening. With glasses filled, we offered the usual toasts, *cheers, bottoms up, here's how, luck.* Then, realizing the Poles had not understood a word, I used the only phrase in Polish I knew. The Poles looked shocked. But, seeing my innocent smile, they laughed and repeated what I had said. I know of no other international gathering that proceeded so amicably when the only exchange between the communists and the other guests consisted of calling each other *you son of a bitch.*

While each day brought new problems, the loading of refugees soon became routine. The pattern was interrupted when our Navy landing ships came to the Briquetrie to load military vehicles. On other days the action shifted to the port proper where commercial ships took on cargos. When not at the embarkation sites, I joined Mike Adler in seeing to the removal of property acquired with American funds. That was Mike's responsibility, but he spoke no French and I often helped him to move things along. I also became involved when the disposition of this property required American shipping.

One such incident began with the visit of a formidable French woman, a real-life *Tugboat Annie*, who knocked on my hotel room door early one morning. She introduced herself as the owner of the lighters serving the port of Haiphong and offered me ten thousand dollars if I could get a landing ship to carry them to Saigon. She appeared unconvinced when I assured her that neither we nor the French wanted such valuable equipment left for the communists and had already arranged with our Navy to move her lighters.

Another break in the routine involved a memorable visit to Hanoi on the last weekend the French flag flew over that city. Hanoi, the pre-war capital of Indochina and over twice the size of Haiphong, had been an important city since the time of Chinese suzerainty. I found its blend of French and Asian influences attractive but was saddened by the sight of furnishings littering sidewalks in front of abandoned European homes and by the strange hush of a city in suspense. We had gone to help close down our aid mission's refugee operation and remained overnight. After a long day, we spent an equally long night trying valiantly to reduce the bar stocks that would fall to the communists on Monday. We accomplished our first task but proved unequal to the second.

As news of the evacuation reached beyond our world, we began to have visitors. Newsman Joseph Alsop, whose interest in the local situation concerned classified matters I could not discuss, was among the first civilians. Cardinal Spellman, who followed, was received by Capt. Nicholas J. Frank Jr., the new Seventh Fleet representative based aboard a destroyer escort anchored in the river. Then it was my turn to arrange the late November tour of retired Gen. J. Lawton Collins, President Eisenhower's newly appointed special envoy, who appeared anxious to learn all he could. I took him through the refugee camps

**VISIT OF REFUGEE CAMP,
HAIPHONG, NORTH VIETNAM, NOVEMBER 1954**

From Left: Lt. Col. Victor J. Croizat, unidentified assistant to General Collins, Gov. Le Quang Luat, Gen. J. Lawton Collins.

USOM Photo

and the port and accompanied him on courtesy calls; the first was to Maj. Gen. Rene Cogny who, as commander of French forces in the North, was responsible for security until the final withdrawal.

Cogny was deferential in his greetings, as a major general should be to one who had worn four stars. Collins responded, with his finger directed at the French general's chest, by emphasizing the importance of getting everything out of the North that could possibly serve the communists. When he paused for breath, Cogny explained that his only obligation beyond keeping the Viet Minh out of the perimeter was to leave municipal services operating. All else would go; even the foundations of military buildings were being destroyed. He also spoke of his efforts to get private businesses to leave. However, he did not mention his frustrations with the policy changes by the succession of short-lived French governments, as he had to me in private.

Another visit, in which I featured as principal rather than escort, began when Governor Luat suggested I accompany his deputy on a Sunday outing. We drove to an isolated camp where a battalion from the "Provincial Brigades of North Vietnam" was drawn up for my inspection. The tour that followed revealed rudimentary facilities. The sickbay had less equipment than a corpsman's medical kit and the armory held only a few automatic weapons. The display, though meagre, was moving. These were men to whom the communist evil was real. Later, when the conversation turned to their need for our support, I regretted having to be noncommittal.

Although I suspected little would come of it, I reported my visit to Col. Edward Lansdale in Saigon.[8] I had to treat such sensitive matters carefully to avoid giving Querville any reason to question my credibility. A short time before, the admiral had curtly summoned me to his office to account for "certain American intelligence personnel, presumably military," one of whom had made "statements against the interests of France." Querville had given me the man's name and insisted he be removed within forty-eight hours. I had relayed his message to General O'Daniel. The MAAG plane had arrived and departed with one passenger, and relations with Querville returned to normal.

We had no Thanksgiving turkey and Christmas was no more festive. My contacts with refugees were hardly cheering. Nor were the French happy to be leaving Tonkin, which they had ruled for seventy-one years and where they had suffered so many casualties. Though long in coming and high in cost, independence was welcomed by the Vietnamese. Yet, I saw no jubilation in either the North or South, only uncertainty over the future. The Geneva Agreements marked a defeat for the West, but the massive exodus from the North had demeaned the victory of the communists. I regret that recognition of the hardships accepted by the thousands who left home, ancestors, and chattels to seek freedom should have faded so easily.

The massive migration south had left Haiphong a moribund city. The refugee camps retained their animation, but elsewhere the tempo of life had slowed to an unnatural pace. I had no regret when, six weeks into the new year, I was recalled to Saigon where events had been stirring. Premier Diem had from the beginning been challenged by General Nguyen Van Hinh, a French appointee eager to replace him. Ambassador Heath, supportive of Diem, thought Hinh should leave. O'Daniel, who had helped Hinh plan the reorganization of the

Vietnamese Army, believed he could be persuaded to cooperate. These differences had soured relations between Embassy and MAAG just when the French were becoming suspicious of America's motives.

While these conflicting currents were swirling in Saigon, the Joint Chiefs of Staff, bowing to pressure from the State Department, had agreed to organize and train the Vietnamese armed forces. Shortly after, on September 8, 1954, the United States signed the Manila Pact, which would give rise to the South East Asia Treaty Organization.[9] Despite these events, the French continued to view American support of Diem as undermining their interests; the Americans to look upon French initiatives as schemes to overthrow the Premier. At the beginning of November, Collins arrived to assess the situation and determine the scope of the American effort to follow, and in mid-month Hinh was recalled to France.

A month later Collins and Gen. Paul Ely, the new French commander, agreed the United States should have responsibility, under French overall direction, for the organization and training of an 88,000-man Vietnamese Army, to become autonomous by July 1955. O'Daniel, anticipating early French government approval of the agreement, had established the nucleus of a bi-national Advisory Training and Operations Mission as 1954 ended; Comdr. Alan R. Josephson was its only Navy member.

The MAAG was limited to the three hundred and forty-two military personnel present at the time of the Geneva Agreements and already burdened by the return of military equipment originally provided the French. It would be difficult for it to assume the training responsibilities envisioned.[10] The matter was held in abeyance until February, when Paris accepted the Ely-Collins arrangements. The urgent need to staff the Franco-American training mission had resulted in my recall to Saigon.

Upon my return, Hamelin and I asked O'Daniel to allow our families to join us. He agreed, and I turned to Lt. Col. Pierre Obier, another French classmate, for help with housing. Pierre came up with a colonial-style villa on Rue La Grandiere, opposite the Grall Military Hospital. I moved in immediately and, while waiting for my family, hired two Tonkinese as servants. I also spent a hundred dollars for ten cases of scotch ordered by British Embassy contacts and acquired a case of chicken soup from departing friends. When I received word Meda, five-year-old John, and three-year-old Suzanne were arriving in Manila, I flew to the Philippines and surprised them by coming out in the pilot boat that met their ship. We then went on to Clark Air Force Base for the flight to Saigon.

✳ ✳ ✳

Despite the progress that had been made at the end of 1954 to harmonize relations, the atmosphere in Saigon as the new year began continued perturbed by the Sect problem. The specific concern was how Diem intended to maintain the loyalty of the French-supported Sect communities while integrating only part of their forces into a national Army, which was itself being reduced. He had gained favor with the Cao Dai and Hoa Hao sects by generous bribes. However, the Binh Xuyen, who controlled gambling and the Saigon police, had more to lose and were less tractable. On March 3, three weeks after I was back in Saigon, they had been denied renewal of their license to operate the Grand Monde Casino and called for the formation of a new government.

The Americans and French had sought to defuse the confrontation, but this had run afoul of the usual suspicions, to which the French added the argument that the Sects did not trust Diem. Unwilling to allow the situation to continue, Diem had replaced the Binh Xuyen police chief on March 29. In response, the Binh Xuyen attacked the police headquarters and shelled the Palace. When the French quickly interceded to halt the fighting, some American officials, including O'Daniel, suspected they were acting to undermine the Diem government. Collins, however, thought these events indicated that Diem could not govern. The French simply thought Diem mad. By the time Collins left for Washington on April 21, he had decided to urge Diem's removal.

Shortly after his departure, the Binh Xuyen again shelled the Palace. This time Diem promptly directed the Army to intervene and, in the absence of French reaction, the Binh Xuyen were driven into Cholon. Bao Dai, Vietnam's head of state, then called Diem to France, but Diem refused to comply and directed the Army to clear the capital of all remaining Binh Xuyen. This second outbreak of violence had started before I left for Manila, but I had not expected it to spread. I could not have been more surprised the morning of April 24, when I saw newspaper headlines reading SAIGON IN FLAMES. The quiet celebration I had hoped for after we got to Saigon was going to be more animated than I had planned. I crossed my fingers, assured Meda there was nothing to worry about, and ushered everyone onto the plane.

Our flight was uneventful, but once in Saigon the smell of burning buildings and rattle of gunfire revealed it was not business as usual. Still, we reached our new home without trouble. Then, as we sat down to our first dinner, of canned chicken noodle soup because firefights had kept the cook from getting to market, the transformer down the street was blown up and the lights and ceiling fans went out. We continued our meal by candlelight against a background of small arms fire, the explosion of an occasional mortar round, and the clamor of ambulances bringing wounded to the hospital across the street. The children found it all exciting; Meda and I were grateful for the scotch.

Our spectacular return to domesticity might have caused lesser women to reverse course for home. Meda, however, took things in stride. The children's safety received priority. Because grenades had been tossed over garden walls, they were forbidden the front garden with its maze of hedges and gravel walks.

To absorb their energies, Meda entered them in a *jardin d'enfants* run by French nuns. This kindergarten opened at seven and provided a haven where they could be with other children and begin learning French. At noon, she would pick them up for lunch and a swim at the *Cercle Sportif*, the venerable French Sports Club where I sometimes joined them. As an added measure, we never left them in Saigon without arranging for a reliable friend to stay with them.

Continual vigilance also extended into matters of health. We respected the schedule of inoculations, boiled all water used for drinking, cooking, and making ice cubes and washed fresh fruits and vegetables in chlorine or permanganate solutions. The children, too, learned their lessons well; long after we returned to Washington they refused to drink tap water. Such precautions kept the children healthy. Meda and I, however, were occasionally troubled by food or drink consumed away from home.

Meda was the first "Navy" wife in Saigon, and Capt. Harry Day, who had replaced Jim Collett, made her the Navy hostess. This involved official functions in addition to dinners with American, British, French, and Vietnamese friends. Madame Ngai, now in Saigon, was among our friends. On our first family call at her newly relocated orphanage we were received with the traditional champagne. Unnoticed by Meda or me, it was also served to Suzanne, who did not like it, and John, who did. He was soon singing, "The room is going around and around." We were more watchful on later visits.

In early July, a change in currency regulations enabled us to sail to Japan at reduced cost. The crew of the *Vietnam* were largely French Navy reservists who treated us well on the outbound leg, but the atmosphere became more personal once Admiral and Madame Querville joined the ship in Kobe. I was pleased to see the Quervilles and we quickly resumed the easy relations of Haiphong, which Meda readily shared. The ship's officers acknowledged our new status by inviting us to join a small circle that gathered late at night for champagne and caviar. My bar bill for the three-week voyage was all of fifteen dollars, but I have since paid dearly to satisfy the taste for caviar it awakened in Meda.

Shortly after our return to Saigon, Meda started teaching in an English language program for Vietnamese officers. She was startled by the courtesy of her students, who stood when she entered the room, and bemused to find herself at eye level with them. They also provided glimpses of their lives. All were in their twenties or early thirties and all had known only turmoil. Some had grown up in the North, some in the South; all had been affected by the violence. They looked upon their fight against foreign and communist domination as a struggle without beginning or foreseeable end. This view, plus the Vietnamese philosophy expressed in the proverb "the reed that bends does not break," contrasted with the attitudes of the Americans, who came for short tours and expected quick solutions.

DECORATING THE DALAT CHRISTMAS TREE, SAIGON, 1955

Again, there was no turkey that Thanksgiving. Christmas, however, was far more cheerful than in 1954, though an incident threatened to mar the occasion. Earlier in the fall, Meda and I had driven from Saigon to Nha Trang by way of Dalat, the resort town in the highlands. When Christmas neared we decided to return to Dalat with the children to cut a tree for the holiday. On our return, I rounded a blind curve in the Blao Pass and hit a truck on my side of the road, leaving us immobilized in an area that had been the site of recent ambushes. Fortunately, a car with American occupants was close behind and they agreed to notify the police, take the children home, and tell a friend of our where-abouts. That done, we waited in the gathering dusk watched by the crowd of men from the trucks unable to pass.

I chambered a round in my 9mm Beretta, placed the pistol on the seat between us, and waited endless black hours until the police arrived and pains-takingly prepared their accident report. To our relief, the men who had made us so uneasy cheerfully pulled our crumpled fender away from the wheel so we could continue on our way. The feeling did not last. A few miles beyond the pass we entered a rubber plantation where a fallen tree blocked the road. Although it had obviously been cut deliberately, nothing materialized out of the darkness. We found a detour and reached home without other adventures. Our Christmas tree was all the more appreciated for the effort and apprehensions it represented.

Saigon in the spring of 1955 was a city worn by four years of Japanese occupation and eight years of war, superimposed on the tensions of clandestine independence movements that had started in the early 1930s. The divisions and strains in the society during those years continued and the future was obscured by the issues awaiting resolution. The Americans were no more at ease than anyone else, but Diem's decisive stand against the Sects had firmed American support for his government. The future, though still uncertain, could be viewed with some optimism.

General Hinh had unknowingly prepared me for my new role in August 1954, when he had given me a staff paper on the Vietnamese Navy's origins. The document revealed that, although authorized on December 30, 1949, the first unit to fly the Vietnamese flag, a naval assault division of four boats under French command, was not organized until April 1953. The delay was the result of differences between the admiralty in Saigon, which favored a river Navy, and the more ambitious views of the Ministry in Paris. While the Vietnamese Navy was slowly taking form, the French Army had organized various Vietnamese river support units, including six commandos that had been assigned to the Navy. Capt. Jean Louis Delayen, a dashing French Marine, headed these commandos in the North in the final year of the war.[11]

When the war ended, the Vietnamese Navy numbered just over a thousand men, manning four naval assault divisions, three auxiliary mine sweepers, and one large landing craft. In addition, a provisional Marine battalion was encamped near the naval training center at Nha Trang. This unit had been created by Delayen who, distressed at the disintegration of the Vietnamese forces, had gathered his commandos into a battalion and obtained French Navy approval to move them south. Shortly after, the government had decreed the formation of a Marine Corps made up of river support units and commandos. Such was the status of South Vietnam's naval forces at the time I arrived.

When I joined the Advisory Training and Operations Mission in February 1955, it was beginning to expand and about to undergo a name change. I attended an informal gathering in O'Daniel's office when the point was made that the acronym ATOM was disliked by Asians because it recalled Hiroshima. As alternatives were discussed, I thought of how little progress had been made to create viable Vietnamese naval forces and questioned the value of American advice channeled through a Franco-American training mission to Vietnamese units under French command.

Moreover, our training methods, language, and motivation differed. For us, this was a beginning; for the French, it marked the end of an era. With these negatives in mind, I suggested we might name it *Supreme Headquarters Instruction and Training*, but O'Daniel thought the acronym lacked dignity. He preferred *Training Relations and Instruction Mission*, and so TRIM was born.[12] The Navy Division of TRIM was headed by a French Navy captain, who also commanded the Vietnamese Navy. Moreover, the French Navy provided all its logistic support, manned the Saigon navy yard, and held all ships and river craft scheduled for transfer to the Vietnamese. The Americans, handicapped by the language barrier and one-year tour of duty, had little to contribute.

Another difficulty was that the Vietnamese Army dominated the general staff, where there was little interest in a Navy. Then too, the prolonged commitment of Vietnamese forces, including the Navy and Marines, to operations against dissident Sect forces, from which we were excluded, seriously impeded advisory efforts. Under the circumstances, Comdr. James Ross, who had replaced Josephson, and I spent our time visiting various units to gain an appreciation of their operational problems and the resources available. A river patrol we participated in gave us a good feel for security problems in narrow waterways. An extended tour of river communities and force bases aboard a newly acquired landing ship with Comdr. Le Quang My and Capt. Jean Recher, new head of the TRIM Navy Division, confirmed the political and economic importance of the delta area.

By mid-year I had seen enough to conclude that French emphasis on a river Navy had been correct, as was the need for a complementary Marine Corps. Both were dictated by the concentration of populations and economic activity in the deltas where the waterways were the principal routes of communication. The growth of a Navy with riverine and coastal capabilities could be anticipated, but the survival of the Marine Corps would require a concerted effort. Its small size, dissimilar units, and lack of headquarters made it vulnerable to the Army's unceasing quest for added spaces. To prevent its disappearance, I believed it necessary to form its diverse units into a cohesive corps. The support of a sponsor who would benefit from the association and could survive the power struggles was equally vital.

The obvious candidate was Comdr. Le Quang My, who had led river forces in several operations in May and June and done well. This choice proved wise when, on August 20, Diem appointed Commander My to head the Vietnamese Navy and My released all French personnel in his command four days later. I wrote of these moves to Gen. Lemuel C. Shepherd, Jr., the Marine Corps Commandant, in a letter of September 17 stating, "...the net result of this action was that the French were placed exactly in our situation, i.e., on the outside looking in....When the smoke had cleared I found myself assigned as naval adviser to the commander of the Navy with an office in his headquarters."[13]

Shortly before this surprising development, I had officially requested a Marine officer as adviser to the Marine battalion at Nha Trang. I had followed this with a note asking the Commandant for Jim Breckinridge, whom I knew as an excellent officer and fluent in French. When I greeted Jim at the airport, his first words were, "Somehow I knew you were behind my sudden orders!" Jim first worked with me in Saigon and, when his family arrived, moved to Nha Trang as the first American adviser based out of Saigon.

In November, TRIM Navy Division advisers and their Vietnamese counterparts submitted a reorganization plan that represented what could be done with the resources available. A month later, when Gen. Le Van Ty, chief of the general staff, convened a meeting to discuss it, we explained we had addressed only the coastal and inland waterways patrol requirements and formed a two-battalion Marine Corps. "Even such a modest capability," we added, "requires exceeding the authorized 4,000-man ceiling." General Ty nodded and asked, "Can you tell me what is needed to carry out essential tasks effectively?" We responded by tabling a plan calling for a 9,000-man establishment, with river, coastal patrol, and transport forces and a three-battalion regiment of Marines.

General Ty concurred in principle, adding that he would support it even if a commensurate reduction in Army forces was required. Commander My's letter to General Ty in December setting forth a phased reorganization of the Marine Corps into a two-battalion regiment with provision for a third was equally reassuring. The Vietnamese Marine Corps had survived and was beginning to take form. Now, it had to be kept alive. In an earlier conversation with General Ty I had noted reference to the Army's Parachute Regiment as the national strategic reserve. I suggested that the Marine Corps offered a complementary capability which increased the flexibility of the intervention forces under his direction. General Ty was noncommittal but interested. I followed up with a formal proposal, which was implemented after I had left the country.

TRIM was an unusual organization, an expedient of limited duration that helped an awkward transition. I recall Captain Recher, looking out our office window at the open field we had dubbed *dysentery acres*, which many Vietnamese used each morning, and muttering, "See those people, at least they know what they are doing." Yet, despite frustrations and occasional misunderstandings, our Navy Division began 1956 satisfied that we had provided a firm base upon which Vietnam's naval forces could be built. That task became a wholly American responsibility on April 28 when, two days after the French tricolor was lowered for the last time over South Vietnam, TRIM was deactivated.

✳ ✳ ✳

FAREWELL CALL ON PRESIDENT NGO DINH DIEM, SAIGON, NOVEMBER 1955
From left: Lt. Gen. John W. O'Daniel, USA; Lt. Col. Victor J. Croizat, USMC; Pres.
Ngo Dinh Diem.

My effectiveness in Vietnam was enhanced by my command of French,
which gave me access to the French and Vietnamese authorities at the levels
needed to get things done. My duties as interpreter for Chief MAAG had begun
in early August 1954 when General O'Daniel became involved in refugee affairs. They resumed when I returned to Saigon in February 1955. The first time I
went with him to the Palais Norodom and met Premier Ngo Dinh Diem, I observed Diem was addicted to tea, cigarettes, and circumlocution. Where General O'Daniel was straight in approach and clear on issue, the Premier preferred
the indirectness of polite Asian manners. Still, they shared similar views on the
subject of force levels, which featured at my first meeting.

The general explained that, knowing of the Premier's concerns over the
modest force levels the United States had agreed to support, he wanted to report
that an augmentation was expected. Diem nodded and spoke of his wish to take
over France's security mission, how the economy would suffer from reductions
in military forces, and how illogical it was to do so when it was necessary to
counter challenges by the Sects and stay-behind communists. The general reminded the Premier that it would take time to organize and train the Vietnamese, and the French were needed during the interim. The meeting had touched
the two broad issues, relations with the French and the organization and training of the Vietnamese Armed Forces, that would continue to be addressed in the
months that followed.

The French at first had viewed their responsibility for the security of South Vietnam under the terms of the Geneva Agreements as an obligation. However, continuing pressure from Diem, now strengthened by his stand against the Sects, and the unwillingness of the United States to fund their presence in the amount requested caused them to accelerate their withdrawal. Their participation in TRIM began to lessen in May and dropped dramatically after mid-year when Vietnamese officers marked the autonomy of their forces by publicly tearing off their French-style rank insignia. By the end of 1955 only 40,000 French military personnel remained in South Vietnam. The second major issue, the organization and training of the Vietnamese armed forces, was equally complicated and more enduring.

It was initially uncertain whether the mission of the Vietnamese military would be internal security, defense against overt aggression, or a combination of both. The answer varied according to the role accorded the French in Vietnam, the likelihood of intervention by American forces or those of the newly formed South East Asia Treaty Organization (SEATO), and the varying views on the nature of the threat. In May 1955, General O'Daniel was authorized to create Vietnamese armed forces totalling 150,000 men. He decided that four field divisions, six light divisions, and thirteen territorial regiments would be able to provide internal security and defend against overt aggression until outside support arrived. I was with him when he briefed Diem on this organization and obtained his agreement.

In September 1955, the Joint Chiefs in Washington concluded that the major threat to South Vietnam was subversion. This view has been used to question the validity of General O'Daniel's organizational concept. This is perplexing. The Vietnamese army had ended the Indochina War as a collection of separate units without cohesion or logistic support capabilities. The simple remedy was to bring these units together in formations of combined arms with a clear chain of command and logistic support base, then task-organize them to meet operational needs.

The argument need not be pursued. Throughout 1955, Diem kept his forces busy seeking out remaining dissident Sect units. O'Daniel would time and again urge him to begin grouping his battalions into regiments and forming these into divisions. Diem would nod politely, O'Daniel would leave hoping...and nothing would happen. Another continuing frustration was Diem's involvement in the promotion of all senior officers. O'Daniel urged him to utilize uniform selection procedures, but Diem never did.

In mid-1955, Diem decided that, since South Vietnam was not a signatory to the Geneva Agreements, he had no obligation to hold reunification elections. Then, having deposed Bao Dai, he called for a referendum whose favorable outcome in October enabled him to proclaim Vietnam a Republic, with himself as President. When O'Daniel offered his congratulations, Diem accepted his compliments and remarked, "Now, I must awaken the political consciousness of the people." I was startled. Eight years of war over their hearts and minds should have stirred up all the political consciousness most Vietnamese needed.

That same month Maj. Gen. Samuel T. Williams arrived and General O'Daniel prepared to depart. I was sorry to see him go. I greatly respected him and had come to understand why he was known as *Iron Mike*. It took a man of that metal to drive ahead with determination, conviction, and tact in a confused atmosphere of differing views and conflicting interests. His successor was no less appreciated. General Williams was a tough Texan, even more direct than his predecessor, and hence more often exasperated by the President's round-about manner. After his first call on Diem, he told me he disliked being at the mercy of an interpreter. I replied that I understood his feelings but, if I knew his subject in advance and the tone he wished to use, I could transmit his thoughts better. He accepted my remark and did so thereafter.

Williams followed the course set by O'Daniel on matters of organization. However, where O'Daniel had considered the territorial regiments the principal internal security force, Williams came to agree with Diem that the Civil Guard and Self Defense Corps should handle internal security and free the military to get on with its reorganization and training. He also agreed with Diem's view that internal security forces should be trained and administered by the Ministry of Defense, but could serve in peacetime under the Ministry of Interior. The argument over these views, which were strongly opposed by our ambassador and the aid mission director, remained unsettled during my tour.

The harmony of views between Diem and Williams made for an easy atmosphere in most of their meetings, though the President's oblique approach was always trying. On one such occasion, after three hours of convoluted conversation, the President was called away. The general turned to me with, "What in hell is he getting at?" I replied, "I don't really know but his subject is sports as a national pastime." When they resumed their talk, it emerged that Diem wanted help in setting up a national sports program to "Take the peoples' minds off politics and give the newspapers something else to write about." I thought it amusing that the President, having *awakened the political consciousness of the people,* was now concerned with finding a less perturbing interest to occupy them.[14]

In April 1956, the President decided to add to his image by bringing the hill people the traditional offering of salt. General Williams was invited and we joined the President's convoy in his staff car. Suddenly the column stopped and an aide asked the general to join the President. Williams said, "Come along," and minutes later I was squeezed into the President's car, translating a long dissertation on the history of the Vietnamese, contrasting their energy to the indolence of the Cambodians and Laotions. It was interesting but most

VISIT TO HILL PEOPLE, SOUTH VIETNAM, APRIL 1956

From left: Lt. Col. Victor J. Croizat, USMC; Lt. Gen. Samuel T. Williams, USA Chief MAAG; aide; Pres. Ngo Dinh Diem.

uncomfortable, and worse was to come. After our welcome at the tribal center by a dignified reception committee in loin cloths and a brass gong band, the *montagnards* stunned a buffalo so that it fell on a fire.

We then followed the President around the village, ending at a pavilion where a bloody hind quarter of singed buffalo was displayed among other fly-covered delicacies. Large jars filled with the local brew, also fly-covered, into which long reeds had been inserted, stood nearby. The general's expression as he surveyed the offerings recalled Christian martyrs facing the lions. Fortunately, as my own stomach began to rebel, a Vietnamese official leaned over and told me we need only bow before the food when offered, As to the drink, the reed should be held below our thumb, which we could then safely suck as if enjoying the brew. I passed the word to the general and was happy to see his color return.

Another of General Williams' memorable trips was the one we made with our wives to Tay Ninh, the *Vatican City* of the Cao Dai. We were guests of General Nguyen Thanh Phuong, commanding Cao Dai forces, who had found the government side more rewarding. The festivities included a service in the brightly decorated cathedral dedicated to Buddha, Confucius, Lao Tse, and Christ, and honoring Sun Yat Sen and Victor Hugo among its saints. The allegiance of the fifteen thousand Cao Dai troops made the occasion even more impressive.

After that adventure, my time in Saigon grew short, and Commander My requested my tour be extended. Williams concurred but left me the option of deciding. I respectfully declined. I had been sent to Saigon for liaison duties with the French. These had not materialized, but other tasks had proven of consuming interest.[15] The French now were gone. There were capable men to take on the American responsibilities. I left Vietnam glad to have witnessed its transition to independence, satisfied at the status of its Marine Corps, and ready to return home and take on new duties.

Six

WASHINGTON
AND THE THIRD WORLD

The transition from Saigon to Washington was eased by six weeks of travel across Asia and Europe that revealed the extremes of human environment. The Vietnam we knew, while poor by the standards of the West, was not hungry. India, however, offered a countryside long exposed to privation, even as it awed us with the splendor of its palaces. The contrasts became less striking as we continued on to Beirut, Istanbul, and Athens. By the time we reached Rome we were back on the familiar ground of our own Western world, albeit with Latin overtones. We embarked on the *Saturnia* in Trieste and were met by a cheerful stewardess who told us she would care for our children. The favorable impression she made extended to the ship and crew in the leisurely days that followed.

We were glad we had not sailed earlier on the more fashionable *Andrea Doria* which, we had learned while in India, had sunk on its approach to New York harbor. We thought ourselves lucky not to have added that excitement to our Indochina adventure. We reached Washington at the end of August; Meda to start setting up yet another home, and I anxious to learn what my new assignment was to be. My question was quickly answered. I would join the Strategic Plans Section of the plans and operations staff at headquarters. Meda's tasks of sorting our worldly goods, some from Saigon, the remainder out of storage, and furnishing the house we had rented took longer.

In my earlier visits to Marine Corps Headquarters I had been disappointed to find a utilitarian building with crowded offices opening onto drab corridors and only a few inspirational displays near the Commandant's office. Little had changed. The Strategic Plans Section, where I would work, dealt mainly with *top secret* matters so needed a secure area. Such facilities were limited, and conditions in our cramped space were aggravated by loud voices competing with ringing telephones and rattling typewriters. Moreover, the dirt on our electronically secure windows made the little sky we could see invariably gray. I missed the open buildings of Saigon and the unforgettable view from my office over *dysentary acres*, though I soon learned there also were people in Washington equally adept at spreading manure.

My duties as an action officer stemmed from a decision made in 1952, wherein the Commandant of the Marine Corps had become a member of the Joint Chiefs of Staff on matters of direct concern.[1] This required action officers to examine the Joint Chiefs' agenda, select the items of direct concern, prepare a summary background for each with the anticipated positions of the other services, and make recommendations for the Commandant's action. The resulting position papers were forwarded to him for review prior to the briefing by the action officers just before he met with the other chiefs. The procedures, while simple in concept, required considerable judgment in execution.

I had been on board a scant two weeks when I was called to the Commandant's office to receive the Army Commendation Medal for my services in North Vietnam. This made a pleasant introduction to General Pate, whom I would be briefing for the next three years. I was soon immersed in demanding duties of exceptional interest. In my time as an action officer, the Joint Chiefs considered an average of sixteen items each week. Most were agreed on. The exceptions extended deliberations over several meetings, as did the occasional crisis when our working days lengthened into the evenings and weekends. The Joint Chiefs' agenda also provided me a new perspective on major world events. Vietnam had been an absorbing experience; in Washington, it was but one among many pressing items.

My initial responsibilities included the Joint Strategic Objectives Plan for 1960, already in preparation. This plan defined types of conflict and listed the forces needed four years hence to respond to anticipated threats. Nothing could have provided a better introduction to the national defense quandary prevailing in the capital, and nothing could have more clearly revealed the effects of the events I had lived through and puzzled over since World War II. While serving in Hawaii, I had witnessed the precipitate emasculation of the combat power of the Marine Corps. By 1947, when I came to Pendleton, six fine-tuned wartime divisions had been reduced to eleven infantry battalions. My tour in Europe had impressed upon me the dependence of that war-torn area on American support.

The community of interests we shared had been vividly demonstrated when we intervened in Korea. As I had observed the costly effort to build up conventional forces to wage war there, I had wondered why, with so many authorities convinced nuclear weapons held the answer to future conflict, our troops were still using the same weapons we had used in the Pacific. Later, when the Korean War became a bloody stalemate, I found myself asking why nuclear weapons continued to be endowed with such an aura of omnipotence, when the political and military limitations on their use were becoming more and more apparent.

My work with the Objectives Plan revealed that the United States had become wedded to a policy of massive retaliation, which offered the promise of quick, less costly wars through the use of nuclear weapons. Under that policy, defense budgets were heavily tilted in favor of the Air Force, a situation aggravated by funding directives that sought to balance rising costs for strategic weapons by reductions in conventional forces. The uncertainties over the future combat capabilities of the Marine Corps were exacerbated by continuing efforts to strengthen the power of the Secretary of Defense. This made it easier for him to impose force levels by administrative action.

In time, I came to realize that our Objectives Plan was little more than an effort to reconcile differences resulting from inadequate guidance, disagreements over definitions of threats and types of conflict, and prescribed shares of a fixed budget.[2] Under these circumstances, the fortunes of conventional forces would continue to wane. Then, when their future appeared the darkest, a crisis would arise that could not be resolved by the threat of nuclear weapons, and conventional forces would live on for another day. I first noted this during the Suez crisis, whose flash point I had observed during our stopover in Beirut in July.

That drama had begun in 1954 when Gamal Abdel Nasser embarked on a policy of militant Arab nationalism, which brought Egypt into conflict with Israel. The situation had deteriorated until, in July 1956, the United States, Great Britain, and France withdrew their support for the Aswan Dam project. An infuriated Nasser had retaliated by nationalizing the Suez Canal. Meda and I were in Beirut at the time on our way back from Saigon and had occasion for a brief visit to Damascus. In Lebanon, the reaction to the Egyptian initiative was generally favorable, but in Syria feelings against the British, French, and Americans ran high. By the time we had reached Washington and I had begun to find my way in the strategic plans labyrinth, affairs in the Middle East had worsened.

The climax came at the end of October when Israel launched an attack in the Sinai. Within the week, British and French troops joined the offensive against Egypt. The Soviets promptly threatened to intervene, and the United States put its forces on alert.[3] The British and French quickly bowed to pressure from President Eisenhower and withdrew their forces. By the end of the year the crisis was over. I observed these developments in the flow of information to the Joint Chiefs. For me, already aware of the volatility of the Middle East, this crisis was further evidence of how difficult it was for the United States to find a path of reason through the maze of combustible personalities, animosities, and emotions of the region.

As these events were unfolding, another crisis exploded on the world scene. This short-lived tragedy, between mid-October and mid-November, revealed that contrary to the tenets of the massive retaliation policy, there were circumstances where limited war with the Soviets could be envisaged. Even before the uprising in Hungary, the Joint Chiefs had directed the planners to look into ways the United States could support an uprising in Eastern bloc countries. Not surprisingly, we had found that time and space factors alone gave the Soviets a decisive advantage, even if we were willing to risk nuclear war.

About this time, the Central Intelligence Agency agreed on the conditions under which its assets would pass to military control. Since few of us knew much about the Agency, a top secret two-week orientation course to acquaint military planners with its organization and functions was provided. I was among those attending. In an embarrassing coincidence, the morning after we had been assured the Agency could provide warning of any uprising in eastern Europe and none was expected, the press headlined VIOLENCE IN BUDAPEST. Frustration at our inability to do more than support refugee reception centers in Austria was evident when the Joint Chiefs met over this crisis. The Soviets, undeterred by our nuclear arsenal or world opinion, loosed their armor; three weeks after it had started, the Hungarian uprising was over.

The year that ended with these two crises had provided strange contrasts. I had left Indochina impressed with the constructive aspects of our military power. There, our assistance and advisory effort appeared to be helping a troubled country pass through a difficult period and offering the promise of better times ahead. In Washington, the disquieting realities of budget ceilings and the paradox of impotence conferred by weapons of unprecedented power disturbed me. Happily, the new year was to bring me a welcome change of pace.

✳ ✳ ✳

It began early in 1957 at a briefing given to the Commandant and staff by the Vertol Company on the employment of their helicopters by the French in Algeria. Like the Marines in Korea, the French had used helicopters in Indochina, but neither had deployed these versatile machines in significant numbers. Now, reportedly, the French were conducting helicopter assault operations and acquiring an experience of considerable interest to the Marine Corps. Maj. Gen. Edward W. Snedeker, head of our plans and operations staff, was impressed by the presentation and contacted the State Department about sending observers to Algeria. He was rebuffed with the excuse that this could appear as support for a colonial war.

When I heard this, I asked the general if he would allow me to seek a solution. His prompt reply, "Go ahead, but don't get the Commandant in any trouble," soon had me in the Pentagon explaining our interest to Colonel Lennuyeux of the French delegation to the NATO Standing Group. The colonel listened sympathetically and offered to query Paris. A few days later he told me our observers would be welcome. I informed General Snedeker, who arranged for us to see the Commandant. On hearing my report, General Pate said, "Fine, General Snedeker and I are going to Europe on a NATO exercise. Come along and work out the details with the French."

On April 2, I was airborne and heading east in the Commandant's plane. The month-long trip provided me with my first glimpse of Scandinavia and a stimulating day with General Snedeker at the home of British military historian Capt. B. H. Liddell-Hart. My welcome in Paris was equally cordial. The French agreed to arrange for our observers to witness helicopter operations in all three of their corps areas in Algeria. They indicated no surprise at our State Department's attitude and offered to receive our observers in civilian clothes or French uniform, if that would ease concerns. They concluded our meeting by asking we have our observers report to Paris, where the French would take over.

On our return to Washington, the Commandant informed the Secretary of the Navy of our talks with the French and his intention of sending two officers in June, subject to the Secretary's concurrence. The next day, General Pate called me to his office and told me with a smile, "The Secretary has approved your trip to Algeria." I was pleased at the personal pronoun but replied, "I appreciate the assignment, but the general knows that I am not a pilot." He waved my comment aside, "I know. I've arranged for a qualified aviator to go with you. Have a safe trip and wear your own uniform."

Major David Riley was an ideal choice for the assignment, being well qualified in fixed and rotary wing aircraft and possessed of a ready wit. On reading our orders allowing us to "visit combat areas" but "to exercise caution in participating in activities which might incur undue risk," he laughingly exclaimed, "We could carry 100 copies of our orders to sit on to protect us from ground fire!" We arrived in Paris on May 28 and went directly to the Invalides, where we were given French travel orders, two first class Air France tickets to Algiers, and wished bon voyage. We next visited our naval attache and explained our mission and how it had been arranged at the working level rather than through diplomatic channels. He assured us he would handle things without ruffling feathers.

At Orly Airport the next morning, my French orders calmed a stir made by my 9mm Beretta and smoothed the way to our aircraft, where I was seated next to a French civilian who asked what was taking me to Algeria. I replied I was an American officer on a mission to observe helicopter operations. He, in turn, identified himself as a "land-owning *colon*." An interesting conversation followed until, just before landing, he invited me to visit him near Orleansville. When I did so, I found a large property that had been settled by his grandfather and now encompassed an attractive native village housing his workers. The well armed security force of native Algerians was equally impressive. My positive assessment of the place and the contentment of its occupants was later confirmed by the sector commander.

We sailed through arrival formalities in Algiers and proceeded directly to Gen. Raoul Salan's headquarters for courtesy calls. Unlike my long visit with Admiral Renar'ch seven years before, our time with the general was short. He welcomed us, mentioned we had access to information up to *secret*, wished us a fruitful tour, and passed us on to his operations staff to settle our program and brief us on the situation. Added to what we had learned in Washington and Paris, this put the complexities and dynamics of the arena we had just entered into perspective. Our activities in Algeria were to focus on the three corps areas which comprised the principal theater of operations, extending some six hundred miles along the coast and two hundred miles inland, where the desert takes over.[4]

In 1957, the Arab-Berber population in this area numbered some nine million largely unskilled, illiterate, and rural peoples. The million Europeans, only half of whom were French, lived mainly in the cities, where they were small

VILLAGE DEFENSE FORCE, ALGERIA, 1957

FRENCH H-21 LANDS BLOCKING FORCE, ALGERIA, 1957

businessmen and professionals. The large landowners were few but, like most of the other Europeans, long-time residents of Algeria, some dating back four generations. These disparities between the communities were further accented by the different laws under which they lived and by the economic benefits that accrued largely to the Europeans. These were the basis of the rebellion by which the native Algerians first sought not independence, but integration and a share of the bounty enjoyed by the Europeans.

The *colons*, whose long residence gave them emotional as well as legal claims to the land, disagreed. They remained adamant in their opposition, even when the government moved to acknowledge the aspirations of the native Algerians. Confronted with this intransigeance, militant native elements called for full independence, which the communist world was only too willing to support. The principal dissident faction was the National Liberation Front, the FLN, which had opened hostilities in November 1954. When we arrived in mid-1957, they had close to 24,000 men in regular units backed by an additional 30,000 irregulars. Their early terrorism had escalated to battalion-size operations, but they were now beginning to suffer reverses.

The French, initially preoccupied by the denouement in Indochina and the negotiations that led to independence for Tunisia and Morocco, had been slow to react. Once these matters were settled, they had turned their full attention to applying the lessons learned in Indochina to the struggle in Algeria. The importance given to psychological warfare, as evidenced by the addition of cognizant staff sections in units down to battalion, was significant. The civic action teams, created in 1955, linking native villages to the French civil authority were equally innovative.[5] In addition, by calling upon resources denied them in Indochina, the French were able to mass 400,000 troops in Algeria, three-quarters in the three corps areas to support the civil administration.

Under the *quadrillage* (grid system) concept these military forces garrisoned population centers and engaged in offensive operations as circumstances required. Such actions most often sought to encircle the area where rebels were reported. This, difficult to accomplish in the lowlands, had been virtually impossible in the mountainous terrain of Algeria until the advent of the helicopter. The helicopter was no guarantor of success, but its flexibility promised an effective counter to rebel activities. In other efforts, terrorism in Algiers was being brought under control, the three-hundred-mile Morice Line separating Tunisia and Algeria was nearing completion, and a naval blockade was helping reduce the supply of arms and munitions to the dissidents.[6]

Intrigued by all we had heard and eager to begin, Riley and I returned to the Aletti Hotel for an early dinner. The strict curfew did not encourage night life and we soon turned in. Early the next morning we were flying over countryside much like southern California, heading for the Army helicopter base at Setif, where we were greeted by Major Crespin, the base commander. We immediately drew field gear and proceeded to a briefing on an operation scheduled for later in the day, in which we were invited to join. After lunch, we suited up and went to the airfield, where Riley left in one of the troop-carrying helicopters and I took off with the operation commander. We would always choose to avoid flying combat missions in the same aircraft.

Three hours later we were back, showered, and at the officers' club where Riley raised his glass "To the start of our first Air Medal." I replied, "I don't think we'll receive any medals on this trip, not even a Purple Heart if something happens." Riley shrugged, "Not to worry, the copies of our orders will protect us." The truth, as we both knew, was that the rebels killed survivors of downed aircraft and our being Americans would make little difference.

The pattern set for our first operation was essentially the same we were to follow throughout our tour. Our host would advise us of a raid or area sweep planned for the day, and we would attend the preflight briefing. One of us would go with the troop carriers; the other with the command group. Once on the ground, Riley and I joined the operation commander, moving about with him as the situation evolved. We saw several minor firefights and were able to observe the care the French used to minimize damage or casualties among the local people. We also noted how discreetly inhabitants in target areas were searched.

**RETURN FROM MISSION, LT. COL. VICTOR CROIZAT
WITH OPERATION COMMANDER, ALGERIA, 1957**

In this manner, Riley and I each logged more than forty hours in the air on preplanned operations and walked away from two unusual landings. Riley also logged a further fourteen hours on visual reconnaissance flights. These were regularly flown in each sector, preferably by the same observer who was able to detect subtle differences indicative of rebel activity. When not engaged in such operations we used our time to visit ground and other aviation units to gain further insights on their activities. The magnitude of resources deployed for what, in most cases, were inconclusive operations was impressive. It was costly and demanding work.

A visit to the ancient Roman city of Djemilla was a break in our operational activities. The general commanding the division in our Zone provided an escort of a mechanized infantry platoon with two armed aircraft orbiting overhead. At Djemilla, the infantry screened our stroll through the ruins and formed a discreet cordon around our lavishly laden picnic table. The mayor of Setif and his attractive wife were guests. I observed the general favoring the lady with longing eye and roaming hand and concluded we should thank her for our splendid outing. My view was confirmed by the general's aide, who admitted the general found the lady enchanting, adding, "...and her husband is pleased because he hopes to be recommended for the Legion of Honor."

Back at Setif, we heard that rebels had been sighted near El Oued, an oasis southeast of Biskra, the gateway to the Sahara. Crespin agreed that this justified a visit and provided a light liaison plane in which we flew to Biskra for the night. Early the next morning we set off for El Oued, our young pilot overflying the

"TAXI STAND" AT EL OUED, ALGERIA, 1957

track that meandered across an undulating sea of sand. On landing we were seared by the heat and, after touring the vicinity, understood why our hosts appeared to welcome any rebel intrusion as a break in the dreadful monotony. We took off for Biskra after a simple lunch, droning northward until a wall of brown dust suddenly materialized before us.

We were soon being tossed about in a violent sandstorm, against which we could make no headway. The track disappeared and static drowned out the radio. This proved too much for our young pilot who was not instrument qualified. Riley, reacting calmly, took control and landed us on the track to wait for the storm to abate. We piled rocks around the landing gear, but the wind defied us and blew the plane into the gloom. By then the storm was in full fury. Our noses and ears were filling with sand and we had no water. Our pilot added cheer by reminding us the rebels always rushed to downed aircraft and murdered survivors. Riley and I thought that unlikely during the *chehili* and hoped our host at El Oued, who had told us surviving in the desert without water was a matter of hours, was an alarmist.

At this low point, a glow appeared to the south. To our amazement we were soon bathed in the lights of an old automobile driven by a badly frightened Frenchman. He lost his pallor when we proved friendly and identified himself as a soap salesman, a strange occupation in that waterless waste. With much light-ened spirits we settled into his car among the soap samples and bucked the wind for some thirty kilometers until the outline of a fort straight out of the old movie *Beau Geste* appeared; we had reached the Foreign Legion post of Oumache. We approached the massive gate, walking in the car's headlights with hands raised, shouting over the howling wind we were friends. The gate parted at last, and a wary Legionnaire waved us in with his rifle.

No sooner had we identified ourselves to the sergeant major in command than he dispatched a patrol to find our plane and set an ambush to snare the rebels who were certain to turn up. That done, he told us his radios were out, his telephone lines down, and his generator not working. He did, however, have plenty of warm beer. We reduced his stocks substantially before the night yielded to a bright clear morning. A short hour after sunrise we were back in Biskra, where a much relieved base commander welcomed us with a shower and break-fast. We later heard the Legionnaires had found our plane but not whether their ambush succeeded.

From Setif we moved west to the Boufarik Air Force Base, home of the helicopter group supporting the Algiers Corps Area. There, Lieutenant Colonel Canepa expanded our operational experience by arranging visits to several vil-lages to meet the leaders, inspect the native *harkas* that provided local security, and gain an insight into ongoing civic action programs. We were indebted to him for this opportunity to see how the French were carrying on their psycho-logical warfare programs and were saddened to learn of his death soon after our departure. He had been shot down flying into the same valley dominated by rebel-controlled heights where Riley and I had been on an earlier operation. Suppressive fires had reduced the hazards of our approach, but the colonel had been less fortunate when he returned several days later.

Our next move was to the Air Force base at La Senia outside of Oran where Colonel Brunet, commanding the helicopter group supporting the Oran Corps Area, took us in hand and assigned Maj. Jean Teisseire to see to our needs. Teisseire, who had lost a leg to a German 20mm at the end of WWII, regularly got us up before daybreak to ensure our days were full. I accepted this willingly for the sunrises were magnificent. They compensated for the usual breakfast of leftover coffee and stale bread.

Brunet's concerns at the time came from a recent order directing that all landing zones be strafed prior to use, Further, no operation was to be under-taken without artillery or tactical air support and sufficient helicopters to land a minimum of forty men in one increment. The fixed-wing aircraft available were poorly suited to ground attack and Brunet was seeking a solution in the helicop-ter. The French were already using wire-guided missiles launched from light helicopters, but he looked to multiply that capability with machine guns, can-non, and rocket launchers mounted on heavier machines.

Our social life included a Sunday treetop flight to the legendary home of the Foreign Legion at Sidi bel Abbes where, as Marines, we received a warm welcome. We were taken on a tour of the base and stopped at the museum to see the wooden hand of Captain Danjou whose heroic death on April 30, 1863, in Camerone, Mexico is honored each year. We then dined at the officers' mess at an immaculate table set with fine china and massive silver, while a quartet of bewhiskered and bemedaled Legion-

**LIEUTENANT COLONEL CROIZAT
AND MAJOR RILEY WITH
ABUSED B-26, LA SENIA AIRBASE, ALGERIA, 1957**

naires played classical music. Another memorable event was Colonel Brunet's cocktail party which Riley and I attended after a spectacular landing in a vintage medium bomber.

We had taken off earlier in the day to look for a rebel supply train coming from Morocco. After hours of nothing but rock, sand, and scrub, we turned for home. On final approach with ordnance unexpended, our intrepid pilot thought to demonstrate his American training by executing a fighter break. He brought us in high and fast over a runway bordered by open drainage ditches lined with empty fuel drums. Instead of going around and trying again, he cut the power, hit the runway, and stood on his brakes. The abused plane blew a tire and headed for the ditch, which it crossed in a cloud of dirt, drums, and plane parts. Seconds later, we were all on the ground, shaken but unhurt. I was touched by the ambulance attendant's offer of a stiff cognac. It prepared me for the gloom I would cast on Brunet's evening.

That ended our tour and we were sorry, yet relieved, when Teisseire flew us to Algiers to begin our return home. We thought the flight uneventful, but years later Teisseire told me that our aircraft had been hit twice by ground fire. In Algiers we made farewell calls at the French military headquarters, where I arranged to visit their Air Force advance helicopter training facility at Le Bourget

LAC DU BOURGET, SAVOIE, FRANCE, 1957

du Lac on our way to Paris. Lastly, we called on the American consul to have our classified documents pouched to Washington. He was initially cool because we had not reported on arrival, but thawed when I told him I had cleared our mission with the Embassy in Paris. Still, just to make sure our precious records were properly handled, Riley and I took his secretary and three of her colleagues to dinner.

We left early the morning of June 27 for an easy flight to Le Bourget du Lac, where the base commander welcomed us and placed his facilities at our disposal. In the course of the excellent lunch that followed, I told him my father's family was from the region and added that I had lived nearby in 1924 before emigrating to America and visited again in 1928. I ended my story asking if I could make a short aerial tour to give my nostalgia full play. He replied by offering me a helicopter whenever I wished.

Early the next morning I rose through the mists to an alpine meadow on the western slopes of Mont Revard, where I had the pilot leave me. There, during an hour of sun-drenched stillness, I watched the mists dissipate and expose a panorama that encompassed my origins, below me the French and behind me the Italian. I thought of my parents who had enjoyed these scenes in a far different world than the one we lived in now. I again wondered, as I had on other occasions, at what my life might have been had I been raised an Italian or a Frenchman rather than an American. In that context, World War II opened many avenues of speculation. I reached no conclusions and was satisfied to be myself when the helicopter returned to take me back to the real world.

An added note from the past was provided by my widowed aunt who came to spend the weekend with me. She was from a world long gone in which one toured Europe's fashionable spas each year. Tante Helene's afternoon walks with her Bedlington terrier were a performance, as was the ease with which she cowed the pompous maitre d'hotel who presided over the dining room at the casino in Aix-les-Bains. I remember little of the helicopter base, but the fresh scent of the alpine meadow is still with me and Riley long remembered Tante Helene. The weekend over, we continued to Paris and boarded a military flight to Washington. The Marines were interested in our report, but the real enthusiasts were Army officers, who saw the armed helicopter as a way of lessening their dependence on the Air Force for tactical air support.

My Algerian adventure had interrupted my regular duties, but I had missed little. In mid-September I was promoted to colonel and made head of the Strategic Plans Section. I then joined Col. Gordon Gayle and Brig. Gen. Richard C. Mangrum on the Joint Strategic Plans Committee and picked up several additional duties. These included adviser to our defense commissions with Brazil and Mexico, and to the Inter-American Defense Board. Membership on the Navy's Cold War Advisory Panel, created to promote relations with noncommunist countries, was more rewarding. One idea I recall with satisfaction became Project HOPE, the Navy hospital ship staffed by civilian volunteer doctors that was to visit many third world countries as a floating medical center.

Later in the year, I learned General Shepherd, now chairman of the Inter-American Defense Board, had recently talked with President Francois Duvalier about a military mission to Haiti. I would soon become involved with that impoverished country. Before then, however, there was the pleasure of our second Christmas in Washington. The house we had rented on our return from Saigon had been cramped and the winter weather had brought a succession of colds. Meda had found us a more spacious house in Alexandria by the winter of 1957 and, no longer troubled by the cold, we had all taken up ice skating. When Christmas came, there was snow outside, a grand fire in the living room, and all the holiday trimmings. Meda's gifts of a power mower and snow shovel reminded me I was back in American suburbia.

✳ ✳ ✳

April in Washington is usually pleasant, but Major Pierre Pressoir and his two associates from the *Armee d'Haiti* were not finding it so. They had been sent to the American capital by President Duvalier with a request for a Marine Corps mission to reorganize the armed forces of Haiti. They had eventually arrived at the offices of James P. S. Devereaux, the Marine officer of Wake Island fame, then serving as a congressman from Maryland. Representative Devereaux listened to their tale and called the Commandant for a French-speaking officer. Shortly after, I was on my way to Capitol Hill trying to recall something of Haiti other than the Marines had gone there during World War I, remained until the 1930s, and had organized the *Guarde d'Haiti*.

I thought the objectives in the memorandum the Haitian officers had delivered to the Department of Defense were ambitious but I was reassured by its invitation for American officers to visit Haiti "for a thorough study of the questions raised." When I briefed General Pate on my return to headquarters, he informed me that General Shepherd had already spoken of the matter and recommended we take no lead in it. However, he directed me to serve as the point-of-contact for the Haitians, but to take no initiatives. He then added, "If State and Defense agree to pursue the Haitian request, I will ask that a team visit Haiti to confirm the need for the mission and determine its size and composition."

On the second of May, the Commandant learned that the Department of State favored the proposed mission and was asked by the Chief of Naval Operations to dispatch a survey team to advise "the manner in which the Marine Corps Mission may be implemented." Within the week he had designated Maj. Gen. James P. Riseley to head a survey team of seven officers with me as his deputy. Fortunately I was able to get Jim Breckinridge as the team's infantry specialist, with Capt. P. X. Kelley as his assistant. Jim's service in Indochina made him one of the few Marines experienced in advisory duties overseas. General Riseley's assignment was also fortunate. He had served seven years in Haiti during the Marine Corps' peacekeeping years and had retained much of his Creole and affection for the Haitian people.

The next ten days were spent assembling the team, developing a work plan, and arranging the visits in Haiti to gather the data we needed. This was all fairly routine. What was not was the Haitian embassy check for our per diem Breckinridge set out to cash. Jim left with his usual cheerful mien but returned dejected. The check was in gourdes, the Haitian currency unit, which was about as negotiable in Washington as the vegetable of the same name. No one had been willing to accept it. Jim persisted and the next day brought our per diem in dollars. I never asked how.

We arrived in Haiti on May 18. A battalion guard-of-honor presented arms while a thirteen-gun salute was fired. We were then greeted by Ambassador Gerald A. Drew and other American and Haitian officials. Soon after, we were

**MAJ. GEN. JAMES P. RISELEY AND COL. VICTOR J. CROIZAT
CALL ON PRESIDENT FRANÇOIS DUVALIER, HAITI, 1958**

settling in at the Hotel Villa Creole, our headquarters for the next two weeks. We planned to spend half our time gathering data in the capital and six provincial towns, and the remainder drafting our report and discussing its findings with American and Haitian officials. The local airline put a plane at our disposal and we began a tour with unusual impact.

The view behind the facade of our reception was an appalling scene of numbing poverty. The second oldest republic in the hemisphere had passed through a year of anarchy until the previous September, when François Duvalier had emerged as President. Since then, this complex man of deceptively mild manner had consolidated his power over a country with a shattered economy...a Haiti the President himself declared to be "rotting in poverty, hunger, nudity, sickness, and illiteracy."

Our data gathering proceeded as planned, our visits fueled with repeated offerings of strong black coffee and authoritative rum. These cancelled each

**PRESIDENTIAL DINNER FOR U.S. MARINE CORPS SURVEY TEAM,
HAITI, MAY 1958**

From left: Dr. Louis Mars, Foreign Minister; Maj. Gen. James P. Riseley, Team Leader; Col. Victor J. Croizat, Deputy; Ambassador Gerald A. Drew; Capt. Paul X. Kelley, Infantry Specialist; Pres. François Duvalier; Lt. Col. Raymond Fening, Communications Specialist; Maj. Gen. Maurice Flambert, Commander Haitian Army; Lt. Col. James Kisgen, Legal Specialist; Madame Simone Duvalier; Maj. Edward Jones, Engineer Specialist; Capt. George Donabedian, USN Medical Specialist; Maj. James C. Breckinridge, Senior Infantry Specialist.

other out but we could do little to make up for the sleep lost to nightly receptions and dinners. Notable among these was an evening at the Palace where our arrival with Ambassador Drew was challenged by a sentry leveling his rifle in our faces while confirming our identity. Once inside, we found little warmth in President Duvalier, the slight physician who was our host, or in Simone, the stately nurse he had married. Playful Jean Claude, who would succeed his father and rule for fifteen years, added little. No wonder there were few regrets among the diplomats that the Duvaliers seldom entertained and hosted no other dinner during his fourteen-year reign.

We left Haiti on the first of June. Eight days later, General Riseley delivered his report to General Pate. In his letter of transmittal, he stated, "There appears to have been little progress made in the development of the Haitian Army since the end of the American occupation in 1934." Then, because the turmoil the previous year had split the army into factions which Duvalier was seeking to bring under control, Riseley noted, "...some thirty percent of the officer corps has been retired....Many of these are the older and more stable elements of the Army." News of these purges had been troubling, but by the time we had arrived in May, the problem appeared to have been settled.

With its exhausted agricultural lands, decaying port facilities, washed out roads, rudimentary telecommunications, undercapacity bridges, and shockingly inadequate hospitals, Haiti needed all the help it could get. Our report supported this view with a recommendation for a military mission "...sufficient in size, skills, and quality of personnel to ensure efficient results." The report also noted the objection of some Haitian officers to advisers serving in the field. However, Breckinridge and I had insisted, citing our Indochina experience, and the report affirmed that "Field advisers are considered vital to the success of the...Mission." Gen. Maurice Flambert, head of the armed forces, had agreed and the mission was organized accordingly.

General Pate sent our report to the Secretary of the Navy in mid-June with favorable endorsement. Then, in July, an eight-man force, with five Americans, invaded Haiti and nearly succeeded in ousting Duvalier. The Haitian Army's performance was so poor that Duvalier decided to strengthen the *Tonton Macoute*, a militia directly under his control. This, and the repressive measures he instituted caused the State Department to defer action on the mission. Duvalier sent Dr. Louis Mars, Minister of Foreign Affairs, to Washington to intercede with President Eisenhower.

The Minister later told me of his conversation with our President and reaffirmed the importance Haiti attached to the mission. Following his visit, the State Department agreed to withdraw its opposition if the Marines would not appear to be returning to interfere in Haiti's internal affairs. In early September, the Department requested I accompany William Wieland, the director of its Office of Caribbean and Mexican Affairs, to Haiti to discuss its concerns. When we left Washington the following week, neither of us had firm instructions on how to proceed. Assuming this left us free to act at our discretion, we drafted a note for Duvalier's signature asserting he would act to ease tensions.

We arrived draft in hand and were met by Ambassador Drew, who took us to the Palace where Duvalier was waiting. Wieland described the State Department's concerns and Duvalier responded reassuringly. Two days later, he signed a Memorandum of Understanding wherein he agreed "... to take all reasonable and necessary measures to allay current political tension in order that the assignment of United States Marine Corps Mission personnel to Haiti would not be construed as intervention by the United States in the internal affairs of the Republic of Haiti."

Ambassador Drew told us that the public announcement of our visit had already quieted fears of another invasion. "Now," he added, "we should find ways to show our concern over any threats to the security of Haiti and test

Duvalier's intention of adhering to the terms of the note he has just signed." I mentioned that one of our aircraft carriers was about to transit the Panama Canal and suggested the Navy be asked to have it call at Port au Prince. Then, I proposed we arrange for the Marine Corps to conduct a thirty-day training program for a Haitian Army unit. The ambassador and Wieland agreed these actions would prove useful. When I delivered my trip report to the Commandant, I informed him that early approval of the permanent mission was likely, as was a request for a temporary training team.

The carrier's visit was an immediate success. In a mid-October note Robert Murphy at State thanked Adm. Arleigh Burke for scheduling "...visits of units of the fleet...[which have]...contributed substantially to improving the political climate in Haiti." My second proposal was also enjoying a favorable wind. On October 30, I was back in Haiti with a ten-man training team headed by Jim Breckinridge, assisted by Capt. Charles T. Williamson. I accompanied them on calls upon the President and other officials, then returned to Washington. At this juncture, I was told I was the leading candidate for the post of chief of mission.

I was pleased at the news. However, I could not avoid reservations over the likelihood it would succeed. The tragic history of Haiti held no encouragement, and American economic aid appeared to have had little effect. Moreover, it was time for me to attend a top level school, after which I hoped to return to the Far East. I declined the offer and suggested Col. Robert D. Heinl, Jr., as a suitable alternate. Heinl, a military historian who spoke excellent French, was knowledgeable in Washington circles. A short time later he was named chief of mission.[7]

On the first of December, I accompanied General Mangrum, and Bob Heinl to review the results of Breckinridge's thirty-day training effort. After a day of official calls and a lavish evening reception, we joined the morning crowd at the Champ de Mars to watch the Haitian infantry company that had just completed training put through its paces. These formalities ended unexpectedly with Breckinridge, Williamson, and me receiving the Haitian Order of Military Merit. I like to think that my award was as much in recognition for the truckloads of surplus medical supplies I had scrounged from our Army and Navy medical services in Washington and delivered to the Haitian Red Cross, as it was for my service to the Haitian Army.[8]

My involvement in Haitian affairs had been intermittent. My visits had been brief, except for my two weeks with the survey team. I thus continued my regular duties throughout 1958. This allowed me to observe the reorganization of the Defense Department that further strengthened the Secretary of Defense by eliminating the Service Secretaries in the chain of command and removing operational authority from the Service Chiefs. Admiral Burke thought this made his title of Chief of Naval Operations meaningless. I was troubled that the Army, Navy, and Marine Corps, all with traditions as old as the nation, were now subordinated to a monolithic entity created in the name of economy and efficiency, whose first act was to double its staff.

Some months earlier, Gen. Curtis Lemay, the Air Force Chief of Staff, arranged for our Strategic Plans Committee to visit Cape Canaveral and the headquarters of the North American Air Defense and Strategic Air Commands. I was impressed by the sophistication of the facilities. War as I knew it was personal, the war the Air Force represented was technical. I was reminded of a previous visit deep inside a mountain where, in a room with enough atomic bombs to end civilization, I had spoken with a young lieutenant whose only duty was to test barometric switches. How far removed he had appeared from a Marine rifle platoon leader; how different the perceptions of the world I was now seeing.

Back in Washington, I found that Lebanon was again in the news. A fragment of the Ottoman Empire, later a French mandate, and independent only since 1943, Lebanon maintained its parliamentary democracy by balancing the interests of its Muslim and Christian communities. This equilibrium had teetered during the Suez crisis, when President Camille Chamoun would not break diplomatic relations with Great Britain and France. Nasser's enmity followed. Then, in February 1958, when Syria joined Egypt to form the United Arab Republic, Muslim leaders in Lebanon clamored to follow Syria. President Chamoun refused and the Muslims called a general strike, which soon became an armed insurrection.

Chamoun then called upon the Lebanese Army to put down the insurgency, but its leaders refused to act, fearing a Muslim-Christian split. At the same time, Syrian units crossed the Lebanese border to help the insurgents. The threatened President denounced the intervention and the United Nations deployed observers. Then, in July, when a pro-United Arab Republic faction toppled the government of Iraq, Chamoun formally requested the intervention of American forces. The day after, our Marines with the Sixth Fleet landed in Beirut. They were quickly joined by another battalion landing team from Camp Lejeune, which was airlifted via Morocco without incident, but not political repercussion.

Meanwhile the situation in Lebanon remained unclear, and the Army alerted its forces in Europe, while the Air Force moved elements into Adana in Turkey to facilitate their deployment to Lebanon. Additional Marine forces were also alerted, as was the Norfolk headquarters of the Fleet Marine Forces, Atlantic. General Pate then decided that Lt. Gen. Edwin Pollock would find a French-speaking officer useful. A French naval squadron off the Lebanese coast reinforced this view. At this point, the Commandant called me in and told me he was arranging for a plane to take me to Norfolk to join General Pollock, who was waiting to move to Beirut to take command of American forces in Lebanon.

I rushed home to pack, wondering what to tell Meda. There was time to tell her only that I was leaving and had no idea when I would return. Before we could discuss any financial or other matters, the staff car to take me to the airfield arrived. A short time later I was in Norfolk being told by General Pollock that he did not know when or if we would leave. The Army had just been ordered to airlift troops into Lebanon and Lt. Gen. Paul Adams was standing by to follow. Late that long night, General Pollock received a message from Adams proposing the Army and Marines share the cost of *Rest and Recreation* facilities in Lebanon. At that, he turned to me and with a wry smile said, "It looks as if the war is over as far as this headquarters is concerned...you may as well go home." My return within twenty-four hours of my dramatic departure was an anticlimax.

Several months later I was ordered to the Navy's base in Port Lyautey, Morocco to determine the status of our efforts to foster cordial relations with local inhabitants. When I finished my call on our naval attache in Rabat, I asked if his secretary would get Lt. Gen. M. Si Kettani on the phone for me. He replied that relations were strained and it was unlikely the deputy commander of the Moroccan armed forces would come to the phone. I told him that Si Kettani had been my classmate at the French war college and a particular friend. As expected, when the secretary mentioned my name, Si Kettani answered. He addressed me with the informal *tu* used between friends, and invited me to share a bottle of scotch he had been saving. Impressed, the attache wanted me briefed by the local CIA staff, but I preferred to let my meeting evolve naturally.

In the course of a pleasant dinner, I asked Si Kettani what had soured relations between our countries. He replied that we had staged a battalion of Marines bound for Lebanon through Morocco without the courtesy of informing the Moroccan government, much less asking permission. Morocco, he reminded me, was an independent Muslim country careful of its relations with Arab states. Our intervention in Lebanon was our affair, but when we used Moroccan airbases for our deployment, Morocco could not disassociate itself from our action. I was disturbed at our insensitivity toward the country with which we shared the longest unbroken friendly treaty relationship in our history.[9] I left no doubt as to my feelings when I reported this conversation.

Early in 1959 I learned we would be moving to Newport, Rhode Island in the summer and I would be attending the Naval War College in the fall. We put down a deposit on an old comfortable house in Newport that came complete with secret passages, then called the landlord of our Alexandria house to confirm our departure. He replied he was selling the house as soon as we moved. In June, we arranged a date with the packers and completed plans for a leisurely drive to Meda's family home for a vacation. No sooner were the packers at work, than I received a call from Marine Brig. Gen. Lewis J. Fields, on the Joint Staff, about a matter on which I might be able to advise him.

The situation, he explained, resulted from an initiative launched by President de Gaulle, calling for a coordinated approach by the French, British, and Americans to the transition of the African colonies to independent nations. Among the issues raised was the creation of an informal group "...to study what defense arrangements exist and...each country's rationale...[on the]...importance of Africa...."[10] Our Joint Staff concluded it would be desirable to find out what forces the French had deployed in sub-Saharan Africa. When Fields asked me what I knew of French dispositions there, I replied that my knowledge was confined to North Africa.

That ended our conversation until, as I was leaving, he asked what I thought might be the best source of reliable information. My flip reply was, "Send someone to find out." Several hours later, Fields called to inform me he had acted upon my advice! Orders were being cut for my temporary assignment to the Joint Staff where I would team up with Army Col. Wert Williams, their Africa planner, for a fact-finding trip to black Africa. Further, in view of the urgency of our mission, my orders to the Naval War College were to be cancelled and I would go to the National War College in Washington instead.

For me, the bombshell was exciting; for Meda, it was disastrous. Our landlord could not extend our lease and she was left with just two weeks in which to find another house and look into new schools for the children. She then had to cope with the packers who, knowing moves within fifty miles were not reimbursable, harassed her over payment. After obtaining authorization to settle the packers' account, she had to make the move, unpack, and revise the plans we had made to vacation at her parents' home. It was some time before she could hear the Marine Corps Hymn with any enthusiasm.

Seven

THE HORIZON EXPANDS

M y orders to the Joint Staff for the mission to French Africa below the Sahara ended my tour of duty at Headquarters, Marine Corps and cancelled our expectations for an orderly move. It was also something of an anticlimax. We had made our farewells in anticipation of moving to Rhode Island and were now staying in Washington. Happily, we were soon settled and Meda, once again her cheerful self, was not disappointed to have another year to enjoy the friends and interests she had found in the nation's capital. For me, the three years just ended could not have been anticipated and my new mission promised to be equally interesting.

Never a dull moment was an apt characterization of my duties at Headquarters. The agenda of the Joint Chiefs of Staff had covered a fair sampling of the nation's major international concerns. Working with these far-reaching issues had been absorbing and, at times, sobering when the consequences of alternative action were considered. This alone would have provided all the intellectual stimulus needed to satisfy most individuals, but I had had more. My month in Algeria had enabled me to observe how well the French were applying the lessons they had learned in Indochina. I had seen that they were as innovative with helicopter-borne assault operations there as they had been with their *dinassauts* on the waterways of Indochina.

My experience in Haiti had been both different and more disturbing. I could not understand how it was possible for a people who had been independent for nearly two-hundred years to be so incapable of governing themselves. Intervention, such as that undertaken by the United States between World Wars was no longer acceptable, and the economic aid given Haiti since had had little or no effect. These perturbing views had played a part in my decision to decline the offer to head the Mission there. That was now behind me, and I was again involved in arranging travel to a remote area.

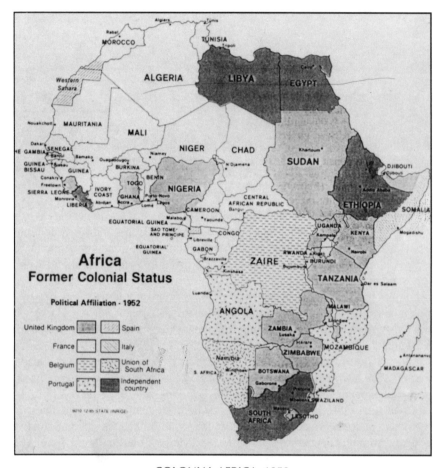

COLONIAL AFRICA, 1952

Department of State Map

By mid-June, Col. Wert Williams and I had met with the French military attache and laid out an itinerary covering all of the French colonies in western Africa. We then discovered we could not complete the trip in the time available using commercial air. Its routes had a north-south orientation linking the colonies with their European capitals, while our plans had an east-west orientation for which there was little or no service. Wert solved the problem by asking European Command headquarters to provide a plane for a thirty-day mission. Upon receipt of an affirmative response we added Nigeria, Sierra Leone, and the Belgian Congo to provide comparisons for our findings in the French territories.

The French, pleased at American interest in the evolving situation in black Africa, arranged for us to meet with the Commander-in-Chief, Central Africa at his headquarters in Paris. There, I found Lieutenant General Cogny, whom I had known in Haiphong, and Brigadier General Nemo, his chief of staff, one of my professors from the Ecole de Guerre whom I had also seen in North Vietnam. Cogny explained that his small headquarters was responsible for contingency planning and would take the field only in a major crisis. He added that he was about to leave on a tour whose itinerary coincided with ours at several locations. We could review our findings as our travels progressed. Further, to facilitate our access to information, he offered us the services of a liaison officer.

On July 14, Williams and I joined the crowd in the Place de la Concorde where we watched President de Gaulle present national flags to the heads of the republics of the newly created French Community.[1] We then went to our Embassy to meet our plane commander and complete final details for our departure the next morning. At the meeting, the young captain appeared concerned at the lack of formal clearance for our first stop in Algiers, a restricted zone. The Air Force attache told him not to worry, the French had approved the flight. The captain, however, appeared unconvinced.

The next morning, after a stop at the Embassy to buy scotch to use as thank-you offerings during our trip, we proceeded to Orly, where a freshly refurbished four-engine transport fitted with galley, office space, bunks, and a comfortable passenger compartment awaited. Four hours later I was being embraced by two classmates from the Ecole de Guerre at the Algiers airport. The presence of staff cars and escorts for the crew, coupled with the personal nature of our reception, caused our plane commander to approach with a smile and tell me he would no longer worry over clearances or any other arrangements I made.

We spent a day in Algiers making calls and attending a comprehensive classified briefing. I was impressed at the apparent success of the military campaign. Later I observed that, where Algiers in 1957 had been insecure and living under a curfew, it now appeared almost normal. I knew the French had been accused of brutality in their pacification operations, but the rebels had, themselves, engaged in terrorism. In 1957, I had been near Melouza when they had cut the throats of all the villagers because they had allowed the entry of French troops. I also remembered how American observers in Indochina had criticized the French for lack of aggressiveness. The French now appeared to have accepted the truism that war is cruel and were waging it accordingly.

We left Algiers early on the seventeenth to allow time for a luncheon stop at Hassi Messaoud, a barren desert area where the French had first found oil. The company camp, even with air-conditioning and other amenities, was a grim place. That night, at Ouargla, we were guests of another of my Ecole de Guerre classmates, who was responsible for the security of that important desert center and a considerable expanse of sand and rock served by the four roads radiating from it. I was awed by the clarity of the night sky and the enveloping silence. The sense of emptiness, which is not easily found in Europe, seemed to explain why French soldiers with long service in the desert often found it difficult to retire in France.

On arriving in Dakar, the capital of Senegal, late in the afternoon of the eighteenth we were met by members of the West Africa headquarters staff and settled into our quarters. My first glimpse of our surroundings reminded me of French cities I had seen in North Africa. However, the people were more striking, particularly the handsome women wearing the large, brightly colored headdresses for which they are known. These vivid images confirmed that we were indeed in black Africa. In the next four weeks, we would cover French territories extending over a fifth of the continent and make brief stops in two British colonies and the Belgian Congo.

The French domain, from the deserts of the north to the tropical forests at the equator, was then inhabited by twenty-five million peoples speaking some hundred and twenty languages. The French, though few in number, had provided the common language and drawn the boundaries that today define fourteen independent countries. When we visited in 1959, all of these countries, less Guinea, were members of the French Community. The eight making up West Africa were administered from Dakar; the five comprising Equatorial Africa from Brazzaville.

The economy was based principally on agriculture but increasing effort was being made to exploit mineral resources. This was a costly and time-consuming process. Little planning data were available and the infrastructure was rudimentary. Soil surveys, meteorological statistics, and population studies were needed, as was trained labor. Transportation was most critical. The entire area was served by only 2,500 miles of railroads, 15,000 miles of surfaced roads, and a hundred eighty-three airfields able to take medium transports. This view of the economy was complemented by the military information we gathered on our visits to major headquarters and field units. Periodic meetings with General Nemo added a touch of history and strategic perspective.

Africa had twice served as a support base for the French. In World War I, 170,000 troops had been recruited in Africa for service in Europe. Then, during World War II, Africa had provided the haven needed to create the French army of liberation. Now, fourteen years later, the French still viewed Africa as a relatively secure rear area that could be called upon to support military operations in Europe. It was believed that this role would be even more important in the event of a nuclear war, whose outcome might well depend on surviving assets in Africa. These would remain available only in a friendly Africa. If Africa were to

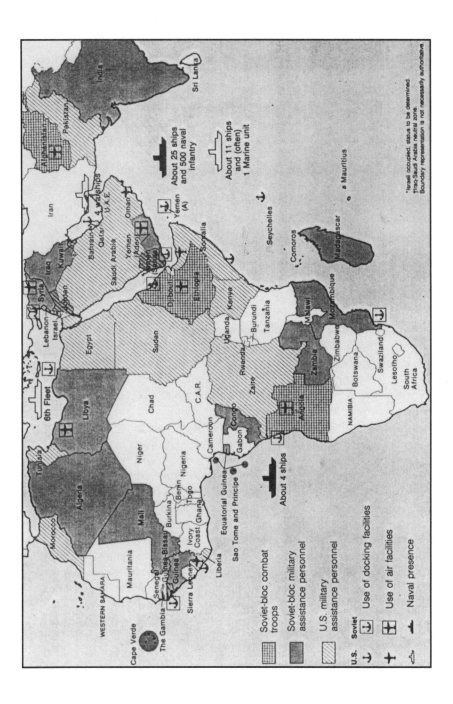

U.S.-SOVIET MILITARY BALANCE

Department of State Map

Legend:

Soviet-bloc combat troops

Soviet-bloc military assistance personnel

U.S. military assistance personnel

Soviet
- Use of docking facilities
- Use of air facilities
- Naval presence

U.S.

About 25 ships and 500 naval infantry

About 11 ships and (often) 1 Marine unit

About 4 ships

*Israel occupied, status to be determined
†Iraq-Saudi Arabia neutral zone.
Boundary representation is not necessarily authoritative.

succumb to Soviet designs, its markets and resources would be denied the West. More serious, it could become a platform for direct military attacks against the United States and Europe.

The French realized it was essential that communist influence be excluded or contained. But, though they accepted the reality of the menace, they saw little direct military threat to the area. In their view, the major effort to safeguard Western interests had to be made in the political and economic domains. Thus, they had created the French Community as a means of orderly transition to independence. In addition, they had poured nearly three quarters of a billion dollars into black Africa since the end of World War II, and their investment was continuing. At the same time, they had deployed over 40,000 troops, half recruited locally, in Community member states. They had also identified three areas of strategic importance whose control was essential to Western interests.

The first of these was the Cape Verde peninsula, the westernmost point on the continent. This peninsula, with its port of Dakar and nearby airfields, is at the crossroads of communications linking Africa with Europe and the Americas. The second area, centered around the mouth of the Congo River, complemented the Dakar complex in controlling communications over the South Atlantic. It also served as the outlet for the mineral resources of the Congo basin, whose exploitation was just beginning. The Chad, with few resources and a sparse population, was less easily seen as the third area of strategic importance.

General Nemo noted our questioning look and affirmed that Chad barred communists in the Middle East from linking up with sympathetic movements in the Cameroons. Were the Chad to become communist, explained Nemo, the continent would be divided and its fragments made more vulnerable to Sino-Soviet penetration. These observations were enriched by many of the personalities we met and the places we visited. Foremost among the officials was Pierre Messmer, the High Commissioner at Dakar. Where French diplomats often appear reserved and painfully correct, Messmer was informal, hearty, and welcoming. A strong Gaullist with a spectacular war record, Messmer emphasized the importance of French, British, and American collaboration in ensuring an orderly evolution of black Africa and fully supported our mission.

While at Dakar, we also made a one-day flight to Atar in Mauritania where we had our first meeting with General Cogny. His comment that the country was well suited to building airfields was perceptive. "All one needed," he asserted, "was paint to identify the runways." Mauritania was indeed stark and in sharp contrast to the Senegalese coastal town of Saint Louis, where we visited two demi-brigades before returning to Dakar. Another tour took us by jeep to Thies to visit an infantry regiment. Along the way, the thatch huts and women pounding grain, rivulets of sweat sparkling on their bodies, created a quintessentially African image.

SENEGAL VILLAGE BELLES, 1959
Note black satin brassiere on headman's wife for photo occasion only.

We left Dakar for an overnight stay in Sierra Leone where we were the first guests of the American consul general in his newly built residence in Freetown. It was singularly lacking in straight lines or right angles, he explained, because the local people aspired to jobs where they could wear white shirts and ties "...like the British." Thus there were many lawyers, accountants, and clerks but few masons, carpenters, plumbers, or electricians. Then he added with a smile, "...the activity everyone is really interested in is diamond smuggling." That the British, unlike the French, relied principally on police for internal security was more pertinent to our mission. Thus where their police numbered 1,500 men, their military establishment comprised a single infantry battalion half that strength.

Upon leaving Freetown, we set course for Bamako on the Niger River. It was strange to think that this country had been penetrated by its first European little more than a century ago. The Frenchman, Rene Caille, passing through the area in 1827, had remarked on the importance of the native village that the French had later made into the capital of their Sudan. He had then continued to Timbuctoo, which he reached a year later after a voyage of incredible hardship and danger. I, too, would have liked to see that fabled city, but I had to be satisfied with merely following the Niger for a short time and then turning southeast to Upper Volta.

SOLDIERS, MAJOR EXPORT OF UPPER VOLTA, 1959

Bobo Dioulasso, the capital of Upper Volta, was a town of picturesque red mud buildings and had little more to offer than the impoverished countryside. I was not surprised to discover that recruits for the French Army were the major export and the pay they received an important factor in the economy. Equally important, when these soldiers returned home after sixteen years of military service, their retired pay and travel-broadened experience made them important members of their communities. Their pro-French attitudes were also appreciated.

Abidjan was a striking contrast to Bobo. An attractive modern city, the capital of the Ivory Coast reflected its relative wealth and the favored position of its leader, Houphouet-Boigny, in French political circles. However, the lands to the north had changed little over the years. The French chief of police told me, over dinner, of a report submitted by a native constable he had sent to a village sixty miles above the capital to investigate a case of cannibalism. The constable had reported that a severe shortage of meat had led the village elders to allow consumption of those who had died of natural causes. This, in the constable's opinion, was not cannibalism and required no action. I was unable to verify the story, but I can affirm the police chief told it with a straight face.

Less challenging to my credulity was a luncheon with the new mayor of Abidjan and his wife. I was seated on the lady's right, and as I ate my lunch of steak and fries I tried and failed to break the awkward silence. Once the indifferent meal had been cleared, a servant brought in several native dishes. I tasted everything, indicating my appreciation as I progressed. To my delight, my hostess broke into a wide grin and responded with an animated conversation in very good French...of sufficient interest for me to ignore her sharply filed teeth. From Abidjan we returned to British colors in Nigeria, where we spent four days visiting the more important facilities and all five battalions of the Queen's Own Nigerian Rifles.

As in Sierra Leone, the 12,000 police in Nigeria were responsible for internal security. These, even with the support of

TOWN HOUSE, KANO, NIGERIA, 1959

the 8,000-man military force, did not seem adequate for a country whose population exceeded that of the whole of French Africa below the Sahara. Yet, everyone I questioned on the point replied that resources met requirements. Moreover, the army's only artillery battery had recently been disbanded. I was further astonished to find the supply department staffed by several dozen native scribes seated at tall Dickensian desks, diligently writing in ledgers with steel-nibbed pens. When I asked my British escort if it could support operations in the field, the major replied, "Heavens no. But it does keep the lads busy."

Among the many conversations I enjoyed in Nigeria, the most memorable was at a reception where I asked Prime Minister-designate Abubakar Balewa what role he envisaged for his populous country in African affairs after independence the next year. Balewa replied that Nigeria was an unwieldy federation and reconciling the differences among its states would occupy him for at least ten years, after which he might look beyond his borders. His task was never completed, for Balewa was assassinated after taking office, and the very differences he sought to end led to the tragedy of the thirty-month Biafran War seven years later.

We spent our last night in Nigeria as guests of the British commander of the battalion based near Kaduna. We had come from Lagos by car and were hoping for a quiet evening. However, our host was commemorating a 15th-century battle in which his regiment had featured. We were swept up in the festivities, which included a formal dinner and dance. The dinner jackets had the green sheen of age, and the evening gowns draped loosely over sun-dried figures. The conversation was animated by alcohol rather than substance, and the music to which we danced was played by native musicians more enthusiastic than faithful to the composers of the nostalgic British melodies. It was a long night. The next morning we flew to Yaounde, in French Cameroon, to make our first call in French Equatorial Africa.

There, Col. du Crest de Neuville was faced with an insurrection of the Bamileke tribe, whose domain was shared with British Cameroon. The British were cooperative, explained the colonel over dinner, but British police and French Army personnel had more than language differences. Meanwhile, the Bamileke used the border to find safe haven on the British side. I asked if his reinforced battalion met his needs. He admitted he could use more troops but hesitated to request them. That would alert the press, and news of the hundred and fifty card-carrying communists among the dissident tribesmen could be blown out of proportion. Meanwhile, he was keeping General Le Puloch in Brazzaville fully informed and was reasonably satisfied that the situation was being controlled.

Major General Le Puloch, commanding 10,000 men deployed throughout French Equatorial Africa, told us that except for the unrest in Cameroon his men had few security tasks. Hence, he was using them in civic action programs to improve living standards among his native troops and their dependents and invited us to look for ourselves wherever we wished. Further, in response to my request, he arranged a train trip to the coast and back. The trip, paralleling the rapids of the Congo River below Stanley Pool, was in a private diesel car. A stop at Dolisie allowed us to speak with American engineers building a link between a mountain of manganese ore in Gabon and the outlet port of Pointe Noire. Other stops allowed us magnificent panoramic views over the African escarpment as we dropped to the coast.

While in Brazzaville, we also met with our consul general who told us that arrangements had been made for us to meet the principal staff officers of the *Forces Publiques* in the Belgian Congo. We took the ferry across the Congo River to Leopoldville and joined a dozen Belgian officers for lunch at our consul's home. The Belgians' enthusiasm was encouraging, as was their conviction that their 25,000-man force would ensure an orderly transition to independence the following year. How different the reality! The *Forces Publiques* were among the first to disappear into the chaos that transformed the Belgian Congo into Zaire.

Our travels out of Brazzaville, Pointe Noire, and Bangui in the French Congo provided several occasions to verify the effectiveness of Le Puloch's civic action programs. In one area we came upon a French *assistante sociale* teaching native women the operation of the foot-powered sewing machine. Elsewhere, another French woman was indoctrinating others into hygienic child care. At yet another base, a French sergeant was explaining the differences among the executive, legislative, and judicial branches of government to attentive native troops. This was a far different army from the one I had known in Indochina.

Our final stop in Chad verified the importance the French attached to that area, where half the forces available in Equatorial Africa were deployed as a barrier to communist encroachment. Our stop also provided an opportunity for a farewell picnic on the Chari River, whose waters were alive with hippopotami. The date coincided with my wedding anniversary, and my telegram to Meda mentioned I had spent my day with many hippos while thinking of her. Five days later I was home explaining that I knew she weighed only a hundred pounds and had unthinkingly juxtaposed words. Her amusement at my taking her seriously made it nice to be back.

✳ ✳ ✳

My class was the fourteenth at the National War College, the nation's top joint services school. It included one hundred senior military officers, seven of whom were Marines, and twenty-two civilian government officials. They were a select group and the curriculum was of comparable quality. Our speakers featured prominent individuals from government, the media, and the industrial, commercial, and scientific communities. Presentations were followed by a lunch at which a designated student group served as host. Most of our afternoons were spent in committee work on national security issues. We also had to prepare individual research papers comparable to masters' theses. My subject, the French Community in Africa, provided an opportunity to reflect upon my travels, whose pace had precluded doing so earlier.

As I worked on my thesis, I was struck by how few the years had been from the Indochina War and the failed vision of the French Union to the concept of a French Community in Africa that accepted the possible secession of its member states. In two short tours of duty I had witnessed the dissolution of a colonial empire three centuries abuilding. This epic was accompanied by declarations of freedom and democracy, conditions that are neither easily nor quickly attained.

In the Western world, it had taken centuries for tribes to become nations. The process wherein autocracy had yielded to democracy had taken considerably longer.

In black Africa, the social diversity was striking. French territories below the Sahara were a linguistic shatterbelt. British Nigeria alone had more than two hundred ethnic groups with their own languages. The only common tongues were those of the colonial powers. Politically, tribal loyalties remained strong even where tribal lands were divided by the national boundaries drawn by Europeans. If the European historical precedent was valid, it would take much time to transform such tribal cultures into nation states. It would take longer still for them to replace their communal patterns of life with demanding democratic practices, notably freedom of choice and the responsibilities that go with it.

The economic development of France's black African colonies had centered on agricultural crops destined for European markets. This had contributed little to the infrastructure these emerging nations needed to diversify their economies and exploit their new-found mineral resources. France was responding with grants and loans for infrastructure and social development. Colonialism was ending on a positive and supportive note. I was glad I had seen this unfamiliar part of the world and learned of the problems inherent in its independence. The effort of the French and British to ease that transition was most impressive.

The highlight of our academic program was a month-long tour of a selected world area. My choice was the Middle East. By the end of winter we had familiarized ourselves with the countries we were to visit and were anxious to start. The trip promised exceptional interest. Our embassies, responsible for hosting our stay, would arrange formal and social occasions for us to meet and speak with our representatives and with upper level public and private figures involved in the country's political, economic, and social affairs. We left Washington on a rainy March day for Tunis, where I enjoyed the familiar aspect of the city. I understood the enthusiasm of Tunisian officials at their recent independence and admired the progress made in social reforms since 1956.

I was less sympathetic when they told us of their clandestine support for the Algerian rebels. Even so, the visit was agreeable and informative, and our tour of Roman ruins outside the city particularly enjoyable. Our departure was less so. We were at the airport, idly watching a mechanic running up the engine on a small plane, while waiting to enplane. Suddenly, the small plane began to move and, before anyone could act, its propeller was chewing at the after end of our aircraft. The damage was slight but we were grounded.

Another plane was sent to allow us to continue our journey, but by the time it arrived, our clearance to Saudi Arabia via Cairo had expired and we had to travel via Khartoum. We were a bedraggled group when we finally reached Dhahran. Regrettably, our stop had to be cut short and we could gain only general impressions of this empty land, where the discovery of oil and introduction of Western technology was impacting on its small, scattered population, which remained rigidly bound by tribal and religious ties.

It was a short flight to Karachi and our introduction to Pakistan, the Muslim state carved out of the Indian subcontinent after World War II. That country then consisted of two segments, West Pakistan where generations of British officers had made and lost reputations on the Northwest Frontier, and East Pakistan where the torrid mudflats of the Ganges delta and monsoon rains make the environment man's principal adversary.[2] Between these two disparate fragments lay a thousand miles of India and most of the resources of the subcontinent. This would prove too great a barrier, and East Pakistan would in time become Bangladesh. Despite the autocratic government of General Ayub Khan, we sympathized with much that we observed.

This view was influenced in part by our military mission, which was then helping modernize Pakistan's armed forces, and in part by our shared interests in two treaty organizations.[3] We enjoyed the pomp with which we were received and entertained. A spectacular dinner at the Pakistan Army Headquarters mess in Karachi featured bagpipers parading around our outsize dinner table. The lunch we enjoyed as guests of the Khyber Rifles in the Northwest Frontier Province was equally impressive. We flew to Peshawar to visit the Pakistan Air Force Headquarters. Then, to see something of the security situation along the Afghan

**THE KHYBER PASS,
LINK BETWEEN PAKISTAN AND AFGHANISTAN**

border, we entered the Khyber Pass to reach a fort still guarding the route made famous by Alexander the Great.[4] Passing through its gate was entry into legend.

We were assembled outside the mess for drinks while the pipers of the Khyber Rifles entertained us with music and marching. When they retired for a well-earned break, Col. Louis Metzger and I followed and asked, if we whistled the tune, could they play the Marine Corps Hymn. They agreed to try. After a melodious interlude, Lou and I rejoined the party and had just replenished our drinks when the skirling of pipes announced the return of the band to the unmistakable music of the Marine Corps Hymn. The surprise of our classmates doubled our delight. I thought I heard those same notes among the echoes carried by the wind when, sixteen years later, I again passed those barren mountains heading to Kabul with Meda in a rickety taxi.

In Delhi, the farthest point on our itinerary, we were received by Jawaharlal Nehru, first Prime Minister of independent India. Cambridge-educated and modern in outlook, Nehru offered us tea and conversation. We found him complex and contradictory. We could understand his anticolonialism but thought his policy of national integration unrealistic in view of the diversity of the people, languages, and religions in India. We could commend his efforts to raise the level of India's economy and the well-being of its people but thought his goal of doing everything at once unattainable. We were also unsympathetic with his policy of nonalignment which did not appear to equate with neutrality but to encourage Soviet Russia to extend its influence.

We were even less sympathetic during our meeting with the Defense Minister, Krishna Menon. That gentleman, known as the stormy petrel of the United Nations, was a socialist and long-standing opponent of Pakistan. Already opposed to his political views, I found his unctuous manner when answering our questions offensive. I did, however, greatly enjoy dinner in a lovely garden that evening where my charming dinner partner solved a question that had puzzled me for years by deftly unscrewing the diamond she wore in her nostril.

It is said that, when the queen-mother of Egypt saw her daughter off to Iran to marry young Mohammed Reza Shah, she was distressed at the prospects awaiting Princess Fawzia in a barbaric land. We arrived twenty years later with a more open mind. By then the Shah had been married for the third time and Iran was in its second Seven Year Development Plan, but still traveling the road to the modern world. The Shah's father Reza, like his Turkish contemporary Mustafa Kemal, had set Iran on that road. His son was continuing the effort, but traditional values and the power of the mullahs in the villages remained strong. Moreover, Iran sheltered over two million independent-minded nomads and shared concerns with Pakistan over the irredentist aspirations of the Baluchi people and with Iraq and Turkey over those of the Kurds.

TEHRAN REACHES UP THE ALBORZ MOUNTAIN BARRIER

Only the urban elite had western interests and educations. The French-educated Iranians with polished European manners we met were but a thin veneer on a highly conservative and rigidly structured Islamic society. The English-speaking engineers, doctors, and other young professionals being educated in the United States and England had not yet returned in large numbers. Unfortunately, the Shah was abroad at the time of our visit. Equally unfortunate was the impossibility for us to see beyond the European facade and gain some understanding of why this Middle East power was familiar yet remote. Still, what we saw impressed upon us the magnitude of the young Shah's task.

In striking contrast to the magnificent mountain backdrop of Tehran, Turkey's capital city of Ankara sprawls in the center of the drab Anatolian plateau. We had looked forward to our visit. Turkey was a member of NATO and a comrade-in-arms in the Korean War. It was also the new home of the Central Treaty Organization.[5] Our ties were many and assured us a warm welcome, but we arrived at a time of troubles which distracted our hosts. Problems were inherent in the creation of modern Turkey. Mustafa Kemal's reforms in government structure after the demise of the Ottoman Empire had been readily accepted, but social change had been resisted by the traditionally conservative masses. Nonetheless, he had been able to continue his authoritarian and paternalistic regime until his death in 1936.

ISTANBUL, GATEWAY TO ASIA AND THE ISLAMIC WORLD

Tight controls had continued during World War II, but greater personal and political freedoms granted after the war had invigorated traditional Islamic attitudes and opened the door to political contention. By the time we arrived, internal tensions had led to violence and martial law. Under the circumstances, our visit was more ceremonial than substantive. I left Turkey thankful for the wisdom of our founding fathers who had separated church from state. That sentiment would gain strength in the arena of the bitter Arab-Israeli conflict, which we entered in Jordan, a country the Arabs remember as the fragment of a broken promise.

In 1915, the British had induced the Arabs to rise against the Ottoman power in return for support of their independence. After World War I, much of the Arabian peninsula did gain that status. However, Syria and Lebanon became French mandates, while the British became the overlords of Iraq and Palestine. Then, in 1921, the British separated the land east of the Jordan River from Palestine to form Transjordan, a barren land of mostly nomadic tribesmen. As it moved toward independence, Transjordan created the Arab Legion to keep the restive tribes under control. Meanwhile, Palestine was receiving a steady inflow of Jews seeking the "national home for Jewish people" mentioned in the Balfour Declaration of 1917.[6] Conflict erupted and no effort to reconcile differences had succeeded.

Finally, in 1947, the United Nations called for the partition of Palestine and the creation of a Jewish state. In the war that followed British withdrawal in 1948, the Arab Legion proved to be the only effective fighting force. Jordan had emerged in possession of 2,000 square miles of land on the West Bank and most of the holy places in Jerusalem. These had been incorporated into the newly named independent Kingdom of Jordan. Jerusalem and the West Bank were significant economic gains, but they were offset by the need to accommodate almost a million Palestinian refugees. Adding to the problem, the Arab farmers and city dwellers from Palestine had little in common with the herdsmen who roamed the Jordanian desert.

We were warmly received in Amman by our ambassador who, after presenting the Arab view of the Middle East, led us to several Palestinian refugee camps on the West Bank. The near-hopeless situation of the people there had already lasted more than a decade. We thought it inevitable, as did other perceptive people at that time, that the empty future of the young would make them prime candidates for guerrilla and terrorist organizations, We also visited Jordanian Jerusalem, where we were shocked to see Christian holy sites neglected because the various religious denominations could not agree on what each should pay for their upkeep. Conflict seemed endemic to the region.

Shortly after we entered Israeli Jerusalem, military officers took us to viewpoints overlooking the same holy sites we had just left. The Israelis spent little time on the history of the area. They concentrated instead on pointing out avenues of approach to commanding terrain and preferred positions for mortars and machine guns. We were fascinated by their military commentaries. They were also indefatigable in presenting their accomplishments. We agreed that their efforts had been great and their achievements many, but we thought the costs had been high. The creation of Israel, where now two million Jews were settled in lands long dominated by Arabs, had intensified the conflict between Arab and Jew.

Moreover, the image of internal harmony promoted by Israel was not realistic. A sophisticated Jew from a great German city does not see the same world as a Jew from a Russian village, and neither has much in common with a Jew born and raised in North Africa.[7] All are linked by Judaism, but even there differences exist. We saw this in Jerusalem where the orthodox community opposed public transportation and services on the Sabbath, to the annoyance of those less strict in their beliefs. Another reality emerged during a visit to one of the long-flourishing kibbutz, where the elders spoke of sons wishing to seek their fortunes beyond the horizon of their fathers. The same complaint had risen in the communes established in New York State after World War I.

The perplexities in the situation and difficulties of reaching a viable Middle East policy were clearly demonstrated at a meeting with our ambassadors at our consulate in Jerusalem. The ambassador from Jordan, who was ending a long career in the Foreign Service, was seated at one end of a long leather couch; our ambassador to Israel, a young political appointee born about the time his fellow ambassador had started his diplomatic career, sat at the other end. With refreshments in hand, we began asking questions. The two ambassadors started their replies calmly enough but, before we had emptied our glasses, they were loudly proclaiming opposing views. We left, unenlightened, with sympathy for the State Department official responsible for devising a Middle East policy from the conflicting reports that crossed his desk.

At the same time our group admired the military prowess of Israel and its agricultural and economic development, we were concerned at the plight of the Palestinians, including the paucity of support given them by the oil-rich Arab countries. Questions of how to justify the cost in blood and resources expended in creating and maintaining independent states to accommodate the many ethnic and religious groupings in the Middle East also troubled us. The Palestinians and Israelis were not the only ones struggling to establish their own countries; the Kurds and Armenians, and others less well known, had also been striving for independence for many years.

Though ill-equipped to pursue these issues, we could readily acknowledge the profound attachment for their homeland of all of these peoples. We gained a sharp view of the Israeli perspective at a luncheon hosted by Golda Meir, the Ukranian-born teacher from Milwaukee who had become a labor leader in Israel and was now Foreign Minister. She would end her amazing career as Prime Minister. We were received at her residence much as if we were family. Her informality and candor made the experience unique. She acknowledged the problems confronting her country, spoke of its need for support, took pride in its development, and looked to the day when the Arabs could accept its existence and live with it in peace. Her performance helped ease, but not remove, our misgivings. I can only conclude Israel is as much emotion as nation.

We completed our Middle East tour with a stop in Athens. My father had often recalled how the ancient Greeks had barred the westward expansion of Persia five centuries before Christ and, by so doing, assured the cultural identity of the western world. I found satisfaction that the United States had helped repay this obligation by saving modern Greece from the communist scourge. It is difficult for me to think of Greece as a Balkan country, four hundred years under Ottoman rule. It had been independent a hundred years when invaded by Italy in 1940 and occupied by Germany shortly after. The communist guerrilla movement that threatened to take over the country once the war ended had been thwarted by President Truman. Greece was a success story of American foreign policy and a fitting place to end our travels.

Laden with brass trays, Indian silks, precious stones, and lesser souvenirs, we headed for home. The long flight allowed time to think over all that I had seen. I had been impressed, first in Africa and now in the Middle East, by the cultural diversity of so many new nations and their dependence on the West if they were to evolve socially and economically. Regrettably, their immaturity was being exploited by the communist powers who sought to dominate these areas. I found it a paradox that the Soviet Union, the most oppressive imperial power of modern times, should be denouncing the Western nations as imperialists at the very time these nations were assisting their colonial holdings to realize a viable independence. Words such as colonialist and imperialist were acquiring new meanings.

Beyond the issue of cultural diversity, the emotional ties to disputed geographic areas among so many tribes and peoples were inhibiting an orderly progression toward nationhood. The confrontation of the superpowers added further confusion and ensured that pragmatic solutions to these many problems would be difficult and long in coming. The only certainty was that we and our successors at Defense and State would have much to do for many years to come.

I had left Washington in the cold rains of a dying winter and returned to the cherry blossoms of the capital at its most attractive season. It was a nice welcome back and a pleasant introduction to our final months of academia. In mid-April, I received orders to report to the 3rd Marine Division on Okinawa upon completion of my studies. The division was part of the Marine Corps' force-in-readiness in the Western Pacific and, as such, subject to immediate commitment. This alert status required that its personnel serve without dependents. For me, duty in a force at the cutting edge of our international interests in the Far East offered a change from the heady atmosphere of Washington.

Meda was not warmed by the prospect of another separation. She understood better than I that the disruptions in the children's lives were increasingly difficult. Her first thought was to remain where they were, but this was expensive with a divided income, and the prospects of an interesting job to supplement it were limited by the one-year commitment she could make. Then, a friend from our Saigon days offered Meda her apartment overlooking the Mediterranean. This appeared a productive and affordable solution. The children could return to French schools and she could reinforce her French with university courses in Nice. Moreover, Tante Helene lived in nearby San Remo. Although they came from vastly different worlds, they enjoyed each other's company. There were also friends in London when she and the children needed to hear their mother tongue. Meda quickly accepted.

The Marine Corps would not pay for her move, but the modest cost for her to live in France would balance this. She and the children would spend the summer with her parents and sail for France in September, where another friend would have a small car ready for her in Paris. By the time her plans were complete, I was envying her the adventure and thinking that somehow the tables had been turned on me this time.

At the beginning of June, with my diploma in hand, we put our household effects in storage, said *au revoir* to friends, and started the long drive across the country. After an all too short vacation at Meda's parents' home, we said our own good-byes and I began my now familiar solitary journey westward across the Pacific.

Eight

STORM CLOUDS RETURNING

My briefings at Fleet Marine Force Headquarters in Hawaii differed from those of 1954. Then, French Indochina was remote and of peripheral interest. Six years later, there was a marked awareness of the region, whose early promise was not being realized. The future, particularly for Vietnam and Laos, was uncertain. I left Honolulu knowing only that I was heading into a difficult situation and possible active operations. During the long flight, I thought back over my twenty years of service. They had given me more than my share of diverse experiences, but these had been acquired at the price of frequent and sometimes long separations that had shifted many responsibilities to Meda.

The compensations for me had been many. Wherever I had been...with the Foreign Legion at Sidi bel Abbes, the Khyber Rifles in Pakistan, the Ecole de Guerre in Paris, or simply in the homes of General Flambert in Port-au-Prince or General Le Van Ty in Saigon...I had been made aware that the Marine Corps was considered an elite force. Maintaining this reputation was largely up to our ready forces, and I accepted the need to make my contribution although, as I had learned in Hawaii, the command arrangements under which I might be employed appeared complex.

The 3rd Marine Division and the 1st Marine Aircraft Wing fulfilled the ready role in the Western Pacific, where they served without dependents. Together they comprised Task Force 79, the amphibious component of the Seventh Fleet. Either could also be called upon, individually or in part, by the Commander in Chief Pacific (CINCPAC) to serve in his Joint Task Force 116, a contingency command that could be activated in crises situations. One such, in Laos, involved intervention under Marine command.[1]

❋ ❋ ❋

HEADQUARTERS FLEET MARINE FORCE, SEVENTH FLEET, OKINAWA, 1960

I arrived on Okinawa on a rainy morning in late July. Col. Jack Scott, the plans officer at the headquarters of Task Force 79, welcomed me as the prospective chief of staff. This unexpected news was soon confirmed, with reservations, by Maj. Gen. Robert B. Luckey, the 3rd Division commander. My classmate Col. Talbott F. Collins, the current chief of staff, had been stricken with a baffling illness. General Luckey asked me to press forward with the planning effort he had been directing, adding, "Tab will probably be evacuated, but until he is, your assignment will have to be temporary."

The basic contingency plan published the year before by CINCPAC had triggered an update of plans throughout his Pacific command. The staff I was joining was preparing plans to support those of the Seventh Fleet. It was also working on the contingency plan for joint operations in Laos. A handful of officers and men drawn from the division and wing were responsible for this weighty workload. In addition, they were the nucleus around which an operational headquarters would be formed if a particular plan was implemented. The work, while demanding, was outside the drum beat directing the activities of the 30,000 Marines in the Western Pacific. As a planning headquarters, the staff had little status and the facilities to match.

Tab Collins was soon evacuated and I was asked to stay on by Maj. Gen. Donald M. Weller, who relieved Luckey near that same time. Weller, like Luckey, was senior to the wing commander and hence recipient of the added command responsibilities that seniority conferred. My position now formalized, I concentrated on finishing the Seventh Fleet planning effort, then went on with planning for the Laos contingency. General Weller, my immediate superior, was a highly competent professional with an incisive mind, who was also sensitive to the human aspects of his celibate command of near 20,000 isolated men. He met that challenge by looking upon his young Marines as he did his son of the same age.

The Army, Navy, and Air Force units occupied the more developed southern half of Okinawa with their dependents; the Marines lived and trained alone in the sparsely populated north. Training and athletics consumed much of their energy, but liberty was difficult and offered few distractions other than the bars. Welcome breaks came during amphibious exercises when there was time ashore in the Philippines; the artillerymen had the added advantage of going to Japan for firing exercises. All hands lived in spartan Quonset huts, the officers and noncommissioned officers less crowded than the other ranks. Colonels had the added privilege of the general's mess. Weller did much to keep our evening dinners animated, but we all welcomed opportunities for official travel or visiting friends in other services.

My planning group was largely spared these morale problems; our concerns came from the flow of generally discouraging intelligence reports. During the first half of 1960, the dissident Viet Cong had demonstrated a disturbing effectiveness that was currently costing the South Vietnamese substantial casualties, plus the armament of one infantry battalion each month. President Diem had continued to resist the advice, first offered by General O'Daniel and repeated by General Williams, to stop interfering with field operations and the selection of military commanders. As a result, he was being blamed for his army's shortcomings.

A national intelligence estimate in August 1960 noted these developments and added that supplies and cadres were being infiltrated south from North Vietnam by both overland and offshore routes. It further acknowledged growing dissatisfaction with the Diem regime among noncommunist elements within the society. That same month our ambassador reported that Diem's government faced two threats, one from the communist Viet Cong, and the other from an internal coup. Three months later, the parachute brigade tried to depose the President. This attempted coup, badly organized and quickly quelled, might have proved useful if Diem had seen it as a warning. Instead, it reinforced his paranoia.

Developments in Laos were no less alarming. The 1954 Geneva Conference had supported an independent Laos as a buffer between Thailand and North Vietnam. It had also recognized the leftist Pathet Lao as a legitimate party in a government of national union under Souvanna Phouma. By 1955, North Vietnam was supplying Pathet Lao forces, while the United States financed the

Royal Lao Army. When the Pathet Lao succeeded in occupying two of Laos' northern provinces, Gen. Phoumi Nosavan took over the government and intensified the fight against the communists. Then, in August, a coup led by a young Maj. Kong Le, seized Vientiane and restored Souvanna Phouma to power, to be replaced again, four months later, when General Phoumi reoccupied Vientiane. Kong Le fled to join forces with the Pathet Lao. At year's end they controlled eastern Laos, thus linking North and South Vietnam.

✳ ✳ ✳

Planning at the national level, as I had learned in Washington, was essentially an allocation of resources to meet specified contingencies. In contrast, the planning I became engaged in on Okinawa had the human dimension I had encountered during World War II. Our intelligence was fresh; the Vietnamese paratroopers that attacked the Palace in Saigon were real, as were the Soviet aircraft landing supplies at remote fields in Laos. In pursuit of this reality, I became involved in a succession of meetings and travels, many with General Weller, that blurred the passage of time. Our contingency plan for Laos conveys something of the preoccupations of our small staff group.

It called for the airlift of a Marine infantry battalion to Vientiane, with the remainder of the regiment deployed by ship to Bangkok, then by road and rail to Laos. Seventh Fleet shipping was familiar; the airlift was not. A visit to the Air Force base at Tachikawa, Japan to meet Brig. Gen. William Kershaw was useful. Kershaw decided to send an officer to Vientiane to check facilities for his transports, and we agreed that an airlift exercise for our Marines was urgent. We sent Adm. Harry D. Felt, the Commander in Chief Pacific, a proposal to that effect. He promptly replied, "Airlift exercise approved, execute without delay." The visit to Vientiane revealed that landing a single battalion would require a dawn-to-dusk operation, and that our aircraft would have to refuel in Bangkok for their return trip.

Our airlift exercise showed our headquarters equipment in poor shape, our communications sets too cumbersome, and our Marines inept but willing. I had just started working on these shortcomings when General Weller dropped by, lit his pipe, and said, "Vic, I'm worried. We're assuming the airfield at Vientiane stays in friendly hands. But, a single truck set afire on its only runway could halt the whole operation. What we need is a unit on the ground to ensure its security before we launch the troop carriers." After discussing our options, we asked Admiral Felt for the only Army parachute battalion in the Pacific command. The request was granted without comment.

Our involvement with the Air Force and Army in joint planning had other ramifications. One was the visit of Brig. Gen. Philip Mock, who had been an Army planner when I was in Washington. I well remembered his tactic, when an

Army-sensitive paper was at issue, of introducing hours of trivia until we were all tired, then slipping in wording that best served the Army's interests. His greeting was cordial, but it was not long before he was back in character asserting the Marines should never have been given command for the Laos operation because the Army units committed outnumbered them. I retorted, "Phil, you leave out the main point. The Marine units are combat-ready and available within hours, whereas few of those on your roster exist, even in Hawaii. Most are reserve units in the States."

Neither of us convinced the other. We parted in friendly fashion, but I was certain this was not the end of the numbers game. The Sunday visit of a gentleman in civilian clothes, whom I was to brief on our Laos contingency plan, was more amusing. I knew he was actually an Army officer on his way to Vientiane to relieve the current head of our supposedly clandestine military advisory group there. Still, I played the game, carried out my briefing, and avoided telling him that the word on the streets of Bangkok was that the Americans had covert military advisers in Vientiane who could be identified by their short haircuts.

Ambassador U. Alexis Johnson's unfamiliarity with the subject when General Weller and I visited Bangkok and briefed him on our plan for moving several thousand Marines through Thailand into Laos was less amusing. His surprise revealed that liaison between our military and diplomats left something to be desired. We extended our time in Thailand to see communist-held Vientiane, against which General Phoumi's forces were then advancing. We arranged to have our Army team in Udorn meet our plane and provide transportation to Nong Khai on the Mekong River opposite Vientiane.

We were among the first to use the new runway at Udorn. Within minutes of landing, we were surrounded by Thai monks in saffron robes fingering the crew's flight suits of the same color. We could not tell whether they thought our Marines were members of an unfamiliar Buddhist sect or bearers of new robes intended as gifts to gain merit in their next incarnation. We left the crew and monks to work out their fraternal and spiritual relations and set off for the Mekong. The closer we got, the fewer the people in the villages. By the time we reached a good viewpoint above Nong Khai we were in a world without people or animals, silent except for the crash of mortar and artillery shells. Phoumi's forces were preparing their entry into Vientiane and we had a front row seat.

The view was excellent and the gunfire obviously stimulating to General Weller. I, however, was troubled by stray rounds falling into the river before us and fresh shell holes in our vicinity. After allowing enough time to satisfy his artilleryman's enthusiasm I told Weller that a round hitting where we stood could seriously foul up command arrangements in the western Pacific. Reluctantly, he replied, "I suppose you're right, let's get out of here." Meanwhile, Jack Scott and

HEADQUARTERS JOINT TASK FORCE 116, OKINAWA, JANUARY 1961

Lt. Col. Paul McNeil, our logistics officer, who had dropped off at Nong Khai to investigate the river crossing facilities, found themselves helping American civilians fleeing the fighting in Vientiane.

From Thailand we flew to Danang to spend a day with Maj. Gen. Tran Van Don, commanding the I Corps. I had known General Don during my Indochina tour and found a warm welcome. He treated us to a candid presentation of the security situation in his corps area and his plans to delay any overt attack from the North. His resources for the task were meagre, and I told him we had a powerful amphibious force in the vicinity that could quickly come to his assistance. He replied, "South Vietnam does count on American help, but the commitment of your forces is a political matter that will be decided in Washington. That will take time, and time is a luxury we won't have. We must plan to do what we can with what we have."

The final weeks of the year on Okinawa were marked by a sense of accomplishment, but also of envy of my Army and Air Force friends on the island who were spending Christmas with their families. My staff group had worked well and hard. Now with our contingency plans completed, I looked to begin the new year in command of a regiment. This would conform to the usual practice

SEATO FIELD FORCE HEADQUARTERS, KORAT, THAILAND, MARCH 1961
Lieutenant Colonel Ottowell (UK), Operations Officer; Colonel Croizat (U.S.), Chief of Staff; Lieutenant Colonel Sawit (Thailand), Intelligence Officer.

U.S. Army Photo

of dividing the one-year tour for officers on Okinawa between staff and command duties. Several weeks earlier our staff group had taken a weekend break at the officers' rest center at Okuma. This had been a great success and I now proposed to repeat it over New Year's Eve. We arranged for a bus, loaded it with beer, choice steaks, and other necessities for a barbecue and headed north. After welcoming the New Year with appropriate ceremony, I retired.

Sometime around two in the morning of January 1, I was recalled to consciousness by an armed messenger with a *top secret* message. Admiral Felt had decided that communist initiatives in Laos required activation of his Joint Task

Force 116 headquarters and the alerting of its assigned forces. A helicopter soon arrived to return us to camp and, in the chaotic forty-eight hours that followed, we created our headquarters in pyramidal tents surrounded by concertinas of barbed wire on the open ground in front of the 3rd Division headquarters. The staff that began to assemble soon after daybreak on New Year's day was as bedraggled as the facilities. Many from commands on Okinawa appeared in the evening dress they had been wearing when the alert was given. Later arrivals from Japan and Hawaii were in more appropriate clothing, but still short of sleep.

As hosts, we did what we could to make everyone comfortable, but we had only slim fare to offer. Still, with a bit of sleep and the restorative effects of coffee the staff began to take form. The various units making up the joint task force, although on alert, had not been passed to our operational control. Nonetheless, I soon discovered how loudly some of these support units could clamor for space on the initial airlift. In typical Marine fashion, we had given priority to combat units. Now, I had to cope with competing demands from such Army units as a propaganda leaflet platoon with a press big enough to print a town's newspaper.

A more serious complication was that many of the combat units earmarked for our joint task force were about to leave on a SEATO exercise.[2] Admiral Felt directed us to carry on with the exercise, then reconfigure the embarkation teams to conform to our contingency plan. Falling out an exercise force and falling in a combat force using the same units and the same ships scattered in various ports was more easily said than done. We addressed the problem directly with Vice Adm. C. D. Griffin aboard his Seventh Fleet flagship in port at Keelung in Taiwan. Then, the admiral's operations officer and I spent the rest of the night ironing out the details.

Col. Hamilton M. Hoyler, the 3rd Division's chief of staff, raised a troubling issue when the division lost the 9th Marines and several of its key officers to our joint task force. Ham had stopped me with the query, "I don't understand why our combat ready division should be fragmented and its parts mixed with units from other services to create a joint force of uncertain quality. Tell me, am I missing something?" I agreed our Laos intervention mission could be given to the division. However, I explained, "To ensure that all services get a piece of the action, we now respond to crises with joint, rather than single service forces, and try to live with the confusion and problems that result."

As we carried on our work, the Army was pressing its case for command of the Laos operation. The Joint Chiefs resolved the matter by replacing our joint task force with the force prescribed in SEATO Plan 5 that used the same units and staff personnel, except that Army Lt. Gen. Paul D. Harkins replaced General Weller, and Marine Brig. Gen. Richard G. Weede replaced me.[3] Weller took the news without comment beyond instructing me to help Harkins settle in. I did so with a deep sense of personal loss. Activation of the joint task force headquarters had denied me my anticipated command. Now that it was working and its combat units prepositioned, I had to step aside. When the Army converted a recreational compound for Harkins' headquarters, we struck our tents, gathered our wire, and closed the book on our brief excursion into joint command.

Sometime later I was in Weller's office when Admiral Griffin was visiting. The admiral was to retire that summer and I had orders to SEATO Headquarters in Bangkok.[4] The mood was relaxed and the conversation rambling. When reference was made to the continuing Soviet airlift into Laos, I suggested to the admiral, "You could retire in a blaze of glory if you ordered a strike against that operation." He laughed and replied, "That would certainly make a splash, but I'll settle for a less spectacular retirement ceremony." General Weller and I were equally willing to end our tours quietly. However, we were back in Thailand in early March engaged in a SEATO exercise near Korat. My duties as chief of staff to Army Maj. Gen. John L. Richardson, the SEATO Field Force commander, were an excellent introduction to my next assignment.

Once back on Okinawa, I was able to look beyond our alert for the Laos contingency. Although wholly absorbing for me, it had been but one of the actions taken to prepare for intervention in Southeast Asia. In another, Weller had shifted the focus of his division's training from amphibious operations to counter-insurgency. In yet another, Lt. Gen. Alan Shapley, commanding the Fleet Marine Force Pacific, had approved the rotation of Marine officers and noncommissioned officers through South Vietnam for two weeks of on-the-job training in counter-guerrilla operations.

In May 1961, the Geneva Conference was reconvened to consider the situation in Laos. Though inconclusive, the resulting cease-fire eased tensions and enabled United States forces to stand down from their alert status. Then, at the end of the year, as the news from South Vietnam continued to be discouraging, President Kennedy sent Gen. Maxwell Taylor to Saigon to appraise the situation. Not unexpectedly, he recommended an increase in our military commitments. By then I had left Okinawa for Bangkok and the diverse political interests of the SEATO Alliance.

✳ ✳ ✳

The French Assembly vote in March 1954 to seek a settlement of the Indochina War, and the conclusion of that conflict at Geneva in July, revived Secretary of State John Foster Dulles' interest in a collective security arrangement for Southeast Asia. The outcome was the Manila Pact, whose signatories each accepted that "...armed attack in the Treaty Area...would endanger its own peace and safety..." Each further agreed "...to meet the common danger in accordance with its constitutional processes...." The wording allowing each member the option to act revealed an inherent weakness. Still, the South East Asia Treaty Organization had taken form, and its Military Planning Office had plans that identified command responsibilities and force commitments.[5]

**ADM. HARRY D. FELT, USN COMMANDER IN CHIEF,
PACIFIC AND U.S. MILITARY ADVISER TO SEATO**

My introduction to SEATO had started on Okinawa. Then, during the exercise in March, I had contacted Col. Henry Koepke, the Army officer I was to relieve as U.S. Military Advisers Representative in Bangkok. Thus, by the time I arrived in Hawaii for my pre-assignment briefings, I had a general understanding of what to expect. I stopped at Fleet Marine Force, Pacific headquarters and then went to the headquarters of the Commander in Chief Pacific where I met the staff involved in SEATO planning. Lastly, I called on Admiral Felt who, as the U.S. Military Adviser to SEATO, would be my immediate superior. The admiral put my mission simply, "Ensure that all SEATO plans parallel ours so that we can take action either unilaterally or through the Alliance." Then, he advised, "Don't form any white man's club," and sped me on my way.

While in Hawaii I received a copy of Meda's travel orders. These routed her and the children by commercial air from France to Dhahran, where she was to transfer to military air for her flight to Bangkok, with an overnight stop in Delhi. Worried this transfer might not go smoothly, I checked the roster of our mission to Saudi Arabia and found its deputy chief to be Army Col. Victor Delnore, who had occupied quarters in the same building as we at Quantico. My mind eased, and not knowing that Meda had decided to include sight-seeing stops in Rome and Cairo in her itinerary, I sent a message asking Vic to help her through Dhahran. He replied that he would be absent, but his assistant would meet her. I could not tell her of this, nor that I would be in Delhi.

Upon my return to Bangkok, I checked in at the American Club, a simple hotel with bungalows used mainly by diplomatic mission families. Meanwhile, Meda started on her way. After a long day sight-seeing in Cairo, she awoke on the ground at Dhahran with two exhausted children and flight attendants telling her to let them sleep. She soon had the confused stewardesses help her deplane. To her surprise she was being paged by Delnore's assistant, who saw her through arrival formalities and to comfortable air-conditioned quarters. The next day he

EN ROUTE TO BANGKOK
MEDA, SUZANNE, AND JOHN, CAIRO, 1961

took them for a visit to an oasis, and the day after put them on the flight to Delhi. Their welcome in India was particularly warm. They had expected the heat but not the presence of a delighted husband and father.

Our month at the American Club seemed endless, although membership at the Royal Bangkok Sports Club where John and Suzanne could work off their energy helped shorten the days. Finally, our thirty-day overlap ended, the Koepkes left, and we took over their house and the five servants Hank had assured me we would need. When our household effects arrived, our servants marvelled at the sleds, snow shovel, and ice skates that had been stored with our other belongings. The cook was even more surprised when I broiled hamburgers on our grill at the children's request. She told me I had used more charcoal than she did in three days to prepare all our meals, which were cooked over charcoal in an outside kitchen.

Having a family and a house was a pleasant return to normal, but being awakened by trumpeting elephants stabled just beyond our wall was an exotic touch we were willing to forgo. We also discovered that our modern house with its large two-story glass windows was like a greenhouse. We never understood why such houses should have become popular when traditional Thai houses with wide overhanging roofs and windows with shutters rather than glass were welcoming to the slightest breezes. Meda immediately began looking for a house more in tune with the environment. She also saw to enrolling John and Suzanne in the International School, plus helping them make the transition from their French curriculum.

Her other immediate task was to establish her role with the servants, all of whom had quarters behind the main house. This included mastering the subtleties of their hierarchy and arbitrating their disputes. We decided to keep the full staff and do much of our SEATO entertaining at home. Despite this economy, Meda thought it wise to supplement our income. We had thought that my official allowance would be adequate until we realized that the eight countries in SEATO translated into guest lists in multiples of eight that were further augmented when visiting dignitaries were being honored. That, and her wish to meet Thais other than officials and servants, plus avoid too much mah jong or bridge, led her to again teach English as a foreign language.

The settling-in process of the family was paralleled at the office. Chief Yeoman Harold Hatch started our work day picking up my message traffic at our military mission's cryptocenter, a necessary chore since virtually all of my communications with Admiral Felt were highly classified. When I arrived at the office, he would have the references needed and a note with recommended actions attached to each message. I had never been so spoiled.

Our weekly Military Advisers' Representatives Committee meetings were characterized by frank discussions in an amicable atmosphere. Nonetheless, it was evident that the United States, which provided the SEATO Field Force commander and the bulk of the forces for each SEATO plan, was the dominant partner. However, I avoided advancing national views unless invited, and relied instead on the American planners on the international staff to reflect our national interests. When not busy with committee work, I was closeted with Lt. Cols. William Luecke and Carl Bailey, our Army and Air Force planners, and with Marine Lt. Col. James Linnan who filled the Navy billet. I also spent at least one full day each week at our embassy, and regularly called at our military mission.

Incident to a visit at the Embassy, I learned that the Navy was threatening to withhold funds from our attache for the 45-foot picket boat he used primarily for entertaining. I responded with lukewarm sympa-

**SEATO ROAD RECONNAISSANCE,
NORTHERN THAILAND, 1962**

thy until I realized my opportunity. With animation, I told him that SEATO regularly reconnoitered the roads in northeast Thailand and had now extended this to other border regions. I then suggested, "If you can let us use your boat, I will propose we also survey the inland waterways and provide you copies of all our reports." The attache was delighted; the SEATO Military Planning Office was equally pleased, and I was able to observe a colorful and unusual way of life.

In this manner we adjusted to a new life that was endlessly fascinating, and particularly demanding for Meda. Beyond her commitment to her teaching, she was responsible for arranging Mrs. Felt's time whenever she accompanied the admiral to Bangkok and was also frequently involved with other official visitor's delegations. Then, as an unusual add-on to her SEATO obligations, she was asked by Begum Akhbar, the wife of my opposite number from Pakistan, to help her and some of the other Pakistani wives adjust to the unfamiliar open social life in Bangkok.

John and Suzanne, meanwhile, were soon at home in the International School among friends of varied backgrounds. Their free time was divided between the sports club and the polo club which sponsored the summer riding camp they enjoyed at Kanchanaburi, site of the real "bridge over the River Kwai." Not surprisingly, they acquired far more Thai than their parents. We also found time to explore Bangkok's network of canals together in a small boat. And, to lighten the heavy social burden we escaped as often as possible to Pattaya, the beach resort south of Bangkok.[6] Pattaya then offered only simple thatch cottages with charcoal pots best left to the cook each family brought along.

While my first six months at SEATO passed in this relative tranquility, I was not isolated from events in Laos and Vietnam. My ready access to all official messages kept me well informed. In South Vietnam, 1961 had ended with the Taylor mission in November and the first deployment of U.S. Army helicopter units in December. Four months later, Marine helicopters would follow. By then, American military advisers had been authorized to participate in combat operations. The ill-conceived Strategic Hamlet Program under the direction of Ngo Dinh Nhu, President Diem's brother, had also been launched. That program, based on British experience in Malaya was poorly executed, and would fail disastrously.[7]

In early February 1962, while in Hawaii for a staff visit, I called on General Harkins to find him leaving for Saigon to head the new Military Assistance Command, which would absorb the existing MAAG. Several days after, I was in Admiral Felt's office when a message listing Harkins' personnel augmentation requirements arrived. The admiral read and began to sputter, "ridiculous," "impossible," "mad." I quickly escaped. I mentioned Felt's reaction when I later saw Harkins in Bangkok, and, at his dismay, explained that admirals think of a headquarters as a few personal assistants who serve him aboard a flagship that has all the necessities a general must take into the field with him.

I suggested he might offer to settle for an amphibious command ship in lieu of additional headquarters personnel. Harkins was taken with the idea but never enough to raise it with Admiral Felt. Shortly after, I was in Saigon and found the staff shaping up without Navy help. My visit was routine, but when I returned to Bangkok I was excitedly asked what had happened. I replied, "Nothing unusual, why?" I then learned that minutes after I had become airborne, several Vietnamese Air Force planes had attacked the Palace where the President had his offices. Later, I was told that Diem had survived this second coup attempt.

Our most pressing issues remained the worsening situation in Laos and Thai concerns that American assistance under SEATO should not require the agreement of all members. These concerns were allayed by the Council Representatives, who held that action by member nations did not require unanimity. This

THAI TRANSPORT
U.S. ARMY BATTLE GROUP, KORAT, THAILAND, MAY 1962
Center: Lt. Gen. John L. Richardson, USA, Commanding Joint Task Force 116, with visiting SEATO Officers.

was confirmed in a joint statement issued on March 6, 1962, by Secretary of State Dean Rusk and Thai Foreign Minister Thanat Khoman. Though this issue appeared settled, fighting in Laos intensified. The United States was actively supporting General Phoumi, even to the extent of airlifting artillery to replace his losses. Despite such efforts, Phoumi's forces were routed at Nam Tha and the way was open for a possible invasion of Thailand.

In response, Admiral Felt again activated Joint Task Force 116 on May 10 under command of Lieutenant General Richardson, whom I had served as chief of staff during the SEATO exercise the year before. Five days later President Kennedy ordered United States forces into Thailand. At the time of these decisions, our Army had a battle group engaged in an exercise at Korat. The unit, promptly assigned to the joint task force, went into bivouac, ostensibly ready for combat...except that it had no ammunition. The readiness of American forces improved later in the month when lead elements of a Marine Expeditionary Brigade began deploying to Udorn. Further strengthening was provided when our Air Force brought in twenty fighter planes and based them at Takhli.

None of these actions had been discussed in advance with either SEATO or the Thai government. However, the deployments corresponded to those prescribed in SEATO Plan 5, in which Alliance forces intended for intervention in Laos were to be initially deployed into Thailand. On the presumption that the United States was implementing that plan, the British moved a Hawker-Hunter squadron to Chiengmai, the Australians sent a reduced Saber squadron to Ubon, New Zealand brought in a Special Air Service detachment to Korat, and the Thai Army reinforced its border forces.

Pakistan, observing these actions, prepared to contribute the brigade which the United States had, in earlier bilateral arrangements, agreed to transport to Thailand. Accordingly, an infantry battalion comprising their initial contingent was moved to Karachi ready to be airlifted. The battalion was paraded for our ambassador and held on alert for thirty days, but our planes never arrived. Meanwhile I was assailed by Pakistani officials, many now personal friends. They refused to believe these deployments were all national initiatives. To them, we were embarked on a devious enterprise from which Pakistan was being excluded.

During this embarrassing period, I was invited to call on Air Chief Marshal Dawee Chullasapya, the Thai Military Adviser to SEATO and Chief of the Thai Armed Forces General Staff, to discuss command relations. I anticipated an awkward meeting and was not disappointed. In SEATO Plan 5, wherein Thailand served as the support base for operations in Laos, two headquarters had been designated to avoid placing American forces under direct foreign command. Thus, Thailand provided the SEATO Force commander to interface with the Council of Ministers, while a SEATO Field Force commander, designated by the United States, was to direct operations.

As expected, Dawee noted that four countries now had combat forces in Thailand, but that no means of coordinating their activities had been established. He proposed an early meeting of all interested parties to settle matters and asked I get Admiral Felt's views. His closing comment was that Field Marshal Sarit Thanarat, the Prime Minister and Commander in chief of the Thai Armed Forces, should be made the commander of Alliance Forces in Thailand. I reported this to Felt who came back promptly with instructions to say nothing, do nothing, and commit nothing pending further advice, which he was soliciting from the Joint Chiefs of Staff.

However, Field Marshal Sarit called a meeting before I received anything more from Admiral Felt. The assembly was imposing. The United States was represented by Generals Harkins, Richardson, and Weller, now chief of staff of Joint Task Force 116. The other countries with forces in Thailand were represented by their ambassadors and each had his SEATO Military Advisers Representative in attendance. Sarit opened the meeting and senior Thai officers began

**AIR CHIEF MARSHAL DAWEE CHULLASAPYA
CHIEF OF STAFF, ROYAL THAI ARMED FORCES,
BANGKOK, THAILAND, 1963**

developing the rationale for Thai command. It soon became evident there was no easy solution. However, I had earlier consulted our manual with guidance on the command of joint United States forces and found a possible solution in the definition of "coordinating authority."

During the coffee break, I took the manual to Weller, who read it and called Richardson. Then they both went to Harkins. All agreed I should approach Lieutenant General Kriangsak, my former colleague at SEATO. Kriangsak, fluent in English, read the definition and exclaimed, "This sounds like it. Let me try it out." When we reconvened, the Thais circulated a paper proposing that Field Marshal Sarit be the coordinating authority between the Thai armed forces and the Alliance contingents and General Harkins act in the same capacity for the Alliance forces. The proposal was quickly agreed to. I left satisfied that I had earned my pay that day. I did not anticipate I would be doing so again so soon.

As before, the occasion began with a call from Dawee who told me that Their Majesties wished to visit the SEATO troops in the field. He went on to say that the King and Queen desired to spend a night under canvas and he thought a hospital tent would be the only suitable accommodation. Further, not all locations they wished to visit were accessible to the Royal plane, and helicopters would be needed. Could I help? I replied I would try. I briefed Ambassador Kenneth Young, obtained Admiral Felt's agreement to do what was necessary, and headed for Udorn to meet with Brig. Gen. Ormand B. Simpson who commanded the Marines there. Orme assured me of his support and I returned to help Dawee finalize the program.

Three days later the show was on the road. The Royal Couple, with aides and ladies-in-waiting, were to travel in the Royal plane. The remaining entourage of some seventy dignitaries was to be distributed among five other planes. The British, Australian, and New Zealand ambassadors and their SEATO Military Advisers Representatives were all invited to join Ambassador Young and me in our air attache's plane. Generals Harkins and Richardson planned to travel independently and meet the group whenever they could. The group was large, the itinerary extended, and the details intricate. Yet, everything went off as planned.

We gathered first at Korat, 130 miles north of Bangkok. The reception was grand, but Their Majesties' visit to our Army battle group was less successful. The bivouac, with troops dispersed in the jungle and equipment camouflaged, was properly professional. But, precisely because it was professional, there was little to see. Their Majesties, young, attractive, and inexperienced in military ways, were polite but disappointed. The Marines at Udorn, however, put on a performance that earned high praise. It began with General Simpson greeting Their Majesties on arrival and introducing them to his staff and principal commanders in formation before a guard of honor. He then escorted the Royal party to freshly built bleachers where two throne-like chairs were centrally placed.

Then, the moment Their Majesties' bottoms touched their seats, a flight of Marine Skyhawks thundered down the runway, circled the field at low altitude, and slammed to a stop in the arresting gear in front of the bleachers. My classmate, Col. Ross S. Mickey, commanding the composite Marine Aircraft Group, had done us proud. Next, Lt. Col. Harold W. Adams commanding the 3rd Battalion, 9th Marines, received the Royal Couple, standing before a camp of carefully aligned pyramidal tents with rolled-up side walls erected on a bare slope. That sight alone was impressive, but what really caused Royal comment were the cots, seabags, and shoes of a thousand Marines all in perfect rows. This, the Royal Couple agreed, was properly military.

MARINES RECEIVE ROYALTY, UDORN, THAILAND, JUNE 1962
From left: Queen Sirikit, King Bhumipol, Brig. Gen. Ormand Simpson, USMC.

The Thais were no less adept at doing things in a grand manner, as was demonstrated in the remote northwestern village of Chiang Rai where a tent city had been erected in a rice field in twenty-four hours. Their Majesties were under canvas in the hospital tent we had provided. The rest of us were assigned more modest tents which, even so, were equipped with flush toilets that worked. The tour was a great success. The Thais, including Their Majesties, were comforted by what they saw, while we were able to see a facet of Thai life usually denied foreigners. I was not prepared for the reverence accorded the King and Queen.

After drinks with Their Majesties in their lavishly furnished tent, I strolled about the camp with the Queen and a few of her attendants to meet with local people, who had gathered to offer delicacies and handicrafts. It was an informal promenade, yet wherever the Queen stopped to speak with someone, that person dropped to the ground. This practice was repeated at dinner, where Their Majesties sat at a table on a raised platform, while the rest of us were at ground level. The trays of food were offered to the Royal Couple by servants on their knees. More impressive, whenever the King or Queen addressed one of the

BLAZING TRAIL FROM KORAT TO THE COAST, THAILAND, 1962

Ministers or court officials, that individual would leave his table and either kneel or prostrate himself while replying. The practice did not appear to encourage small talk.

In the weeks that followed, diplomats in Vientiane and Geneva moved toward a resolution of the crisis in Laos. With this development, the Marines began withdrawing. Then, after the Declaration of Neutrality of Laos was signed at Geneva on July 23, our joint task force was deactivated and our remaining troops left. How far the Alliance members' deployments influenced the neutralization of Laos is uncertain. What is clear, is that the experience gained in moving troops into Thailand led to further improvement of the Thai infrastructure.

After the difficulties encountered landing a reinforced battalion in Bangkok and moving it to Udorn by road, rail, and transport aircraft, it was evident that reliance on the port of Bangkok had to be minimized. Among the alternatives examined, Sattahip, on the Gulf of Thailand where the Thai Navy and Marines had large installations, appeared promising. Unfortunately, there was no nearby airbase nor was there a road leading inland. That summer I led a SEATO reconnaissance team, augmented by U.S. Army engineers, from Korat south to the coast. Subsequently, the 508th Engineer Battalion was brought into Thailand to build a by-pass road around Bangkok, Sattahip was improved as a staging area, and work began on an air base at Utapao.

The British, too, lost no time in making their own contribution to SEATO capabilities. Shortly after our joint task force was deactivated, I was briefed by British Army engineers from Singapore on plans to build an airfield on the Thai side of the Mekong River opposite Savannakhet to facilitate deployment of their forces. I was also told that London would approve funding only upon United States assurance such a base would significantly contribute to military capabilities in the region. Shortly after, I conveyed Felt's reply that I should encourage the British or any other ally willing to spend his own money to improve military capabilities, to the British ambassador in somewhat more diplomatic language. The project was duly funded and the airfield built.

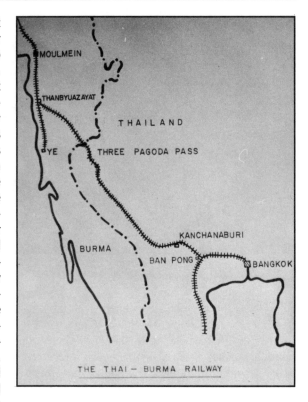

THAI-BURMA RAILWAY, 1943

Another consequence of the crisis merits notice. During one of Felt's visits soon after the Royal Laotian forces broke at Nam Tha, the admiral and I went to the Laotian Embassy, where General Phoumi had been summoned. There, the admiral read, and I translated into French, a personal letter from President Kennedy to the general which voiced extreme displeasure at the general's performance. I had difficulty finding appropriate words to convey the President's harsh sentiments. At this same time our undercover military assistance group in Laos was withdrawn.

At the fall meeting of the Military Advisers, the French representative stated that the neutralization of Laos made Plan 5 superfluous. Admiral Felt argued that this was SEATOs most advanced plan and incorporated many agreements that served as useful precedents for other plans. But Lieutenant General de la

RAILWAY ALONG THE KWAI RIVER, THAILAND, 1962

Chenelliere insisted on its cancellation. At the break, Admiral Felt asked me to find out how rigid the general's instructions were. If he appeared flexible, I was to find out if he would agree simply to shelve the plan and exclude it from periodic updates. De la Chenelliere gladly accepted Felt's proposal and the plan was retained but in an inactive status. Our interests and efforts were then directed to the preparation of a new SEATO Plan 7 to assist Vietnam.

As the year ended, Laos had been neutralized and the buildup of our advisory and support efforts had begun in South Vietnam. For me, the year had been of consuming interest. I had observed the workings of high councils and twice followed in the traces of the Japanese forces that had crossed Thailand to enter Burma in 1942. First, I had traveled what remained of the infamous railway paralleling the Kwai River and briefly linking the two countries. Pushed to completion by the Japanese in thirteen months, the railway had cost the lives of 16,000 Allied prisoners and uncounted thousands of Asian laborers.

That adventure had required one day by train, two days by fast motor boat, and another day by elephant to reach the Three Pagoda Pass on the Thai-Burma border. When he heard of it, our naval attache was sufficiently intrigued to ask how far up river I thought we could get his 45-foot picket boat. I replied, "Probably as far as the last police post at Sang Klaburi, but only in the rainy season." Sure enough, when the rains came, I returned to the Kwai with the American, British, and French attaches on a river trip that brought us to that post within seven miles of the Burma border. It was a very wet journey, the flow of scotch almost equalling that of the monsoon rain.

TO THE BURMA BORDER BEYOND THE KWAI, 1962

Christmas 1962 was spent in our new house, a spacious dwelling with teak floors, shuttered windows, and shaded terraces. Its high walls enclosed a garden and pond large enough for my kayak and the gardener's geese that kept the snake population down. Our folding Christmas tree lacked the drama of the one cut in Vietnam's highlands but had accompanied the children from France. We enjoyed Christmas Eve carol services, lunch with friends on Christmas day, and escaped to Pattaya for the rest of the holiday. Meda and I then spent three days in Singapore with our SEATO colleagues as guests of Vice Adm. Sir Varyl Begg, the British Commander in Chief, Far East. It was a festive occasion marred only by the insight provided by the Royal Marine Brigade commander on the fighting between British and Indonesian forces in Borneo.[8]

Once returned to Bangkok, I devoted myself to preparing for the SEATO Council meeting in Paris in March. Among the instructions I carried with me were a request from John and Suzanne for artichokes and from Meda for caviar, both tastes developed in our nomadic lives. Though wet and cold, I found Paris particularly welcoming. Our host, the Minister of Defense, was the same Pierre Messmer who had received me so cordially in Dakar when I visited there in 1959. The SEATO meeting went well, thanks to the long hours the staff spent preparing position papers after informal negotiations on agenda items during receptions and dinners. The formal sessions then were used mainly to approve what had been worked out earlier by the staff.

BANGKOK HOME, 1963

Back in Bangkok, the planning group working on Plan 7 had concluded it should support South Vietnam's own national security plan. The other Advisers Representatives agreed, but Admiral Felt, aware that Vietnamese government planning was not sufficiently advanced, urged that work continue under existing guidance. He later directed me to brief Ambassador Frederick Nolting and General Harkins in Saigon on the plan. I mentioned to Harkins I had been hearing much on the British experience in Malaya but little on the French in Indochina. "The French," I continued, "prepared a lengthy critique of their operations against the same enemy we are confronting. I believe it is more relevant to our interests." Harkins appeared to nod agreement, then said, "But the French lost their war and, besides, their reports have to be translated."

I called on the ambassador at nine on a Saturday morning to find him in relaxed dress, though his manner was not. When I commented on his obvious preoccupation, he replied that Secretary of Defense Robert McNamara had asked for a means of measuring progress and he had yet to find a satisfactory answer. Nolting's use of the word "progress" was significant for it reflected the prevailing view that additional resources invariably led to improvements. That was not the way lower echelon personnel saw it. This was emphasized in an unexpected encounter with Lt. Col. John Stockton, my Army friend from the Ecole Militaire, who commanded one of the first Army helicopter units in Vietnam. John had

Lt. Col. Frank Clay, adviser to the 7th Vietnamese Division, staying with him, and I joined them for dinner.

I spent most of the night listening to a wide-ranging discussion of the situation. Both officers were witness to Vietnamese military operations in the Mekong delta, and both were vehement in condemning the callous disregard of these forces for the population. In their view, increases in American support simply meant more civilian dead. Unlike the Viet Cong, South Vietnam's forces appeared determined to alienate the people. This disdain was further shown in May when the government refused to allow Buddhist flags to fly on Buddha's anniversary. Violence followed and, in Hue, twelve Buddhists were killed. The climax, emphasizing the schism between the Diem government and the Buddhist majority, occurred in August when the national police conducted nationwide raids on temples and pagodas.

At this time, SEATO was engaged in an exercise involving some 26,000 troops. Its final day was marked by a field demonstration at which I was pleased to find the Vietnamese generals, Duong Van Minh and Tran Van Don, among the dignitaries. After our greetings, they asked to meet me privately. We had lunch at my home and talked of many things, but the key point they made was that they knew SEATO was working on a plan to come to Vietnam's assistance and wanted to contribute to its development. I reported this to Felt, who instructed me to refer all queries from Vietnamese officials concerning SEATO planning activities to Harkins in Saigon. I did so, and heard nothing more. I still find it strange that this second initiative to involve the Vietnamese in helping to plan their defense should have been rejected.

In Vietnam, the Buddhist crisis increased tensions to the flash point and on November 1 Generals Duong Van Minh, Tran Van Don, and Le Van Kim seized power in Saigon. The following day, President Diem and his brother Ngo Dinh Nhu were dead. I had never met Nhu but was dismayed at Diem's death. I thought him a frustrating man, opinionated and inflexible, but personally honest. He had settled the Sect problem after the Indochina War and brought a measure of stability to his country. There were many reasons why that had not endured, but the responsibility was not all his. United States policy was not always consistent nor had we denied him support for disruptive and unrealistic population resettlement programs. In any event, I could not see where Diem's assassination served any useful purpose.

Twenty days later, halfway around the world from Saigon, President Kennedy would meet the same fate at another assassin's hand. Though saddened at Diem's death, I did not think that extraordinary in the context of South Vietnam. However, it was incomprehensible to me, as it was to many others, that the President of the United States, an economically advanced and politically sophisticated country of free peoples, could be gunned down by other than a madman.

Sometime after these disturbing events, I had the opportunity to ask Tran Van Don in a private conversation about the assassination of Diem. I recalled that he had always respected his President and found it difficult to believe he had allowed him to be killed. Don assured me that the assassination had not been planned and he had been distressed when it had happened.[9] Our conversation then turned to the prospects for South Vietnam. Unfortunately, his role in these was to be limited for, on January 30, 1964, General Nguyen Khanh arrested Don and the other leaders of the Military Revolutionary Council and seized power, which he in turn soon lost to the coup that followed.

South Vietnam's future at the end of 1963 did not appear bright. The Strategic Hamlet Program had failed and been replaced by a less ambitious resettlement effort. A strengthening of the paramilitary forces associated with this move might have had a positive effect had the Viet Cong confined its struggle to the rural areas. But, by then, the communists' use of the Ho Chi Minh trail in Laos to reinforce the Viet Cong was enabling them to conduct operations in the South at the regimental level. Moreover, the personnel changes in the leadership of the South Vietnamese military forces and confusion following the November coup had severely impeded the pacification effort. These troubles were compounded by American plans to begin turning over military responsibility to South Vietnam.

The coup in January, which removed the triumvirs who three months earlier had overthrown Diem, brought more changes in the Vietnamese armed forces and a further decline in their effectiveness. The communists were quick to exploit these developments and the United States felt compelled to respond. In March, Secretary McNamara called for a 50,000-man increase in the Vietnamese forces. President Johnson agreed. Then, in June, Harkins was replaced by Gen. William Westmoreland, who promptly asked for 5,100 additional advisers to support the planned increase in South Vietnam's forces. In this manner, both sides were building up to more violent confrontations.

Meanwhile, SEATO was losing effectiveness, and its promising start fading. Though it had prepared plans that embodied commitments for coordinated action and had exposed officers from widely different countries to the discipline of combined endeavor, its accomplishments were being diminished by the lessening interest of Pakistan and France. Pakistan's own security concerns were along its borders with India. France, now free of Indochina, had many problems close to home. More serious, as the United States commitment in South Vietnam grew, its capability for unilateral action increased and it became less inclined to have its freedom of action circumscribed by an international council. SEATO would continue to survive, but the burden for the defense of Southeast Asia was rapidly becoming American.[10]

These disquieting indicators that all was not well had little effect upon my personal activities. My year had begun with the visit of General Wallace M. Greene, Jr., the newly appointed Commandant of the Marine Corps, who, after dinner at our home, asked where I would like to go next. Meda and I had already discussed the subject and I was quick to reply, "Washington, Sir." The general was equally quick in saying, "Sounds reasonable, I'll see what can be done." That matter seemingly settled, I turned to preparations for the annual SEATO Council meeting to be held in Manila in mid-April.

I went to Manila early to ensure everything was in order. This was complicated by Admiral Felt's insistence we save travel funds by staying at Sangley Point Naval Air Station. Since the meetings were to be held in the city and Sangley Point was down Manila Bay, we had to organize two motor pools and obtain high-speed boats for shuttle services. None of this was insurmountable, but it precluded our joining the informal after-hours exchanges with the other delegates during which agenda problems were worked out. This was a serious failing. Altogether, the meetings were a great deal of work for little return. My reward came in meeting the chief of staff to the Commander U.S. Naval Forces, Philippines and arranging passage home on a President liner.[11]

In Bangkok the farewell parties had begun for the many expecting to leave in the summer. All were pleasant affairs. However, at a gathering hosted by Ambassador Graham Martin for General Harkins, the clearly depressed general confessed to me his bitterness at the brusque manner in which he had been relieved. I was sorry that our last meeting should end on such a note. I had always found him a considerate gentleman. I did not always agree with him, but the problems confronting him were not simple. The optimism for which he came to be criticized was simply a reflection of the prevailing view that success would follow increased commitments of resources.

I received my orders shortly before we were to leave Bangkok and discovered that I was not going to Washington. I suspected General Greene had concluded my irregular service might hinder my promotion so was sending me to the 1st Division at Camp Pendleton where, presumably, I would have the regimental command I had missed on Okinawa. We were surprised at the news. I had also just learned I would be in the zone for promotion that summer. Command of a regiment was coming a little late. Yet, with ten colonels vying for each star, the chances were slim at best, and a command qualification might help next year if I missed the first round. The question remaining was how we all would adapt to the life in southern California. For Meda and me, the setting would be familiar, for John and Suzanne, now fourteen and twelve, it would be new and different.

They had long outgrown the warm clothing they had brought from France. To correct this, we took a military flight to Hong Kong to outfit them for the sea voyage home and the chill of San Francisco. John greeted the first cool breezes he had felt in nearly three years with, "How clever. The Chinese have air-conditioned the whole city." The shopping was a great success and compensated in some part for the exceptional turbulence of our return flight. At one point, an abrupt down-draft had many passengers falling back on collapsed seats. No one was seriously injured, but it was not an experience to repeat...even for a trip to Hong Kong.

Preparation of farewell letters to the military advisers, whom I had come to know on a personal basis, was among my last efforts in Bangkok. The response from Air Marshal Sir Frederick Sherger, Chairman of the Australian Chiefs of Staff Committee, best reflected my own sentiments. He wrote, "I always felt that the Military Advisers and their staffs missed a priceless opportunity of getting together outside of formal meeting hours by not staying at one hotel." Then he added, "I always sensed that America was and is a little unhappy at the apparent lack of support she is receiving in South Vietnam..."

A final reception in the Thai Government lounge at Don Muang airport launched us homeward in proper style. A few hours later we were at Clarke Air Force Base as guests of Maj. Gen. Samuel Maddox, with whom I had worked when he was Admiral Felt's chief planner. The next morning we moved to Sangley Point where we enjoyed a brief stay before boarding the *President Roosevelt* This ended a unique period in each of our lives. We were all truly sorry to leave, but we also found a pleasant excitement at the first throb of engines that started us on our way home.

Nine

AT THE TWILIGHT'S LAST GLEAMING

The first leg of our return journey from Manila to Hong Kong provided welcome leisure...no commitments or obligations, just rest and time for easy conversations. These revealed we were already nostalgic over the life we had so recently left and uncertain at what awaited us in California. We also found ourselves less enthusiastic at the thought of going home than we had expected. In the seventeen years we had been married, Meda and I had come to think of home as where we lived. Moreover, our experience of the regulated military life had been minimal.

At Camp Pendleton, after we were first married, I had commanded a schools battalion. Later, at Quantico, the academic atmosphere of the Educational Center encouraged pursuit of wide-ranging interests and my duty in Washington had centered on international security affairs. These interests had grown, during seven years of residence abroad, as had Meda's. Our children had shared in this life; the world they knew best was international. Their first real memories were of Saigon where they had started school.[1] Their education had continued in the cosmopolitan atmosphere of Washington, shifted to France, then to the International School in Bangkok. Given this background, we all wondered how we would fit into the life we would find at Camp Pendleton. John and Suzanne had no idea; Meda and I had lived there, but the years since had changed us greatly.

I had spent the past four years in war planning at national and international levels and extended my familiarity with Southeast Asia and its key personalities. I thought this experience could have been put to greater use in meeting the storm gathering over Vietnam had I been assigned to Washington. However, it would also serve me in the 1st Marine Division. I put these serious thoughts aside when we reached Hong Kong, our first port of call. We had traveled there by ship and plane over the years and had always enjoyed its animation and spectacular scenery, the attractions of its restaurants and the temptations of its myriad shops. After an all too short excursion ashore, we were back at sea on course for Yokosuka, where we enjoyed a traditional Japanese dinner with old friends.

The long run from there to Honolulu remains a fond memory for John and Suzanne. There were other families aboard returning from duty in Asia. A teen club was soon rocking, deck games organized, movies screened, and tables set aside for them in the dining salon. Suzanne, two months shy of the magic age, was included. We too found agreeable companions. One, a Foreign Service wife shepherding her young children home from Cambodia, had just congratulated herself for having everything she would need with her, including a hammer to hang pictures, when she realized she had packed her tickets and passport in her hold baggage. We sympathized with her confusion and agreed on the importance of having one's own pictures, music, and books to make home wherever one was.

Shortly after arriving in Honolulu, I was in Admiral Felt's office enjoying the sweeping view of Pearl Harbor, while making my farewell call. Ours had been an unusual relationship; a colonel directly subordinate to a four-star admiral, while separated by 5,000 miles of ocean and the international dateline. Yet, throughout our three-year association, I never raised an issue to which he failed to reply within hours. I had always found him willing to listen, a quality which often diminishes as rank increases. Even more, I was impressed by his grasp of issues. He was demanding but unfailing in his support and fully deserving of my respect. Our association must have worked. I left his headquarters with the Joint Services Commendation Medal and an invitation to use his beach house during our stay in port.

San Francisco was as cold and gray as the news that my name was missing from the promotion list...proving that *out of sight, out of mind* is a more rational saying than *absence makes the heart grow fonder*. Then, even as I found consolation in the thought I would have another chance the following year, the sun came out to restore my spirits, a process aided by buying a new car and leaving for a visit with Meda's family before heading for southern California.

✳ ✳ ✳

Camp Pendleton appeared little changed since our hasty departure in 1949. We were offered the choice of an apartment in a converted barracks or fending for ourselves on the local market. We opted for the latter, and Meda soon had us settled in a house on a ridge with a view of the back country. The school situation was less satisfactory. Academically ahead, John and Suzanne had already completed the courses for their grade levels at the local high school. Moreover, though younger, they had a broader view of the world than their classmates and higher educational goals than most of them. Both adjusted, but our two years at Pendleton did not leave them with many pleasant memories.

COMMANDING OFFICER, 5TH MARINES
COL. VICTOR J. CROIZAT, CAMP PENDLETON, 1964

Maj. Gen. William T. Fairbourn greeted me with command of the 5th Marines. I had expected a command but had not thought it would be the regiment in which I had served as a lieutenant fresh out of Basic School and then as a *salty* captain on Guadalcanal. A few days later, I received the regimental colors, whose cascade of streamers told its story in battles fought, victories won, and hazards endured. The first had been awarded for service in Haiti in 1914, the year the 5th Marines had been formed. They had multiplied rapidly during World War I. Then, a single streamer for the years in Nicaragua marked the interval until World War II, where the Asiatic-Pacific campaign streamer and its honors for Guadalcanal brought a rush of memories.

Those had been exciting days, when I had looked upon regimental commanders with awe. Now, I felt neither remote nor awesome, though I was again to learn that command becomes increasingly lonely as one rises in the hierarchy. Command of a platoon is intensely personal. Ties begin to loosen at company level, and a battalion commander must be as ready to allow his company commanders to carry on without interference, as he is to appear when needed. Regimental command further lengthens the distance. Yet, command requires mutual understanding which can only be attained by close association. I gained this by adding the role of observer to my usual duties. My excellent regimental staff handled the day to day paper work, leaving me free to visit the firing ranges and maneuver areas to follow the incessant training.

Late in 1964 I went to Twenty-nine Palms, a vast desert training center where tanks and artillery were free to maneuver and fire. This was my first experience in command of the regiment with its usual reinforcements: a battalion of artillery, a company of tanks, and a miscellany of other supporting units. I returned much impressed by the realities of time and space. That winter, I went to the high Sierras to observe the cold weather training. This was designed to build confidence in the men that they could survive and fight in a hostile environment. I had reservations over twice trucking a thousand Marines from their sea-level barracks several hundred miles to the high country. The exercises, however, proved to be of great value.

By this time, I had found much satisfaction in the status of the command and instituted the practice of holding commendation masts on the premise that a commander should be as ready to recognize superior performance as he is to punish malefactors. A series of talks I gave to my officers and noncommissioned officers to further their understanding of the conflict in Vietnam was also well received. Since I strongly believe that an informed wife makes for a better Marine, I was pleased when the Officers' Wives Club invited me to address them on the same subject. Meda contributed by organizing a series of coffees to help the noncommissioned officers' wives meet and develop the mutual support useful in handling the problems of family separation. General Fairbourn told me her efforts were much appreciated.

The new year brought SILVER LANCE, the largest training exercise since World War II, which was to involve our division and the Hawaii-based 1st Marine Brigade. Lt. Gen. Victor H. Krulak, commanding the Fleet Marine Force, Pacific, directed the exercise, which focused on many of the problems in the intensifying conflict in Vietnam. Unexpected drama was added when the 1st Brigade embarked for California, only to be redirected to Okinawa to replace the brigade that had just been ordered ashore in South Vietnam. My regiment's enthusiasm was heightened by its responsibility for providing the insurgents, guerrillas, agitators and other hostile elements making up the aggressor forces. General Krulak encouraged our initiatives and the effort succeeded. The press, which turned out in force, agreed.

The observers from RAND, the military research organization, who attended SILVER LANCE invited me to visit their offices in Santa Monica. A short time later, I was with them at a luncheon that included several Air Force officers from their Systems Command. When I asked an Air Force colonel what he did, he replied, "I'm on my way to Washington to present a project proposal which should be of interest; we just spent thirty-five millions in its preparation." I looked at him in amazement and said, "You live in a different world from mine. I command a regiment of 3,000 Marines and my annual operating budget is one-sixth the cost of your proposal." The colonel did not reply, but I thought I detected a look of sympathy...obviously directed at me, not at the taxpayer.

I returned to find an invitation to replace General Fairbourn as speaker at a breakfast meeting of the Boise Chamber of Commerce. The general provided me a copy of the standard prepared speech, heavy in generalities and thin in substance. I thought anyone willing to listen to a speech with his breakfast coffee deserved more than packaged cliches, no matter how laudatory of the Corps, so I added some observations on our interests in Vietnam. This was well enough received to earn me a press conference later in the day. Vietnam had become a popular subject.

Back at my headquarters, I started on an amphibious exercise in which my regiment provided the infantry component of a brigade. The embarkation at San Diego went well. Then, while steaming slowly up the coast toward our landing beaches at Camp Pendleton, I received an exercise message that the ship on which the brigade commander was embarked had been sunk and I was now the landing force commander. I suspected that Brig. Gen. Hunter Hurst, in command of the brigade, was reciprocating for the hard time my aggressor force had given him during SILVER LANCE. I had no time to verify this; I was totally engaged with the landing which, happily, succeeded with neither accident nor adverse comment.

* * *

The emphasis we had been placing on Vietnam in our training was being justified by the worsening conditions in that country. I had arrived at Camp Pendleton at the time of the encounter in the Gulf of Tonkin.[2] The congressional resolution authorizing the President to commit United States combat forces to assist the South Vietnamese had come as I assumed command of the 5th Marines. Then, while American forces began limited air strikes against North Vietnam, the Viet Cong engaged its forces in what they identified as the general counteroffensive phase of the conflict. The intensification of the ground war was matched by turmoil in the government of South Vietnam. General Khanh was finally deposed in December, but it was February 1965 before Gen. Nguyen Van Thieu became the country's leader.

That same month, communist forces attacked the upland town of Pleiku and an Army billet in Qui Nhon, where twenty-three Americans were killed. The government in Washington then shifted emphasis from retaliatory air raids to a policy of sustained pressure in which continuing, but limited, air action was complemented by naval and small-scale ground operations. Because Danang was vital to the implementation of this policy, the 9th Marine Expeditionary Brigade from Okinawa was landed on March 8 to defend the Danang air base, and the 1st Brigade from Hawaii replaced them on Okinawa instead of joining us in SILVER LANCE. Coincident with this move, General Westmoreland decided to reexamine the entire American effort in Vietnam.

One of the three courses of action considered was the deployment of five divisions, three American, across Vietnam and Laos just below the 17th parallel. This was rejected because facilities and communications were inadequate. I found this interesting for I had spoken of such a deployment, though on a more modest scale, with General Weller and Ambassador Martin in the early 1960s.[3] The course actually adopted was to bring in two American divisions, one to the highlands and another on the coast. As a result, the III Marine Expeditionary Force headquarters was in place in Danang in May 1965, as was the advanced command echelon of the 3rd Marine Division and 17,500 Marines.

In California, the arrival of summer brought the departure of General Fairbourn and the replacement of Hunter Hurst by Brig. Gen. William A. Stiles, who assumed temporary command of the division as it prepared for deployment to the Far East. At this same time, I received the unwelcome news that there would be no star in my future. This, under the "two strikes and you're out" regulation meant I would be retired the following year. I was glad that the press of events did not permit the difficult moment to linger. In mid-August, I turned over the regiment to Col. Charles Widdecke and assumed duties as chief of staff. I then turned to the task of mounting out the division.

Unlike my earlier experience with the newborn 4th Division during the hectic days of 1943, the departure of the veteran 1st Division was an orderly process. The 7th Marines moved out first. The forward echelon of the division headquarters followed when Maj. Gen. Lewis J. Fields assumed command. Stiles and I stayed behind with the rear echelon to direct the departure of the remaining division units.[4] I went to Long Beach to say good-bye to the 5th Marines. I had seen many a troopship sail in my quarter-century of service, but none with the emotional burden I was carrying. I had spent a year preparing the regiment for a role I would not see it perform. Even worse, I looked upon its departure as the end of my active career as a Marine.

Camp Pendleton without the 1st Division was eerily quiet. Where a few months before it had been impossible to roam its 132,000 acres without hearing the crash of artillery and mortar fires or the rattle of small arms, the countryside had now reverted to the tranquility of the original Santa Margarita Ranch. This was aesthetically appealing, but being left behind was a new experience and my world was full of ghosts. At the same time, there was the irony of retiring at the very moment my unique experiences in Southeast Asia could be most useful to the Corps.

These sentiments had barely taken form when I received orders to report to Fleet Marine Force Headquarters in Hawaii. General Krulak greeted me cordially and immediately turned to the news that Westmoreland was planning to deploy a riverine force in the Mekong River delta. The Marine Corps had been approached to provide the ground component for the force, but the Commandant had replied that all his resources were committed in the northern I Corps Tactical Zone. The mission had then been assigned to the Army. Westmoreland had called for a conference at his Saigon headquarters to review the experience of the French and Vietnamese and develop the organizational and operational concepts needed by the American river force.

General Krulak concluded by directing me to attend the meeting as his representative, adding, "Marine Corps involvement in river warfare does not appear imminent, but I believe we should understand such operations. I also want you to stay after the conference and update yourself on the situation, then come back and prepare an interim doctrine for our use if we have to fight in such an environment." My "Aye, Aye, Sir" was heartfelt. I spent my remaining time in Hawaii reviewing files. The basic literature, still mainly French, was familiar. Official reports of recent events brought me up to date and confirmed how intimately the history of the region was tied to its waterways.

✳ ✳ ✳

When the French returned to Saigon in 1945, they had included a naval brigade and an armored combat command among the initial elements of their expeditionary corps. Lt. Gen. Philip Leclerc, former commander of the 2nd Armored Division that had liberated Paris, promptly dispatched his armor to secure the river town of Mytho as a prelude to regaining control over the delta. It set off confidently for its objective sixty kilometers south of Saigon early on October 15 but, impeded by downed bridges and other obstacles, it had gone less than half the distance by nightfall. It reached Mytho the evening of the sixteenth, to find that a unit from the naval brigade had arrived by boat and taken the town the day before. The lesson was not lost on General Leclerc.

The naval brigade, eventually reorganized into naval assault divisions, the famous *dinassauts*, had gone on to play an important role in restoring French authority over Indochina.[5] That legacy had been passed to the Vietnamese Navy which, by 1965, had a River Force of nine River Assault Groups, as the *dinassauts* had come to be called. The early emphasis on a river navy had been justified as long as the French patrolled the coast. When the French withdrew, the Vietnamese Navy was not prepared to take on this added responsibility. We had started a Vietnamese coastal patrol force in 1955, but its resources had been totally inadequate and the effort remained ineffective. Not surprisingly, a U.S. Navy survey made in early 1964 had found that maritime infiltration was not being controlled.

When a communist trawler carrying arms was intercepted in South Vietnam's coastal waters in 1965, the United States had joined in patrolling offshore. Later that year, it also organized a river patrol force in the southern delta where it now proposed to deploy a riverine combat force. The Vietnamese opposed this initiative, citing among their reasons the absence of land for a base. This was confirmed by Westmoreland's engineers, who recommended a base be developed with fill dredged from the river. Meanwhile, the riverine force could be based afloat. This recommendation had been accepted, and the decision had been made to hold the conference I was to attend in January 1966. Such was the situation when I again headed west across the Pacific.

✳ ✳ ✳

I wondered what Saigon would be like. When I had last been there in 1964, the Saigon of the French was already gone and a new tempo of life was evolving from the demise of the midday siesta. General Williams had exemplified the Americans' inability to accept this custom. Soon after arriving, he had requested a meeting with a French official immediately after lunch. When I reported the official had declined, Williams exploded, "Damn their siesta; it's a wonder anything gets done in this town." His reaction to my explanation that he would be welcome at seven-thirty that evening was equally vehement, "Why don't these people keep proper office hours; who wants to meet at dinner time?" He came to admit that the French worked as long as the Americans, but never accepted that the siesta made sense in the humid heat when there was no air conditioning.

**U.S. NAVY INSHORE COASTAL PATROL BOAT
SOUTH VIETNAM, 1966**

U.S. Navy Photo

I expected to find the American presence making its mark. This, I thought, should be particularly evident in the Vietnamese Navy and Marine Corps whose progress reminded me of my debt to General Williams. In response to his brusque request that I tell him "about this damned Marine Corps of yours," I had summarized the economic and political importance of the delta area and concluded, "General, it makes no difference whether the security forces there are army or navy as long as they are organized, trained, and equipped to operate in that unique environment." Williams had listened, nodded his head, and never again raised the subject. The two-battalion regiment I had left in 1956 was now a five-battalion brigade under Brig. Gen. Le Nguyen Khang, who was also responsible for the security of Saigon.

The drive to my billet confirmed that the Americans had indeed accelerated the cadence of the usual Asian bustle. Further observations would have to wait. The next day, in company with officers from Washington, Coronado, and Hawaii, I arrived at Westmoreland's headquarters to begin a heavy conference schedule. His operations officer summarized the situation and outlined the concept of the river force we were to develop. The preliminary staff work had been thorough and my colleagues were well informed.

U.S. AFLOAT BASE, MEKONG DELTA, SOUTH VIETNAM

U.S. Navy Photo

My principal contribution would be in relating French river force organization and equipment to their operational experience and tracing the lessons they had learned to the more recent activities of the Vietnamese Navy River Assault Groups. In doing this, I reviewed how the French Navy had adapted World War II landing craft and ships to the riverine environment. I further noted that virtually all of the modifications had been done locally and considerable ingenuity displayed, even to using turrets from Italian tanks to convert tank lighters to monitors. Lastly, I observed this same materiel was continuing to serve the Vietnamese Navy.

Still thinking of how the French had made do with what they had, I was dazzled by my colleagues' proposals for factory modification of tank lighters and the design of other specialized boats. They also planned to rehabilitate and air-condition landing ships. The plan to dredge a base at Dong Tam near Mytho was equally wondrous to me.[6] The conferees were recreating the *dinassaut*, but on a grander scale. Moreover, the concept of an afloat base and the utilization of helicopters with river forces promised to multiply operational flexibility. How delighted Admiral Querville would have been at these remarkable developments! [7]

When the conference ended, I stopped to see Maj. Gen. William Rosson, who had been General O'Daniel's right hand during my time in Saigon and was now Westmoreland's Chief of Staff. I also ran into an officer I had met at the

THE RUNG SAT, SOUTH VIETNAM

U.S. Navy Photo

Vietnamese officers' school at Quang Yen in North Vietnam in 1954. He was now in intelligence working on estimates. I asked if he noted any differences in the estimates prepared by Americans and Vietnamese using the same data. He replied unhesitatingly, "Oh yes, to you time and space factors are specific. We are satisfied with the generality that a unit is moving and will arrive when it can." I smiled in parting, "That is a difference we tend to forget."

Later, General Khang invited me to spend a couple of days at his headquarters compound. I had known Khang in late 1955 as an unassuming young captain with an excellent reputation. His fame had started in November 1960 when he rushed two Marine battalions to the defense of the President's Palace during that coup attempt. Two years later, Khang had become Commandant of the Corps. In a quiet conversation during which we spoke of the old days, Khang, recalling my efforts to have the Corps made part of the nation's strategic reserve, observed that he had since made good use of his Marine battalions outside the delta. He

U.S. NAVY RIVER PATROL, MEKONG DELTA, SOUTH VIETNAM, 1966

U.S. Navy Photo

then added, "Such operations were necessary, but they weakened Marine ties with the Navy. Our Corps is now an independent service." I agreed that the Vietnamese Marine Corps had proven itself and no longer needed Navy help to survive.

When Khang then spoke of the Viet Cong threat in the Rung Sat, I mentioned I had crossed that roadless mangrove swamp in a small boat my second Sunday in Indochina in August 1954. I told him I thought its four hundred square miles a perfect example of the land that time forgot, a steamy home for prehistoric monsters. Khang smiled and replied, "The Viet Cong, who threaten shipping in the channel to Saigon, use its maze of lesser waterways to move their troops and supplies in and out of their bases on the isolated islands. They are more dangerous than any monsters."

Our conversation reaffirming the importance of the Rung Sat prompted me to ask Khang to arrange a visit. Early the next morning, I was at Nha Be, headquarters of the Navy's Rung Sat Special Zone, being briefed. Then, wondering why I had volunteered to serve as a target in the Rung Sat, I set off in a small patrol boat for a long day, which passed without incident. I found the place unchanged; it remained a formidable obstacle that limited the mobility and fields of fire of friendly forces, while offering the enemy excellent concealment. It was a difficult combat environment.

After leaving General Khang, I called on Rear Adm. Norvell G. Ward, head of the Naval Advisory Group, to obtain his approval for the visits I wished to make. In response to his query about what I had been doing, I told him of my visit to Nha Be and added that the two boats he had helping the Vietnamese Navy patrol the Rung Sat were not enough. He agreed but explained that delivery of a hundred and twenty river patrol boats was due to begin the following month; forty for the Rung Sat and the remainder for the delta. Then he continued, "Our coastal surveillance capability is also growing. The Coast Guard brought in seventeen 82-foot cutters last year, and the Navy has ordered eighty-four SWIFT boats for inshore coastal patrol. The first of these 50-foot boats arrived this past fall, the last is expected in October." I told him how hard it was for me to compare these developments to the situation I had known in 1954.

In the week that followed I visited most of the main river towns, ground I had covered ten years earlier. Then I had traveled in Vietnamese Navy boats and had once gone to Cantho in a French Navy seaplane. Now, thanks to Admiral Ward, I had a helicopter to ease my travels and return me to Saigon each night. I was surprised on my first flight by our high speed vertical takeoff, which the

RIVER BASE, MEKONG DELTA, SOUTH VIETNAM, 1966

pilot explained was to get us out of range of automatic weapons. Thereafter, every time we took off or landed I was reminded of Algeria and Dave Riley's suggestion we sit on multiple copies of our orders.

Vinh Long, Cantho, Mytho, and the lesser communities appeared animated. Yet the barbed wire, troops, river force bases, helo pads, and defense posts all gave an ominous aspect to the surroundings. This show of strength should have been reassuring, but for me it underlined how insecure these localities had become. At the same time, I was struck by how well American troops were adapting; I also recognized the price they were paying. The year before, Lt. H. Dale Meyercord, adviser to a river assault group, had become the first American naval officer to be killed in action. Now, though security was more precarious and others were dying, these young Americans were responding to the challenges with the same courage their fathers had shown in the Pacific War.

✳ ✳ ✳

When my mission in the south ended, I flew to Danang, once a quiet provincial town the French had called Tourane. Now, it was reeling under the impact of our Marines. The port was crowded and the airfield rapidly converting to a major airbase. Military trucks, jeeps, staff cars, and troops were everywhere. The animated scene was strangely familiar; I knew the stage and many of the players. I was welcomed by Maj. Gen. Keith McCutcheon, a remarkable officer largely responsible for our close air support procedures, who invited me to share his billet. He was temporarily in command, while Maj. Gen. Lewis Walt was in Washington getting his third star, and suggested I join in his tours and strike out on my own as I wished.

I attended the situation briefing each morning, then visited the coastal force units patrolling the lagoons into which the short, swift rivers of central Vietnam flowed. The threat to the local traffic in these discontinuous inshore waterways was limited, but the potential for trouble was real should the Marines begin using them to support their own forces, as they later did. One evening at dinner I mentioned my visits to Brig. Gen. Marion E. Carl, a friend from Quantico now deputy commander of the 1st Marine Aircraft Wing, who proposed we spend the next day viewing the lagoons near Hue and Quang Tri. I readily accepted. I knew Marion as a pilot of international fame and an adventuresome outdoorsman, but I did not anticipate how much he would enliven my day.

The thrills began when I arrived at the pad and found him settling into the left seat of his helicopter. A sergeant had just loaded the machine guns projecting out of both doors and was prying the lid off a case of hand grenades. Marion waved me to the right seat, blasted off, and quickly levelled out at low altitude. Once my stomach was back in its rightful place I enjoyed the flight. Danang from the air is most attractive, as is the mountainous terrain to the north. Once

over the Hai Van Pass, the coastal plain sweeps to the horizon, offering a panorama of rice fields, hamlets, and the coastal lagoon. This spectacular view
culminates in the citadel of Hue, the ancient imperial capital on the banks of the
Perfumed River.

The sights were of such interest I forgot the war and the hazards of flying
low until we passed over an artillery battery lobbing shells toward the mountains. That encouraged me to ask Marion if the flight altitude limits set in IV
Corps differed from those in I Corps. Marion replied, "No, but don't worry, the
sergeant will shoot back at anyone who fires at us and we have grenades to
drop." At that point my mind went back to the tragic story of Col. Frank Schwable
who was shot down by ground fire in Korea while on a reconnaissance flight.
He was chief of staff of the 1st Marine Aircraft Wing at the time and became the
senior Marine prisoner of war.

The North Koreans had worked him over until he admitted being involved
in germ warfare. After the war, a Court of Inquiry recommended no disciplinary
action but noted that his usefulness as a Marine officer was seriously impaired.
It had been a sad ending to a brilliant career. I decided to remind Marion of
Schwable later. I might not have waited had I known that after a fuel stop at
Quang Tri he intended to continue to the demilitarized zone before returning to
base. When I noted our course, I asked where we were going. Marion repeated
his not very convincing "Don't worry. I've been wanting to see the DMZ and I'm
sure we'll know when to turn back." Sure enough we flew on until we saw a
small military post flying North Vietnam's red flag with yellow star, before turning for home.

After dinner that evening, I again thanked Marion for the tour and casually
mentioned Schwable. Marion nodded slowly and we went on to speak of other
things. Later that night I thought of courage. Marion, who had qualified as an
ace three time over in the skies over Guadalcanal, was a brave man. So was Jack
Cram who had made that unforgettable torpedo run in a lumbering patrol plane.
Erskine Wells, who had led a bayonet charge and Perry Ayres, who had set up
an aid station on a fire-swept beach, were also brave men. They had been recognized for their valor, but the many who had simply endured the unendurable
while performing their duty, had not. Courage indeed has many faces. I found
comfort in the thought as sleep silenced the night sounds.

✳ ✳ ✳

While my main purpose in Danang was to round out the data I needed to
draft an interim doctrine of river warfare, I also learned something of our command relations. I was dismayed to find the question of unity of command unre-
solved. While their units often fought side by side, formal ties between the Americans and their Vietnamese counterparts were through the advisory system.

General Walt, commanding the Marines in the I Corps area was the senior adviser to Maj. Gen. Nguyen Chanh Thi who commanded Vietnamese forces in the same area, but Walt did not exercise command over Thi.[8] And, though the United States funded the war effort and had major forces engaged, Westmoreland did not command the Vietnamese Armed Forces.

The more substantive Marine accomplishments in this early period were achieved by small unit actions and the development of personal relations with the people. An effort to encourage the population to withhold support for the insurgents had started in mid-1965, when the 4th Marines, confronted with defending an ever-expanding area with the same number of troops, had turned to South Vietnam's Popular Forces. The Marines had taken these ill-equipped and poorly trained local security units and integrated them with specially selected Marines to create what had become the Combined Action Companies. These had cleared the enemy from numbers of villages and enabled the return of normal activity. Coordination of this military action with relief agencies for medical services and infrastructure repair had further gained the confidence of the people.

I thought the participation of our young Marines in this effort remarkable. Already impressed by how well Americans had adapted to living in the delta, I was discovering others moving deeper into the Vietnamese culture. I told McCutcheon that the French had placed their main reliance on the use of force during the Indochina War. Only later did they admit their large-scale operations had done little more than alienate the people. "In Algeria," I continued, "they applied what they had learned in Indochina and organized *Sections Administratives Specialisees.* These, like our Combined Action Companies, had emphasized the psychological aspects of all of their actions. That is the way we should go."

McCutcheon pointed out that Westmoreland thought our Marine approach resulted in a dispersal of forces that invited attack. He believed that the Marines should conduct large scale operations against Viet Cong base areas half of the time. These differences were never settled. The consequences of Westmoreland's preoccupation with the big picture were only just appearing at the beginning of 1966, but Krulak and Greene were even then sounding warnings at councils in Hawaii and Washington. However, they were unable to convince Westmoreland or effectively counter his authoritative voice. I was well outside of this controversy but could understand the frustrations it created.

I was encouraged by the manner in which the Marines were going about gaining the support of the people. That this effort was to be diluted and diverted in pursuit of conventional engagements was still unclear. The 1st Marine Division was still in the process of being phased into the country, and even the 5th Marines that I had seen depart from Camp Pendleton had yet to arrive. The conflict was in its early stages and much of what I had seen appeared promising. Although evidence suggesting that the promise would not be fulfilled was already apparent, it was far too early to contemplate such a conclusion.

My time in South Vietnam came to an end in February. I had been a month traveling over much of the country, listening to people and gathering information. It was time for farewells and the long flight back across the watery battlefields of World War II. On arriving on Oahu I was told that General Krulak wanted to see me immediately. I was rumpled from the trip and would have enjoyed a shower and a change; however, I went directly to his headquarters. He waved a greeting and told me to take the next plane to San Diego, where the Amphibious Force Pacific staff was planning an operation in the Rung Sat and needed inputs from someone who had been there recently.

A young Navy officer met me and rushed me off to an eight o'clock conference. I did not look or feel my best, but I did have some practical inputs. I explained that the Rung Sat was a large sieve. If the Marines were to land in conventional fashion, the enemy would simply slip through the mesh and disappear. To increase the likelihood of entrapping the Viet Cong, they would need to coordinate the landing with blocking operations by the river patrol forces. After long discussion, I was able to get home for an early supper and a good night's sleep. The next day I returned to Hawaii. My concept was never validated. The operation ran afoul of command problems, coordination with local forces was lacking, and little was accomplished.

Before leaving for Vietnam in January, I had drafted a detailed outline of my study to guide my data collection. Now, again in my temporary office in Hawaii, I organized my notes, modified my outline, and fit everything together in two volumes. The first was a background of the French experience and the on-going operations of Vietnamese river force units; the second contained what General Krulak in his introduction was pleased to identify as "a first step in the progressive distillation of doctrine for the landing force aspects of river warfare."[9]

My task completed, I returned to California to join Meda in settling our affairs and make a final nostalgic tour of Camp Pendleton. My command of the 5th Marines was too recent for me to linger in its regimental area. I turned to a more distant past at Camp Del Mar where, in 1943, I had lived the impossible month granted me to form a new amtrac battalion and sail off to combat, and where, in 1947, I had returned with Meda. I also thought of the qualities of the young crewmen and mechanics who had helped make the story of the amphibian tractor possible.

I had been in good company during my twenty-six years of service. I had found comradeship in the Corps and, in my years of travel and life among the warriors and leaders of many lands, I had found numerous kindred spirits. Saddened that my journey was ending, I drove out the main gate of Camp Pendleton on June 30, 1966, to begin a new life.

EPILOGUE

I left Camp Pendleton on June 30, 1966, a Marine colonel with over eleven years of foreign service and the conviction that my journey among warriors was at an end. Eighteen months later, as a civilian working for the RAND Corporation, I was again in Saigon in time to witness the Tet Offensive and observe the promising future I had envisioned for South Vietnam being shattered in the blast of rockets striking the capital each night. Meda, alone in Santa Monica now that Suzanne had followed John to college, was preparing to join me. Instead, our inability to communicate during that period made us realize it was not the time to chance being inaccessible to our children, and I returned to California.

Our curiosity about the remote areas of the world had not lessened and within two years we were living in Iran. Though based in Tehran, my task to assist the Imperial Iranian Gendarmerie organize a surveillance system along the Persian Gulf coast required travel in much of the country. Meda joined me in many of these trips through history, from Abadan and Bushire to Persepolis, Shiraz, and Isfahan. However, she was not allowed to travel with me in the eastern border region of Baluchistan, where a military escort was required, nor could she participate in my ground reconnaissance of Iran's 1,400-mile Persian Gulf coast because of security restrictions.

We returned to Santa Monica in 1972, impressed by the Shah's efforts to move his people into a more modern world, but concerned that the opposition of the clergy and the abuses accompanying his efforts might have adverse reactions. We had found the Middle East a fascinating contrast to the Far East. Three years later we were back in Tehran, this time with me engaged in marketing throughout the Middle East for an American aerospace company and Meda working for the Iranian government.

By then, Tehran had become a cosmopolitan city, though much of the countryside retained traditional attitudes. The striking changes in Iranian society were

212

paralleled in neighboring countries. Their transformation, fueled by oil riches, had accelerated after November 1971, when Great Britain abrogated its treaties with the Arab states of the Persian Gulf. With the demise of these treaties under which Great Britain had been responsible for their security and external affairs, they began to complement their new-found sovereignty with their own military forces.

We traveled throughout much of the Middle East during this period, observing these developments and the replacement of mud villages and crowded souks by communities of multistoried buildings and air-conditioned shopping centers. The impact of these changes on the people varied greatly but, in all cases, exposing conservative Muslim societies to the practices of the western world created difficulties. Near the end of 1977, after a torrid August in Saudi Arabia looking into the feasibility of establishing an office in Riyadh, we were transferred to Germany.

Moving our Middle East marketing office to Munich appeared strange, but it was better than explosive Beirut, where we were first scheduled to go. Not surprisingly, our office was soon transferred to London, from where travel to the Middle East was easier, within the year. We were unprepared for the stratified society in England but found the black, Asian, and Middle Eastern faces on London's streets less unexpected. We particularly enjoyed the opportunity afforded by our four years in England to renew friendships formed in the Far East.

In 1981, our office was again transferred, this time to Paris. This twist of fate brought us to our final assignment overseas in the city where my unconventional service had begun thirty-two years earlier. Paris, though changed over the years, remained familiar and, as in London, we enjoyed seeing old friends. Our three years in Paris passed quickly. By 1984, having spent another eleven years abroad, we agreed it was time to return to Santa Monica. By then, both John and Suzanne had married and settled in California with their own families. How welcome this closing chapter, after having voyaged so far and seen so much.

NOTES

CHAPTER ONE

1. Legend has it that the jewel-encrusted sword given to O'Bannon for his deeds in the war with Tripoli is the model for that carried by U.S. Marine officers to this day.

2. The house in Ceyzerieu, built in 1682, passed to my great-aunt when my grandmother Marie Chaley died.

3. Capt. Sam Puller was killed shortly after he landed on Guam in 1944; it was his first operation. His brother Chesty would retire a lieutenant general with five Navy Crosses after a final hour of glory in Korea.

4. Navy funds for landing craft research and development totalled $40,000 in 1935 and $400,000 in 1940. At the beginning of that year the Navy had only thirty-five personnel boats and eleven tank/artillery lighters. The following year the Navy settled on the 36-foot LCVP for landing light vehicles and personnel, and the 50-foot LCM for landing tanks, artillery, and other heavy equipment. These were procured in large numbers for use throughout WWII.

5. Production of the LVT(1) begun in Dunedin in 1941 and ended in 1943 after 1,225 machines had been built. The LVT(2) designed by the Food Machinery Corporation became available that same year. Five variants of that model were manufactured...

   - The LVT(A)2, armored cargo vehicle for the U.S. Army, 450 built; only cargo amtrac with an "A" designation.

   - The LVT(4), cargo vehicle with stern ramp, 8,348 built.

   - The LVT(A)1, armored vehicle mounting 37mm gun in light tank turret, 509 built.

   - The LVT(A)4, armored vehicle with open turret mounting 75mm howitzer, 1,890 built.

   - The LVT(A)5, same as the LVT(A)4 except for powered turret traverse and gyro-stabilized weapon, 269 built.

The only amtrac used during WWII not built by the Food Machinery Corporation was the LVT(3), a cargo vehicle with stern ramp built by Borg-Warner. First used in the invasion of Okinawa (April 1945), the vehicle was retained after the war and fitted with an armored cover. It was used during the Inchon landing (September 1950) and through the Korean War.

6. H.M.S. *Bedfordshire* was torpedoed by the U 558 on May 11, 1942, and lost with all hands.

7. Vice Adm. Robert L. Ghormley, Commander South Pacific, established his headquarters aboard the *Rigel* in Auckland harbor on May 22, 1942. He moved ashore on June 19, where, six days later, he first heard of the coming Solomons campaign. Joint Chiefs of Staff confirmation followed on July 2.

CHAPTER 2

1. The name Guadalcanal is not in the Joint Chiefs of Staff directive of July 2 which identifies the three tasks to be undertaken in the South Pacific. General Thomas, Vandegrift's operations officer and later his chief of staff on Guadalcanal, remembers that Tulagi was the only name in the initial warning message.

2. I attended the July 19 meeting and well recall our complete surprise at General Vandegrift's opening remarks. My memory of what followed is less precise. Neither Vandegrift in his biography, nor Thomas in his oral transcript mentions the occasion. What I give here follows the usual format for an operations briefing and is not verbatim.

3. Vandegrift remembers that Fletcher "seemed nervous and tired...lacked interest in the operation (and) did not think it would succeed." Turner reportedly told Fletcher on July 25 that if the landings went well, the transports could be withdrawn the night of August 8. However, at the *Saratoga* meeting, Turner wanted the carriers to remain five days.

4. A salvo from the cruiser *Quincy* struck the *Chokai's* operations room and killed thirty members of Admiral Mikawa's staff. Soon after, the Japanese commander decided to retire.

5. Vandegrift considered the airfield his main objective and was determined to hold it; Turner thought the Marines should conquer the whole island.

6. A recent study concludes "...had the planners for Guadalcanal demanded the same assurances of success and lack of risk that we seem to require today, the campaign would never have been launched, let alone seen through to its conclusion..."

7. At the end of the first month on Guadalcanal, combat casualties were still under one thousand men. However, twice that number were suffering from malnutrition, exhaustion, fungus infections, and dysentery. Malaria, slower to start, was claiming an ever increasing number of victims when suppressive treatment finally began on September 10. Incomplete entries for the division list 8,580 admissions for disease from August to December.

8. The President's October 24 message reads in part: "My anxiety about the Southwest Pacific is to make sure that every possible weapon gets into the area to hold Guadalcanal, and that having held in this crisis, munitions, planes and crews are on the way to take advantage of our success."

9. Evans Carlson, envied because of his access to President Roosevelt following a tour with the Marine detachment at Warm Springs (1935–1937) later aroused suspicions when, after duty in China, he resigned his commission to accompany the Chinese communists in their operations against the Japanese. Jealousies were added when James Roosevelt became Evans' second-in-command and his Raider battalion enjoyed exceptional freedom in equipment and personnel selection.

CHAPTER 3

1. The effects of prolonged tension were soon confirmed when several of us failed flight physicals because of high blood pressure and pulse rate.

2. We replaced the 41st Infantry Division which had been sent to New Guinea for the Buna operation.

3. Adm. Chester W. Nimitz issued his plan for the invasion of the Marshalls on October 12, 1943. The plan did not specify objectives, and details on the seizure of Kwajalein were not issued until December 14.

4. The code names and actual names for the islands we landed on were:

   Abraham....Ennugarret   Ivan.........Mellu

   Albert.....Ennumennet   Burlesque....Roi

   Allen......Ennubirr   Camouflage...Namur

   Jacob......Ennuebing

5. The early WWII LST (542 Class) carried 17 amtracs on its tank deck, 500 tons of cargo, and 150 troops.

6. Each unit designated officers as censors who read all mail and deleted items concerned with operational activities.

7. The LVT(2) used in the Marshalls was a metal box 26' long, 8' high and 10' wide, open to the sea. It weighed 12 tons, had a crew of three and carried about 20 troops or 3 tons of cargo. Thin armor plates were attached by using units. Loading and unloading over its 10' height was difficult.

8. The 4th Division had anticipated problems with its amtracs. Brig. Gen. William W. Rogers, chief of staff of the division in the Marshalls, wrote after the war: "...the 4th Amtrac Battalion was withheld entirely on D-day...to be able to land the 23rd Marines on Roi on D+I either from the outside or from the inside of the lagoon...the [division's] mission could have been accomplished by the capture of Ivan and Jacob and the subsequent landing on Roi...even if the landings on the east side of the lagoon had not been possible on D-day. This would have invoked the subsequent capture of Namur by assault from Roi...."

   Admiral Conolly, referring to the plan for D-day, simply stated it was "too complicated."

9. Peck's Company, attached to the 22nd Marines, landed on fourteen other atolls of the Marshalls between March 7 and April 5. The company then went to Guadalcanal and later landed on Guam with the 4th Amtrac Battalion.

10. Sgt. Harry Elliott, who had selected the three amtrac bridge sites on Guadalcanal, was killed in the landing.

11. Maj. Gen. Ralph C. Smith, commanding the 27th Infantry Division on Saipan, was later relieved of command by Maj. Gen. Holland M. Smith. The unfortunate repercussions outlasted the war.

12. Construction of B-29 bases on Saipan began June 24, 1944.

13. The allocation of amtracs was made by the 1st Provisional Amphibian Tractor Group Headquarters established under Col. William W. Davies after the Marshalls operation.

14. The defense of Tinian cost the Japanese 5,500 dead. The Marines lost 355 dead and 1,675 wounded in taking the island.

15. We had fifty old model LVT(2) and fifty new model LVT(4) at Iwo Jima. The latter were the same as the LVT(2) but had a stern ramp that increased troops capacity by 25 percent.

16. Harry Marshall went aboard the control vessel for the Yellow Beaches, over which the 23rd Marines would land. Our two task company commanders went aboard the control vessels for Beach Yellow 1 and Beach Yellow 2 with representatives from the headquarters of the two assault infantry battalions.

17. Our amtracs carried ladders for scaling terraces.

18. By war's end 2,250 B-29s manned by 24,761 airmen had found safe haven on Iwo Jima. The Marines had suffered 5,885 dead and 17,272 wounded in taking the island.

CHAPTER 4

1. In 1945 the Fleet Marine Force's Supply Service comprised a headquarters, two field service commands, two base depots, four field depots, six service battalions and one depot company. The Service Command in 1946 included two service depots, one service regiment, and two service battalions.

2. The V Amphibious Corps deployed to Japan in September 1945. Its 5th Division was disbanded in February 1946; the 2nd Division moved to Camp Lejeune in mid-year.

3. The two-battalion Fleet Marine Force West Pacific left to guard 7th Fleet facilities was deactivated in February 1949.

4. The LVT(3) with stern ramp had a cadillac engine in each pontoon, which gave it the largest cargo space of any amtrac in WWII. First used on Okinawa in April 1945, it was the only cargo amtrac retained after the war. Fitted with an armored cover, the LVT(3)C saw service in Korea.

5. The curriculum of the Ecole de Guerre extended over two cycles, the second restricted to French officers. The first cycle included three hundred fifty-one hours

of lectures on national and international security affairs, and eight months of exercises at division, corps, and field army level.

6. German ground forces totalled one hundred and thirty-five divisions equipped with 2,700 tanks and 7,710 artillery pieces. Allied forces comprised one hundred and thirty-two divisions, 3,000 tanks and 11,200 field guns. Only in tactical aviation was there an imbalance of 3,200 German planes against 1,275 French.

7. My report of January 3, 1951, to the Commandant of the Marine Corps reports on visits to twelve Army and Navy schools and nine other military and naval facilities, and identifies ten reports, with added data on nine Algerian and four Tunisian ports, forwarded separately.

8. Before WWII our graduates of the Ecole de Guerre were sent to Quantico as instructors. This policy was continued in my case though Marine Corps would have benefitted from having representation on the NATO staff from its beginning.

CHAPTER FIVE

1. Indochina included the colony of Cochinchina acquired in 1862 and the protectorates of Cambodia (1863), Annam (1884), Tonkin (1884), and Laos (1893). Vietnam today comprises the former Cochinchina, Tonkin, and Annam.

2. The Geneva Agreements signed on July 20, 1954, by France and the Democratic Republic of Vietnam went into effect on July 27 in North Vietnam, on August 1 in Central Vietnam, on August 6 in Laos, on August 7 in Cambodia, and on August 11 in South Vietnam. Under the terms of the Agreements, the French were to evacuate the Hanoi perimeter within eighty days and clear the Hai Duong area twenty days later. The remaining French-held zone centered on the port city of Haiphong was to be evacuated at the end of the 300-day period. Functioning public services and facilities were to be left in working condition. Vietnam had been similarly divided in the 17th and 18th centuries; the Dong Hoi wall marked the separation.

3. The Cao Dai and Hoa Hao were religious sects whose adherents controlled large parts of the Mekong delta and had security forces totalling 15,000 and 12,500 men respectively. The Binh Xuyen were not a religious sect but an ultra-nationalist movement centered in the suburbs of Saigon.

4. The French surrendered 4,500 wounded and 5,500 able-bodied men to the Viet Minh at Dien Bien Phu. Earlier losses among the French forces included 1,142 dead, 1,606 missing, 4,436 wounded, and 1,161 deserters. Viet Minh losses are estimated at 23,000 of which 8,000 were killed. The French losses represented 5 percent of the Expeditionary Corps and 3.3 percent of the total French and Associated States' forces in Indochina.

5. General Hinh was aware of the political implications in refugee resettlement and would have been willing to take charge of the effort. But, as a political rival of Diem, he was never given the opportunity to do so.

6. The International Control Commission, made up of respresentatives from India, Canada, and Poland, was responsible for the implementation of the Geneva Accords.

7. The book, entitled *Deliver Us From Evil*, was challenged by six Americans who had served in Haiphong when Dooley was there; their critique was communicated to the Embassy Public Affairs Officer in Saigon who recommended to Washington "that the [U.S. Information] Agency...stop at once any further exploitation of the Dooley book..."

8. Lansdale headed the Saigon Military Mission, a special CIA team. He also served as head of the National Security Division of TRIM.

9. The South East Asia Defense Treaty was signed September 8, 1954, by representatives of Australia, Great Britain, France, New Zealand, Pakistan, the Philippines, Thailand, and the United States. The South East Asia Treaty Organization was established in Bangkok in 1956; its Military Planning Office was created the following year "to establish continuity and to expedite detailed defense planning."

10. The Pentalateral Mutual Defense Assistance Pact signed on December 23, 1950, by the United States, France, and the three Associated States of Indochina set the ground rules for military assistance. The Collins-Ely agreement of December 1954 provided for a survey of American equipment to decide upon its disposition. This led to the estimate that property worth 150 million dollars could be salvaged if the 342-man limit on the MAAG was raised. In June 1956 a 350-man Temporary Equipment Recovery Mission (TERM) was brought in.

11. Jean Louis Delayen, of a French military family, grew up in Saigon and was a brilliant commando leader in the war.

12. TRIM began in March 1955 with 68 American and 209 French officers. In May it peaked at 121 American and 225 French. By the end of 1955 there were 142 Americans and only 58 French. In March 1956 the French were gone and TRIM was deactivated the following month.

13. My assignment as advisor to the Navy staff was verbal. General Williams later requested written confirmation.

14. Bui Diem, a stern critic of the President and ambassador to the U.S. (1967–1972), states that "by the late 1950s practically the whole country had been politicized by Diem's arrogant authoritarianism..."

15. My last personal contact with Le Quang My involved his request for help in planning an operation to retake the Paracel Islands from the Chinese. I suggested it might be useful to begin with a reconnaissance. The U.S. Navy sent two destroyers to the area in June which reported no signs of military activity. The Vietnamese later landed an occupation force.

CHAPTER SIX

1. The Commandant of the Marine Corps became an unrestricted member of the Joint Chiefs of Staff in 1978.

2. The military budgets for the period 1955 to 1959 reveal consistent sharing on the basis of 46 percent for the Air Force, 28 percent for the Navy and Marine Corps, and 23 percent for the Army; the balance going to the Defense Department.

3. The end of American nuclear supremacy in 1955 brought a nuclear stalemate that reduced the freedom of action of the two superpowers. This appeared to grant lesser nations greater latitude to pursue their interests. However, as the Suez crisis demonstrated, local disagreements could involve middle-level states and bring the superpowers into play. This sequence, repeated throughout the Cold War, revealed that the freedom of action attributed to lesser nations was illusory.

4. The French operated twelve squadrons of light surveillance aircraft in the three corps areas. In addition, Army Helicopter Group 2 based at Setif with ninety helos supported operations in the Constantine Corps Area. Helicopter support in the Algiers and Oran Corps Areas was provided by the Air Force operating forty-two helicopters in each area.

5. The *Bureau d'Action Psychologique* passed to army control in 1955 with the mission to mount an offensive targeting the Muslim population. This included using mobile medical teams, reopening schools in secure areas, establishing technical training programs for Muslim youths, and undertaking public works projects using native labor.

6. Paradoxically it was the success of the French military in Algeria that led to the resentments, even sense of betrayal, that was voiced by many officers when President de Gaulle decided to support Algerian independence.

7. The mission began arriving in Port au Prince in January 1959. It gained the enmity of the President in 1961 when Heinl refused to include *milice* personnel (Tonton Macoutes) among officers sent to Quantico for training. Relations deteriorated thereafter until, in March 1963, Duvalier asked for Heinl's recall...two months later the mission was gone.

8. I was appalled at the rudimentary medical services I saw in Haiti. To help, I gathered excess medical equipment and supplies from military facilities in the Washington area and took them with me on my trips.

9. The treaty of friendship between the United States and Morocco dates back to 1787. Moroccan sensitivity over the American air bases, built by agreement with France without Moroccan involvement, was well known. On gaining its independence in 1956, Morocco had requested the withdrawal of American forces. That was done in 1963.

10. A message from our Paris embassy to Washington of May 13, 1959, refers to tripartite talks on Africa and supports a French proposal to create an informal military group stating it is of "..fundamental importance for military conversations to get under way soonest...".

CHAPTER SEVEN

1. The French Community created by the Constitution of the Fifth Republic included all overseas territories as member states with individual and shared Community powers and the right of secession; Guinea was the first to leave in 1958.

2. West Pakistan included four provinces: Sind, Punjab, Baluchistan, and the North-west Frontier. East Pakistan became Bangladesh, after the India-Pakistan War of 1971.

3. Pakistan was a member of the Southeast Asia Treaty Organization and the Central Treaty Organization.

4. Alexander the Great approached what is now Pakistan in 327 B.C. with 35,000 men, half moving through the Khyber Pass, the remainder through the hills to the north.

5. The Central Treaty Organization began as the Baghdad Pact in February 1955 with Iraq and Turkey as members. Iran, Pakistan, and Great Britain joined a few months later. The headquarters moved from Baghdad to Ankara in 1958. When Iraq withdrew in 1959, it became the Central Treaty Organization. The United States participated as an "observer."

6. In 1917, the British Foreign Secretary declared that "Great Britain viewed with favor the establishment in Palestine of a national home for the Jewish people [with the understanding] that nothing shall be done which may prejudice the civil and religious rights of existing non-Jewish communities in Palestine..." In the Arab view Palestine was a refuge for Jews. The Jews, however, saw the Balfour Declaration as support for an independent Jewish State.

7. The Roman emperor Hadrian (A.D. 117–138) ended the political history of the ancient Jewish state and dispersed the Jews. Those settled in Germany and eastern Europe became "Ashkenasi," from the Hebrew for Germany. Those who settled in Spain and Portugal and were later driven to North Africa and the Middle East are "Sephardim," from the Hebrew for Spain. The former speak Yiddish; the latter speak Ladino.

CHAPTER EIGHT

1. CINCPAC's contingency plan 32-59 for Southeast Asia was to be implemented by Joint Task Force 116 (JTF 116) utilizing designated units of the Army, Navy, Air Force, and Marine Corps. In that the forces to be used in an intervention in Laos were primarily Marine, command of JTF 116 was given to the senior Marine Corps officer in the Western Pacific. Other phases of CINCPAC OPLAN 32-59 were under Army command since that Service would be providing the preponderance of forces.

2. Twenty-three large scale SEATO exercises were held between 1955 and 1962. Exercise "Tulungan" held in the Philippines involved seventy-eight ships, four hundred aircraft, and 37,000 troops.

3. SEATO plans paralleled those of the United States, providing us the option of taking action unilaterally or through the Alliance. This CINCPAC OPLAN 32-59 II Laos was the same as SEATO Plan 5 except for the command designations.

4. In June 1961, SEATO was headed by a Secretary General under whom there were nine Offices staffed by 140 people. Of the eight on the civil side, only the Office of Counter-Subversion was headed by a Special Assistant. The Military

Planning Office was headed by a two-star officer with a one-star deputy and a colonel/captain chief of staff who directed the international planning group made up of three lieutenant colonels/commanders from each member nation. Policy guidance was provided by a Council of Ministers, which met annually. Implementation of its guidance in civil matters was the responsibility of the Council Representatives, the member nations' Ambassadors in Bangkok, who met monthly. They were assisted by a Permanent Working Group of senior Embassy officials who met weekly. The Military Advisers, usually of four-star rank, met with the Council to advise and report on military matters. They also met one other time during the year in Bangkok to pass on the activities of the Military Planning Office. Military Advisers Representatives of colonel/captain rank at SEATO headquarters met weekly to monitor the progress of planning and related matters. Adm. Harry D. Felt was U.S. Military Adviser; I was his Representative in Bangkok.

5. These included Plan 5 for intervention in Laos and a new Plan 7, which involved SEATO intervention in South Vietnam. In my three years in SEATO I worked on these and other SEATO plans but most particularly with the development of Plan 7.

6. Our official social obligations were determined by the national holidays of the eight member nations, embassy functions sponsored by other than SEATO countries, Thai government affairs, and U.S. Military visitors to SEATO. Altogether, we averaged one official function per day throughout the 36 months we lived in Bangkok.

7. The early successes of the "Chinese Terrorists" in Malaya were largely due to the support of 423,000 Chinese squatters. The British resettled these squatters in four hundred villages built over a period of eighteen months with careful attention to site and construction. The Vietnamese Strategic Hamlet Program sought to build 12,000 villages in a twenty-four-month period. Moreover, the Chinese in Malaya were an ethnic group distinct from the Malays and Indians making up the remainder of the population and quite satisfied to be resettled. The Vietnamese, in contrast, were the principal population and unwilling to leave their lands.

8. The U.S. Marine Corps had an officer exchange program with the British Royal Marines which allowed it a close view of that conflict. Indeed, Major P. X. Kelley, who had been with me on our Survey Team to Haiti, was serving as commanding officer of C Troop, 42 Commando in North Borneo in 1961.

9. In 1966 I discussed the assassination of Diem with Maj. Gen. Le Nguyen Khang, Commandant of the Vietnamese Marine Corps. Khang assured me that Diem's death had been part of the coup plan. Don denies involvement and blames General Duong Van Minh.

10. The Tonkin Gulf Resolution of August 1, 1964, was valid for one year. Thus, in early 1966 the United States shifted emphasis away from the Resolution and back to SEATO to explain the obligations under which it was continuing its intervention in Vietnam. This helped SEATO survive until, in September 1975, the Council directed the Secretary General to phase out the Organization and dispose of its assets.

11. Commander Naval Forces Philippines controlled the few spaces available for military personnel on commercial ships under government subsidy agreements.

CHAPTER NINE

1. Years later, Suzanne recalled that when she arrived in Bangkok in 1961 the languid heat and smells of that city recalled Saigon and made her feel she was back home. She does not remember having a similar reaction any place else.

2. In August 1964 North Vietnamese patrol boats clashed with U.S. ships in the Gulf of Tonkin. This precipitated retaliatory air strikes against North Vietnamese naval facilities and led Congress to pass a joint resolution authorizing the use of U.S. forces to assist South Vietnam.

3. The exercise I had prepared at Quantico in 1953 involved a landing in the Quang Tri area of South Vietnam. Later, in Saigon, I had obtained approval to make a reconnaissance up the Mekong River to the vicinity of Savannakhet, thence east on the all-weather lateral road (French Colonial Route 9) just below the 17th parallel to Quang Tri. I had to cancel the trip in the press of my duties. Later, I studied the feasibility of deploying a Marine Division along Route 9 to block communist infiltration routes. I thought that if this were accompanied by an announcement that any offensive action by North Vietnam would be considered an act of war against the United States, this could have provided the South Vietnamese the time and opportunity to eradicate the Viet Cong in the South without our direct participation. This concept, worth considering in 1961, was no longer valid under the circumstances prevailing at the time of the Military Assistance Command, Vietnam (MACV) estimate in March 1965.

4. The 7th Marines reached Vietnam in 1965. The remainder of the 1st Division went to Okinawa to replace 3rd Division units sent to Vietnam. The 1st Marines arrived in Vietnam in January 1966. Division headquarters followed at the end of March. The 5th Marines, the last unit to leave Camp Pendleton, did not reach Vietnam until the end of May 1966.

5. *Dinassauts* were French Navy boat units with flexible organization used for riverine operations involving landing of up to a battalion of infantry. They often had an infantry platoon or company attached for counter-ambush operations when engaged in routine patrolling or transport duties. These units were gathered into the Vietnamese Marine Corps at the end of the Indochina War.

6. U.S. Engineers estimated that with the dredge equipment available, it would take seventeen and a half dredge years to fill a base area for a division. Steps were taken to order additional dredges but these were not expected to arrive until the end of 1966.

7. The initial requirement for the afloat base was for five self-propelled barracks ships (APB), two LSTs for logistic support, two harbor tugs (YTB) and two landing craft repair ships (ARL). Each River Assault Squadron was to have 26 LCM(6) as armored troop carriers (ATC), 2 LCM(6) as command and control boats (CCB), 5 LCM(6) as monitors, 16 assault support patrol boats (ASPB), and 1 LCM(6) refueler. The afloat base requirements were subsequently scaled down, but the River

Assault Squadron (RAS) organization was eventually approved as recommended. The first of the afloat deployments, which eventually involved two infantry battalions, was made on June 11, 1967. Mobile Riverine Force operations then continued for two years. In mid-1969 responsibility for such operations was turned over to the Vietnamese and the U.S. 9th Division was withdrawn. When the Communists gained control over the whole of Vietnam in 1975, the navy booty acquired included:

Inshore Coastal Patrol	*River Force Boats*
25 Coast Guard WPB	293 PBR boats
107 SWIFT Boats	84 Aslt. Patrol
	64 Monitors
	100 Troop carriers
	8 Command (CCB)
	27 Patrol (RPC)

8. Maj. Gen. Nguyen Chanh Thi was the parachute brigade commander who led the unsuccessful coup against Diem in 1960. General Khang thought him brave but "too political."

9. The river warfare study I prepared at General Krulak's direction never directly served the Marine Corps. However, much of the material was later used in the preparation of NWP-13, *A Doctrine for Navy/Marine Corps Joint River Operations.* More immediate use was made by the Army's Combat Developments Command which met with the Navy in Coronado between November 7, 1966, and January 10, 1967, to outline the draft of the Army's FM 31-75, *Riverine Operations.* I participated in that effort.

Index

225